Also by Thomas Quinn

MODERNISING THE LABOUR PARTY
Organisational Change since 1983

Electing and Ejecting Party Leaders in Britain

Thomas Quinn
Lecturer in Government, University of Essex, UK

palgrave
macmillan

First published 2012 by
PALGRAVE MACMILLAN

Palgrave Macmillan in the UK is an imprint of Macmillan Publishers Limited, registered in England, company number 785998, of Houndmills, Basingstoke, Hampshire RG21 6XS.

Palgrave Macmillan in the US is a division of St Martin's Press LLC, 175 Fifth Avenue, New York, NY 10010.

Palgrave Macmillan is the global academic imprint of the above companies and has companies and representatives throughout the world.

Palgrave® and Macmillan® are registered trademarks in the United States, the United Kingdom, Europe and other countries

ISBN 978-0-230-21961-8

This book is printed on paper suitable for recycling and made from fully managed and sustained forest sources. Logging, pulping and manufacturing processes are expected to conform to the environmental regulations of the country of origin.

A catalogue record for this book is available from the British Library.

A catalogue record for this book is available from the Library of Congress.

10 9 8 7 6 5 4 3 2 1
21 20 19 18 17 16 15 14 13 12

Printed and bound in the United States of America
by Edwards Brothers Malloy

For my father

Contents

List of Figures

List of Tables

List of Boxes

Acknowledgements

This book would not have been possible without the assistance of numerous individuals and the databases of various organisations. The series of interviews conducted for this study provided crucial information on how parties select and remove their leaders. I thank all of the current and former politicians and party officials who agreed to speak with me, whether on-the-record or off-the-record. In addition, I thank the central-office officials who responded to my requests for information on their respective parties' selection rules and leadership-election results. Lord Spicer of Cropthorne, chairman of the Conservative Party's 1922 committee between 2001 and 2010, provided me with the committee's detailed rules on Conservative leadership elections and confidence votes. His successor as chairman, Graham Brady MP, investigated a number of queries I had about the rules on confidence votes. Charles Clarke kindly provided me with a timetable he had drawn up for a possible Labour leadership election in 2009 (reproduced in Appendix M). Steven Huntingdon of the Electoral Commission was extremely helpful in explaining the database on donations to candidates in leadership elections (Appendix L). Nigel Copsey of Teesside University provided information on leadership-selection rules in the British National Party (Appendix F).

This book makes use of a considerable amount of polling data. Particularly useful was YouGov's archive, which contains many polls on the attitudes of individual party members during leadership contests. Ipsos-MORI's long-running leader-satisfaction series was also used extensively. Data on voting intentions were taken from YouGov, Ipsos-MORI, ICM and Gallup.

As this book went to press, a number of regional parties covered in the appendices announced that they would be holding leadership elections. The results of these contests, along with others listed in this book, can be found at my website at http://privatewww.essex.ac.uk/~tquinn/.

Parts of this book have previously been published elsewhere. The analyses of the 2001 and 2005 Conservative leadership contests in Chapter 4 and the 2006 and 2007 Liberal Democrat leadership contests in Chapter 5 appeared in abridged forms in my article, 'Membership Ballots in Party Leadership Elections in Britain', *Representation*, 46:1 (2010), 101–17 ((c) 2010 Taylor & Francis).

A number of people read through earlier versions of chapters or sections of the manuscript. I would like to thank John Bartle, Ben Clements and in particular Nick Allen, who each made valuable suggestions for improving the argument. Any remaining errors are mine alone. Amber Stone-Galilee and Liz Blackmore of Palgrave Macmillan provided helpful assistance throughout this project. I would also like to thank my friend and former colleague, Frank Grundig, who was a great source of advice and motivation. Finally, I am hugely grateful to my father, Tom Quinn senior, whose wonderful support and encouragement helped me enormously. At key moments as I worked on this book, he proved again to be my biggest supporter. All of my accomplishments are partly his.

Thomas Quinn

List of Abbreviations

AM	Assembly Member (National Assembly for Wales)
ASLEF	Associated Society of Locomotive Engineers and Firemen
AUEW	Amalgamated Union of Engineering Workers
AV	Alternative vote
BBC	British Broadcasting Corporation
BECTU	Broadcasting, Entertainment, Cinematograph and Theatre Union
BFAWU	Bakers, Food and Allied Workers Union
BNP	British National Party
CLP	Constituency Labour Party
CWU	Communication Workers Union
ENC	Effective number of candidates
ENP	Effective number of parties
MEP	Member of the European Parliament
MP	Member of Parliament
MSP	Member of the Scottish Parliament
MU	Musicians' Union
NEC	National Executive Committee (Labour)
NHS	National Health Service
OMOV	One member-one vote
PLP	Parliamentary Labour Party
PPB	Parliamentary-party ballot
SDP	Social Democratic Party
SNP	Scottish National Party
TGWU	Transport and General Workers' Union
TSSA	Transport Salaried Staffs' Association
TUC	Trades Union Congress
UCATT	Union of Construction, Allied Trades and Technicians
UKIP	United Kingdom Independence Party
USDAW	Union of Shop, Distributive and Allied Workers

Introduction

In recent years the perception has grown among British politicians, academics and media commentators that the role and importance of party leaders has increased. Tony Blair's ten years as prime minister fostered the belief that high-profile and dominant leadership was vital in the modern era. Political scientists have debated 'presidential' trends in the British political system.[1] In the field of voting behaviour, an important and on-going debate is addressing the question of how far party leaders affect the way people vote.[2] Meanwhile, news-media outlets successfully lobbied for a series of set-piece debates between the party leaders during the 2010 general-election campaign.[3]

Given the importance of leaders in the political process, it is natural to ask how politicians come to be leaders and how they remain so. This book explores the methods that the major British parties use for electing and ejecting their leaders. It does not offer a comprehensive analysis of all facets of party leadership, nor does it do more than touch upon issues such as prime-ministerial power and related debates. Instead, the primary focus of this book is on the role of intra-party institutions in affecting the types of leaders that parties choose and the security of tenure they ultimately enjoy. In short, this book connects to a broader question in political science of whether 'institutions matter'.[4]

The rise of all-member ballots in UK party leadership elections

Until the mid-1970s, all three of the major parties in Britain left leadership selection exclusively to their MPs. By 1998, all three gave some weight to all-member ballots in their leadership elections. The Liberals were the first to switch to one member-one vote (OMOV) in 1976.

Labour created a tripartite electoral college in 1981 and gradually extended the use of balloting in the individual members section. In 1998, the Conservatives adopted a hybrid system in which the final choice between two candidates was left to party members. Each of these systems and some of the contests recently conducted in them are examined in this book. The major parties are not alone in moving towards OMOV. The Green Party, the United Kingdom Independence Party, the British National Party, Plaid Cymru and the Scottish National Party all formally prescribe OMOV for their leadership elections. (The main features of these parties' selection systems and details of recent contests are provided in the appendices of this book.) All-member ballots have become the norm in British leadership elections, although Labour and the Conservatives continue to provide important voting rights to MPs.

The enfranchisement of party members in Britain is part of a broader trend towards more 'open' forms of leadership selection in other Western democracies.[5] A less deferential and more participatory age since the 1960s was bound to affect political parties. The bitterest battle to extend the intra-party franchise in Britain occurred in the Labour Party in the 1970s and 1980s. An influx of middle-class, university-educated and politically radical young members, together with a new assertiveness by the major trade unions, helped to bring about a transformation in the distribution of power in the party.[6] Voting rights in leadership elections were extended from MPs to activists and trade-union officials, although the party's new electoral college in its earliest incarnation was more a manifestation of activist democracy than all-member democracy. Although this 'new left' was ultimately defeated, its campaign for democratisation was not rolled back by a new generation of Labour modernisers but instead extended from the small groups of activists in local parties to all party members, including those who rarely attended meetings.

The battle for democratisation was less bloody in the other main parties. The Liberals had few MPs and as the party's profile increased in the 1970s, demands grew for the membership to have a say over choosing the leader. In the Conservative Party, a more deferential culture existed but it was undermined by the party's landslide election defeat in 1997, blamed on the MPs by the party membership. After considering an electoral college, the party opted for a two-stage method in which MPs presented two candidates to the members, who made their choice in a postal ballot. The Conservatives, like Labour, changed their selection system when they had returned to opposition after a crushing electoral defeat, a frequent combination when parties undertake such reforms.[7] At these moments, the parliamentary party is at its weakest and least able to resist the demands of angry grassroots members.

Paradoxically, intra-party democratisation has occurred during an era when party-membership levels have fallen dramatically. In 1974, Labour had 692,000 individual members, the Conservatives 2.15 million and the Liberals 190,000. By 2005, Labour's membership had fallen to 198,000, the Conservatives' to 300,000 and the Liberal Democrats' to 73,000.[8] This long-term trend towards lower levels of party membership calls into doubt the legitimising role that OMOV plays in leadership elections. The obvious next stage would be open primaries of party supporters, but these have yet to be deployed in British party leadership elections and are beyond the scope of the present book.

The shift to OMOV raises important questions about the selection of party leaders. Do party members choose different types of leaders than MPs do? Are they ideologically more radical? Or do members and MPs use similar selection criteria and choose similar leaders? A comprehensive comparative analysis of different selection systems is beyond the scope of this book. At any rate, parliamentary ballots in the British parties have been extensively analysed in previous studies. The present study focuses primarily upon membership ballots or the hybrid systems in which they occur. It undertakes a number of case studies to examine the selection criteria that party members and other intra-party selectors use in choosing leaders. In doing so, it replicates the approach of what is arguably the most important book written on leadership selection in British political parties, Leonard Stark's *Choosing a Leader* (1996).[9] Stark argued that a simple hierarchy of selection criteria – acceptability, electability and competence – was effective in explaining the outcomes of most leadership elections. The present book deploys the same explanatory schema to analyse more recent contests not studied by Stark and in the case of the Conservative Party, contests that were conducted under a different selection system. It explores whether individual party members select leaders on the same basis that MPs do. In doing so it addresses the question of whether institutions matter since different institutions enfranchise different types of selectors.

At the same time that British parties opened up their selection systems, they also sought to increase leaders' institutional security of tenure. Thresholds for triggering leadership contests or confidence votes were increased in the Labour Party in 1988, in the Conservative Party in 1991 and 1998, and in the Liberal Democrats in 2005. This push for greater protection of incumbents has coincided with several serious attempts by MPs to remove leaders representing all three major parties from power. Leader eviction is a key theme explored in this book. It is normally relegated to a secondary issue in studies of leadership-selection systems, but the present analysis regards it as a serious question in its own right.

Methodology

This study has relied on five principal sources of information. First, existing secondary materials, such as books and articles on leadership elections, as well as politicians' biographies and autobiographies, were used to obtain information about the course and history of various leadership contests, as well as details about selection rules.

Second, internal party documents were consulted, particularly as they related to the changing of parties' leadership-selection systems. These included party constitutions, other documents setting out rules (e.g. the Conservative Party's 1922 committee's rules and procedures for leadership elections), and reports of party conferences.

Third, contemporaneous newspaper articles provided important accounts of day-to-day developments in leadership contests. Given the recent dates of the contests covered in detail in this study, most of these articles are freely available online, including through the Nexis database.

Fourth, opinion-poll data is essential in the analysis of OMOV elections. Data from the pollsters, YouGov, was particularly useful because that organisation regularly conducts surveys of individual party members. These data are most complete for the Conservative leadership contest of 2005, during which at least five surveys were carried out. There are also excellent data for the Liberal Democrat leadership elections of 2006 and 2007. The Labour leadership election of 2010 saw two detailed YouGov polls of party members and affiliated trade unionists, while the centre-left website, *Left Foot Forward*, kept a tally of endorsements by MPs. In addition to these sources, Gallup, Ipsos-MORI and ICM have standard opinion-poll data on the parties, while Gallup and Ipsos-MORI also have long-running data series on the party leaders' satisfaction ratings. ICM's and Ipsos-MORI's databases are available online.

Finally, a series of semi-structured interviews was conducted with politicians, including candidates in leadership elections, non-candidate MPs and party officials. These individuals were essential sources of information, as they were participants or observers of the events being analysed. There is the risk that interviewees may forget important facts or distort them in order to present themselves in the best light.[10] However, there is no way around the fact that these actors are vital sources, particularly in relation to the various attempts, successful or otherwise, to remove incumbent leaders. Leader eviction remains largely in the hands of MPs, with little input from party members. Where possible, information provided by interviewees was cross-checked with other interviewees, as well as press articles. Although some of these interviews were off the record, these were mainly used for background information and most of the references in the text are to on-the-record interviews.

The format of the study requires explanation. Although a chapter is provided on leadership elections in which only MPs could vote, the primary focus in this book is on the newer systems of membership ballots. A chapter is devoted to each of the three main British parties, and the structure is similar in each case. After a description of the selection system and an account of how it came into being, the remainder of each of these chapters is devoted to recent leadership contests and evictions. Past contests conducted under the system are briefly recounted but the major focus is on one or two case studies of the most recent elections. The benefit of this approach is that it enables in-depth analysis of the dynamics of one or two contests, and in any case, there have been only three contests conducted under the Tories' new selection rules.

There are clearly limits to what a few case studies can reveal about the functioning of institutions. Each new leadership election brings events and developments that were not anticipated before. Nevertheless, there are many things that individual contests can reveal that are of broader significance. The utility of the two main frameworks of analysis deployed throughout this study – Stark's hierarchy of selection criteria for leadership contests and a cost-benefit model of politicians' incentives for leader evictions – is that they provide ways of drawing out similarities between cases and understanding why they differ in certain respects. Some of these similarities and differences are drawn out in the final chapter.

Structure of the book

The first chapter considers key questions in the selection and ejection of party leaders. It begins by examining the approach of Stark in his 1996 study of leadership selection in Britain. The chapter then sets out the major questions surrounding the ejection of party leaders, which is sometimes, although not always, distinct from the election of leaders. It discusses institutional and non-institutional means of leader-eviction, including formal leadership challenges, confidence votes, frontbench coups and backbench revolts. These various methods are assessed in terms of the costs and benefits to the leader's opponents of moving against him. This framework is utilised in the analysis of leader-eviction attempts throughout this book.

Chapter 2 explores leadership elections in the era of parliamentary ballots. It discusses features of selection by MPs in relation to the British parties during the periods in which they used such systems. Parliamentary ballots were used exclusively to choose leaders in the Conservative Party until 1998 and the final such contest, which saw William Hague selected in 1997, is the chosen case study for this chapter. This contest is analysed in terms of Stark's selection criteria of acceptability, electability and competence, and it is shown to fit this explanatory framework neatly. The chapter then examines leader eviction by MPs. The principal case study is the removal of Margaret Thatcher by Conservative MPs in 1990. A comparison is provided with Labour MPs' failure to remove Harold Wilson in 1968–69 to demonstrate the importance of eviction institutions in political parties. Ejection rules were easy to operate in the Conservative Party in 1990 but did not exist in the Labour Party in the 1960s when the party was in government.

Chapter 3 examines leader selection and ejection in the Labour Party in the era of the electoral college. After a brief history of the college's formation and reform, details of leadership elections between 1983 and 2007 are briefly recounted. The major case study in this chapter is the 2010 leadership election, which saw Ed Miliband emerge victorious. Polling data is provided to show how the five leadership candidates rated on the key selection criteria. It is argued that this contest is one of the few where selection rules were crucial in determining the winner: without a concerted effort by the trade unions to mobilise support for Ed Miliband, he would have been defeated by his brother, David. The chapter then analyses two cases of attempted leader eviction: Tony Blair in 2004–06 and Gordon Brown in 2008–10. Both leaders survived these attempts and in the case of Brown, it is argued that Labour's cumbersome eviction rules played a vital role in saving him by making it harder for his opponents to mobilise others.

Chapter 4 turns to the Conservative Party and examines the operation of the selection and ejection rules introduced in 1998. After briefly recounting the formation of the new system, the chapter analyses the leadership elections of 2001 and 2005. In the case of the 2001 contest, it is shown that party members rationally selected a leader on the basis of whether he could unite the party. This argument challenges the conventional wisdom in relation to the selection of Iain Duncan Smith, namely, that Tory members foisted an electorally unappealing ideologue on a sceptical parliamentary party. David Cameron's victory in 2005 is also shown to fit Stark's hierarchy of selection criteria. The chapter then turns back chronologically to examine Duncan Smith's removal as party leader in 2003, when he was defeated in a confidence vote of Conservative MPs. It is argued that eviction institutions played *some* role in Duncan Smith's ejection, primarily by making it possible for key shadow-cabinet members to retain public distance from the plots to remove him.

Chapter 5 completes the survey of the major parties by analysing selection and ejection in the Liberal Democrats. It begins with the forced resignation of Charles Kennedy in 2006. Kennedy's eviction offers an interesting case study because it was achieved by non-institutional means. However, its clumsy nature also illustrated the difficulties of organising frontbench coups, especially when the most senior members of the shadow cabinet wished to retain distance from the manoeuvres. The Liberal Democrat leadership elections of 2006 and 2007 are both examined and each is shown to fit in with Stark's hierarchy of selection criteria.

Chapter 6 draws together some of the main lessons of the preceding analysis. It begins by showing that all-member ballots have not hugely affected leadership selection in British parties. On the whole, the candidates who were preferred by MPs were also preferred by party members, although Labour's electoral college complicates the picture because it enfranchises a third group, trade-union members. On the question of leader eviction, it is argued that incumbents' institutional security of tenure is weakened by secret ballots, low thresholds for triggering votes, and the sequential separation of the processes of ejecting and electing leaders. The parties vary in the degree to which they possess any of these institutions, with eviction much harder in the Labour Party than it is in the Conservative or Liberal Democrat parties. The study concludes that institutions are probably more decisive in leader ejection than they are in leader selection.

The book ends with a series of appendices. These include leadership-election results in the major parties, selection systems and results in the minor parties, and financial donations in recent leadership contests.

1
Electing and Ejecting Party Leaders

In 1998, the Conservative Party's leader, William Hague, pushed through a package of reforms to his party's organisation, of which the most eye-catching was a new system for selecting the party leader.[1] Since 1965, the Conservative leader had been elected by MPs alone, but the new system created a two-stage process by which MPs would choose two candidates to put to a postal ballot of individual party members. In doing so, the Tories became the last of the three main British parties to extend the franchise in leadership elections from MPs to members.[2] The Liberal Party had been the first in 1976, when it abandoned parliamentary ballots and moved to a complicated system of membership participation based on local ballots (see Chapter 5). A 'pure' system of one member-one vote (OMOV) was used by the Social Democratic Party (SDP) and the Liberal Democrats, the successor party after the Liberals merged with the SDP in 1988. Labour also abandoned its exclusive use of parliamentary ballots, in 1981, when it adopted an electoral college that split votes between MPs, party activists and affiliated organisations such as trade unions. Initially, only activists who were members of their local general committees could vote, but the franchise was later extended to all party members in postal ballots. Votes in the affiliates section were also removed from union executives and conference delegates to individual union members (see Chapter 3). With the Conservatives' adoption of their own form of OMOV in 1998, the extension of voting rights to members in the major British parties was complete. Like many changes to leadership-election rules, those in the Conservatives Party were implemented in opposition and followed a heavy election defeat.[3] Labour had done the same in 1981 and again, to a lesser extent, in 1993.

At the same time that British parties have extended the franchise, they have also sought to tighten parliamentary control over the instigation of contests. Even under their old system of parliamentary ballots, the Conservatives had begun a process of raising the barriers to those looking to enter leadership contests, most notably by making it more difficult to instigate ballots. Under their present system, incumbent leaders cannot be challenged but must be defeated in a confidence vote, which itself takes place only if 15 percent of Tory MPs formally demand it. Labour raised the nomination hurdle for candidates from 5 percent of MPs to 20 percent in 1988. The Liberal Democrats increased their nomination threshold from two MPs to 10 percent of MPs in 2005. OMOV has given party members voting rights, but the opportunities to exercise these rights are more tightly controlled by MPs. A major factor in this development has been the desire of incumbent leaders to increase their own institutional security of tenure.[4]

This book analyses the effects of these changes. In particular, two main questions are addressed. First, has the use of membership ballots influenced the types of leaders that British parties choose? Second, to what extent have institutions given British party leaders security of tenure? These questions subsume a number of others that are examined in this book. Do party members choose leaders who are ideologically radical? What are the members' criteria in selecting leaders? To what extent do MPs retain control of the selection process despite membership ballots? Which types of institutions provide incumbent leaders with the greatest security of tenure and which provide the least?

This chapter sets out some of the main concepts used in this book. It begins by asking whether there are reasons for supposing that MPs and individual party members prefer different types of leaders. Next, it situates the present analysis in the context of an earlier major study of leadership contests. The following section examines politicians' incentives to evict their leaders and the final substantive section sets out the various institutional and non-institutional means by which leaders can be removed. The extent to which eviction rules make it easier or harder for intra-party actors to remove incumbent leaders is a vital question but tends to be relegated to secondary importance in many discussions of selection systems.[5] Here it is analysed in detail.

MPs, party members and ideology

When the Conservative Party allowed individual members to participate in leadership elections in 1998, some critics complained that Tory members were unrepresentative of voters as a whole and would invariably choose right-wing leaders.[6] The election of Iain Duncan Smith in the first such membership ballot in 2001 appeared to confirm these fears. Similar criticisms were expressed in the early 1980s when Labour adopted its electoral college in which party activists controlled 30 percent of the votes. The fear of the Labour right and the hope of the Labour left was that the new system would enable the left-wing former cabinet minister, Tony Benn, to become leader.[7] At the root of these beliefs was the assumption that party activists and members are politically more radical than MPs. This claim is an important one given that all of the major British parties use membership ballots. If it is true, the expectation would be that leaders elected by party members and activists will be ideologically more radical than those chosen solely by MPs.

The belief that party activists tend to be more politically radical than other party actors has a long history in political science, going back at least as far as Ostrogorski.[8] However, its most famous expression was in John May's 'special law of curvilinear disparity'.[9] May makes two main assumptions. First, party actors can be allocated to organisational positions ranging from high to low levels, with leaders at the top, voters at the bottom and activists occupying an intermediate position. Second, different types of organisational actors have different incentive structures. Leaders are office-seekers, driven by the pursuit of income, power and status that follow from winning elections and forming governments. In contrast, activists are less concerned with winning governmental office, but are instead driven by the pursuit of ideological goals. This ideological orientation is reinforced by social pressure from other activists, who co-exist in the tight-knit milieus of local party organisations, where they all regularly attend the same meetings and social events.

Activists tend to be ideologically radical, occupying the extreme flanks. However, most voters are assumed to occupy fairly centrist positions, reflecting their lack of concern for abstract ideological goals. These different preferences produce a curvilinear relationship between organisational level and ideological position on a unidimensional left-right scale. Since politicians must win the support of voters to win elections, they too prefer more centrist positions, but their dependence on activists' efforts in election campaigns ensures that they cannot ignore the demands of the latter, so they end up taking a position somewhere between activists and the party's voters. In Figure 1.1 (below), these relationships are depicted for a leftist party and a rightist party. In each case, the activists have radical preferences (L_A and R_A), the parties' voters are more centrist on average (L_V and R_V), and the parties' leaders are somewhat closer to voters than activists (L_L and R_L).

Figure 1.1 Curvilinear Disparity

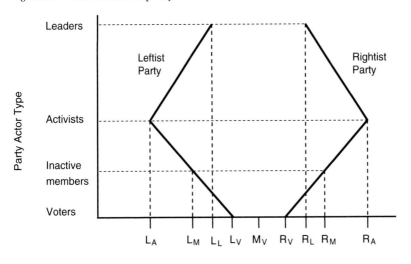

Ideological Position (Left-Right)

May's law has been criticised for being empirically inaccurate.[10] How-ever, its simplicity probably goes a long way towards explaining its durability and its frequent invocation in relation to British politics. The belief that activists were extremists was one of the underlying assumptions of Labour's early modernisation in the 1980s. Indeed, Labour modernisers believed that a major step on the way towards political moderation was to remove the right to select parliamentary candidates from small cliques of activists and extend it to all individual party members in a reform that came to be known as 'one member-one vote', or, OMOV.[11] As well as being greater in number than the activists, ordinary members were more passive, less well-organised, more likely to take direction from above, and crucially, politically more moderate. In terms of Figure 1.1, they occupy an organisational position between activists and party voters, and their preferences, although non-centrist, are not as radical as those of activists (L_M and R_M).

One of the peculiar features of May's law in its original form is that it emphasises the preferences of voters who support a given party. However, the identity of a party's average supporter is not usually of strategic interest.[12] In two-party systems, it is the median voter in the electorate at large that is strategically important to parties, since it is this voter that successful parties must capture.[13] In Figure 1.1, the median voter is at point M_V, which is considerably more centrist than any of the partisan actors. Office-seeking politicians will want to position their policies close to this point. If this argument is correct, any system of intra-party democracy that enfranchises not just activists, but even inactive party members, risks producing policies and candidates that are considerably more radical than the median voter.

Leadership selection criteria

To understand who parties choose to be their leaders, it is necessary to know *how* and *why* leaders are selected. The 'how' of leadership selection is one of the principal themes of this book and concerns institutions. It is important because institutions determine which intra-party actors, such as MPs and individual members, get to choose the leader. The 'why' of leadership selection concerns the criteria that selectors use in choosing leaders. It is connected to institutional rules to the extent that MPs and individual members may judge those criteria in different ways.

In his analysis of leadership contests in Britain up to 1994, Leonard Stark, following Gunnar Sjöblom, identified three principal goals of major parties in parliamentary systems: unity, electoral victory and policy implementation (see Table 1.1).[14] Internal unity is the first-order goal because it is a prerequisite for everything else parties do. Without unity, parties find it difficult to win elections, because voters dislike and distrust divided parties. They also struggle to agree on a coherent set of policies. If a new leader is to achieve intra-party unity, he must be broadly acceptable to the main groups and factions in his party. Thus, the primary selection criterion in leadership contests is *acceptability*. A party's second-order goal is winning elections because only then can it form a government and implement policies. Moving out of the intra-party arena into the electoral arena, the corresponding criterion for selectors choosing between rival candidates is thus their

Table 1.1   Strategic Goals and Selection Criteria in Leadership Contests

Order	Arena	Goal	Criterion
First	Internal	Unity	Acceptability
Second	Electoral	Victory	Electability
Third	Parliamentary	Policy	Competence

Source: L. P. Stark, *Choosing a Leader: Party Leadership Contests in Britain from Macmillan to Blair* (Basingstoke: Macmillan, 1996), p. 126.

electability. Finally, there is the parliamentary arena, where the third-order objective of parties, once they are unified and have won elections, is to implement policies in government. Formulating effective policies requires selectors to assess the candidates' *competence*, which is thus the third selection criterion.

Stark argues that, although the first-order goal of unity is a party's priority, it is usually an explicit consideration only in parties that are badly divided, as Labour was in the 1980s.[15] In these instances, the desire for unity trumps all other considerations. Michael Foot was deemed better able than Denis Healey to unite Labour in 1980, even though Healey was more appealing to the electorate and would have made a better prime minister.[16] Similarly, Neil Kinnock was regarded as being more likely than Roy Hattersley to unite Labour in 1983, but Hattersley was stronger in the electoral and parliamentary arenas.[17]

More often, parties are not dramatically divided and so leadership elections turn on the candidates' electability and competence. Recent leaders of British parties, including Tony Blair, David Cameron and Nick Clegg, were chosen primarily on the basis of their perceived electoral appeal, Stark's second-order criterion. Ideological extremists are not usually attractive to most voters, whereas ideological centrists are generally more appealing. However, if a candidate is regarded as the most electable while at the same time being seen as a divisive figure inside the party, he might not be chosen – such was the fate of Kenneth Clarke in the Conservative Party between 1997 and 2005. If rival candidates are seen as more or less equally electable, the decision is likely to be based on considerations of competence.

Competence is crucial, not merely in Stark's narrow sense of designing policies, but also in terms of general leadership skills. This point is most apparent when a leader is evidently *not* competent, as was frequently alleged of Iain Duncan Smith. Selectors must consider essential skills and attributes when choosing a leader. Competent leaders need, among other things: the ability to perform well in parliament; the appearance of being an effective prime minister (or an effective government minister in the case of Liberal Democrat leaders); managerial skills; and sound judgement, decisiveness and the right balance between strength and flexibility. Experience is also highlighted by those leaders who possess it, as past performance may be a guide to future performance.

Skills and attributes have consequences not only for candidates' competence but also for their perceived acceptability and electability. For example, communication skills are crucial in modern politics if leaders are to enjoy electoral success. Those with poor communication skills risk losing their parties votes as they struggle to get their message across to voters. Honesty and trustworthiness are important for electability: if leaders are dishonest and untrustworthy, electors may feel that their pre-election promises will not be honoured later. Honesty and trust-worthiness are also important for leaders to be acceptable to their parties. 'Acceptability' partly refers to candidates' political conduct. For example, politicians who are seen as disloyal to incumbent leaders may come to be seen as divisive figures who cannot unite their parties, and thereby deprived of the leadership when they seek it. Michael Portillo suffered from this perception of disloyalty to successive leaders when he ran for the Tory leadership in 2001.[18]

Ideology is usually a crucial factor underlying strategic goals and selection criteria. This point was alluded to earlier in relation to electability because radical leaders may find themselves unpopular with voters. However, ideology is normally a central consideration when selectors determine the extent to which candidates are acceptable and able to unite their party. Foot and Kinnock were seen as more acceptable than Healey and Hattersley because they were from Labour's ascendant centre-left, whereas the latter two candidates were from the weakened centre-right. Ideology was the crucial factor impeding Clarke's attempts to win the leadership of the Conservative Party: most Tory MPs and activists believed that only a Eurosceptic could unite their party, and Clarke's views were deemed divisive.[19] However, party unity can be sought in different ways. Sometimes, a compromise candidate is required for unity in order to hold the factions together. At other times, one faction is much stronger and seeks to unite the party on its own ideological terms, as with the election of the Eurosceptic Duncan Smith in the Conservative Party in 2001.

If it is the case that the ideological distribution of party actors varies according to the hierarchical level they occupy in the party, as predicated by the 'law of curvilinear disparity', then it is reasonable to expect that different types of actors will interpret selection criteria differently. That is particularly important in relation to the first-order criterion of accept-ability: if party members are ideologically more radical than MPs, they may have different opinions about what constitutes an ideologically acceptable leader. Labour's deputy-leadership election of 1981 appeared to demonstrate precisely such a split: constituency parties voted four-to-one for Benn over Healey in the second ballot, whereas MPs preferred Healey by two-to-one. Although this contest was not for the top job, there is little reason to suppose that preferences would have been different if it had been.

Ideological and organisational differences could also impact on the other two main selection criteria. It is sometimes suggested that ideologues may be less willing than moderates to trade-off principles for electoral success.[20] If so, the criterion of electability will trail a long way behind acceptability. If party members are more ideological than MPs, then they should be less likely to prioritise candidates' electability.

On the criterion of competence, MPs usually know more about candidates' managerial and leadership qualities than individual members do, because the former see the candidates at close hand on a daily basis. As Peter Shore, a former Labour leadership candidate, put it, '[y]ou can't help but know better than anyone on the outside who are the guys who've got the clout, the authority, the imagination, and the rest of it'.[21] Most party members do not observe candidates closely and so they must make judgements about their competence on other bases. These include public performances by politicians, such as speeches and interviews, and media commentary on the candidates offered by opinion formers, such as newspaper columnists. The latter may make their own judgements partly based on ideology, rather than their own close observation.

Ideology is an important factor that candidates bring to leadership contests, but it is not the only one. There are numerous qualities and characteristics that candidates possess and which may have some bearing on their chances of winning under particular systems. For example, experience is often seen as a crucial attribute in leadership contests. If candidates have enjoyed long parliamentary careers and held important senior positions in their parties or in government, they could be seen as more likely to make better leaders than those without experience. Younger candidates usually have less experience than older ones. On the other hand, younger and less-experienced candidates might be seen as fresher and more likely to provide a break with the past. Chapter 6 assesses the early evidence from OMOV contests in British parties in relation to leaders' ages on election to establish whether there is a trend towards younger leaders.

Ejecting party leaders

Party leaders leave their posts for a number of reasons. Frequently, they stand down of their own volition, particularly after an election defeat. Sometimes, they resign because of ill health and occasionally they die in office. However, the most interesting cases are leaders who are forced to stand down against their will by their parties, usually because of poor electoral performance, contentious policies or a divisive leadership style.

The means of ejection might be a confidence vote, a leadership challenge or a parliamentary coup. These cases of eviction are the focus of attention in this book.

Recent years have seen the removal or forced resignations of a number of British party leaders. These include Iain Duncan Smith (2003), Charles Kennedy (2006) and arguably Sir Menzies Campbell (2007). Before them, Margaret Thatcher (1990) and Edward Heath (1975) were also forced out. However, there have been numerous instances of under-pressure leaders who managed to survive, including Gordon Brown (2008–10), Tony Blair (2004–06) and William Hague (1999–2001). Going back further, John Major (1995), Neil Kinnock (1988), Michael Foot (1982–83) and Harold Wilson (1968–69) all survived challenges, endured talk of coups or resisted pressure to depart. All of these survivors, with the exception of Blair, held on despite their parties languishing in the polls. Clearly, there is nothing inevitable about the dispatching of underperforming leaders.

One way in which to understand the conflicting factors that intra-party opponents of leaders consider before attempting to eject them is through a cost-benefit analysis.[22] In principle, all intra-party actors can make a rough estimate of the benefits of retaining the incumbent or switching to a new leader and the costs of forcibly removing the incumbent.

Benefits of leadership change

First consider the benefits of leadership change for the leader's opponents. Models of politicians typically regard them as being driven by some combination of office and policy incentives. For Anthony Downs, politicians were purely opportunistic, being 'motivated by the desire for power, prestige, and income' that came from elected office.[23] Other accounts have incorporated politicians' policy preferences in explanations of their actions.[24] Here it is assumed that both policy and office incentives motivate politicians, whether they are would-be leaders or backbenchers. (Office incentives are usually much weaker or even non-existent for individual party members, but since they are rarely crucial in leader ejection in Britain, the present discussion focuses on politicians.) Both policy and office incentives may come into play during leadership elections and ejections.

Politicians who want to be leader stand to increase their office benefits from a successful leadership challenge or putsch because of the greater 'power, prestige and income' that the post of leader brings. Assuming that the post also enables them to exert greater influence over policy, it can increase their policy benefits too. Other politicians can increase their policy and office benefits if their party changes its leader. For example, a new leader might shift policy to a position closer to their ideal points than the current policy position. A new leader might also be more likely to offer promotion to these politicians, thereby increasing their office benefits. On the other hand, a change of leader might move policy away from some politicians' preferred positions and it might reduce their chances of patronage if they were too closely associated with the previous leader.

Sometimes, parties look to change their leaders to boost their electoral prospects. This consideration is also related to individual politicians' policy and office benefits, largely because electability improves a party's chances of entering or staying in government. For would-be leaders, the post of prime minister is much preferable to that of opposition leader. The premiership is politically more powerful and therefore offers higher policy and office benefits to a leader than does the post of leader of the opposition. The latter might offer the prospect of higher benefits if the opposition looked set to win a general election, but if it did, then presumably the incumbent leader would not be under pressure.

Other politicians stand to increase their policy and office benefits from electoral success and the access to office it provides. In government, a party can implement policy and not just talk about it as happens in opposition. Most MPs and party members prefer policies implemented by their own party to ones implemented by other parties and thus, being in government increases policy benefits for all or most MPs and members. Strong electoral performance increases politicians' office benefits over the longer term because those with marginal seats have a better chance of holding on to them. Meanwhile, those with frontbench posts accrue more power, prestige and income from holding government jobs than unpaid shadow ones.

The anticipated benefits from a change of leadership for the incumbent's opponents must be set against the chances that a challenge or putsch might not be successful. Leader eviction entails major political risks for all involved. If challengers lose leadership contests, their political careers may end up being damaged, perhaps fatally so. A defeated challenger's supporters or the participants in a defeated coup may be sacked from their current jobs, denied promotion or even deselected as parliamentary candidates. In terms of policy, a defeated challenge may give the re-elected incumbent the confidence to push policy further in the direction he prefers. Alternatively, if the incumbent is defeated by a different candidate from the one that instigated the challenge, the new leader might change policy to a position that the original plotters prefer less than the *status quo ante*.

Costs of leadership change

In addition to anticipated benefits, an incumbent leader's opponents face significant costs in trying to remove him. Forcibly ejecting a leader requires the mobilisation of wider intra-party opposition by a *rival coalition* of politicians, such as a challenger and his allies or a looser group of plotters without an agreed replacement leader. Achieving that is difficult because politicians usually have strong reasons not to become involved in such a risky enterprise as overthrowing the leader. If an attempted eviction fails, the ring-leaders may be punished by a withdrawal of patronage and backbenchers may be overlooked for promotion. The easier option is to leave the plotting to others, but if everyone thinks that way, the incumbent will be safe. It is a classic example of a collective-action problem, or free-rider problem, in which a group of individuals want the same outcome but where acting to achieve it is risky or costly for each individual. If this outcome also benefits those who do not participate in bringing it about, as is the case with a leadership change, it may be better to let others shoulder the costs. However, if all individuals decide to free-ride, no one acts to achieve the outcome and so the *status quo* is maintained.[25]

The risks facing politicians in moving against the leader ensure that the rival coalition faces significant information and mobilisation costs in an attempted eviction. Time and effort must be expended by leadership challengers or coup plotters in mobilising their parliamentary colleagues. However, politicians will be wary of joining a venture that could harm their careers if it goes wrong. They will normally need to be convinced that others will join in too, as there is greater safety in numbers. That is not easy, as many politicians may be cautious in revealing their true opinions lest the leader's allies find out. The rival coalition will have to expend more time and effort discovering the opinions of colleagues. It may also need to work in conditions of secrecy, but that will slow down and hinder the attempt to mobilise against the leader.

Institutions affect the size of these costs: there may be a minimum number of MPs that must call for a confidence vote or to nominate a candidate to instigate a leadership challenge. The higher these hurdles are, the greater the mobilisation costs to the rival coalition. Institutions that force the rebels to identify themselves in non-secret ballots entail higher costs than those that permit secrecy. The costs of mobilising opponents can be reduced if the rival coalition has strong leadership, e.g. a candidate around whom to rally or a 'plotter-in-chief' who does not want the top job but has the desire to see a change of leadership and the skills to organise a revolt.

In most circumstances, it is likely to be more difficult – and therefore costlier – to eject a prime minister than an opposition leader. The authority and importance of the post ensure that an attempt to remove a prime minister is never taken lightly. Prime ministers need to take important decisions every day and even their opponents may decide that it is better to leave them in post rather than risk leaving the country effectively leaderless for the duration of a leadership contest. It may, therefore, be harder to mobilise MPs to move against him. Opposition leaders do not have the same gravitas as prime ministers and so the costs to the rival coalition of mobilising against him are likely to be lower.

In some circumstances, however, the mobilisation costs of evicting a prime minister may be lower. An important factor that can encourage MPs to rebel against an unpopular leader is the fear of losing their parliamentary seats at the next election unless there is a change at the top. In normal circumstances, governing parties tend to be at risk of losing more seats than opposition parties do, unless the opposition has become even more unpopular than it was at the previous election. Otherwise, even a poor poll rating might not necessarily point to a loss of seats for an opposition party, even if it does portend another election defeat. Poorly-performing governing parties, in contrast, could have scores of MPs fearing for their seats, and they may be more amenable to a leadership change that saves them.

In addition to mobilisation costs for individual members of a rival coalition, leadership ejection entails 'party costs', which are collectively borne by the party. Three types of party costs are particularly important. *Disunity costs* arise from rival factions or candidates publicly attacking each other and damaging the party's public image. It is conventional wisdom in British politics that voters punish divided parties. *Decision costs* are opportunity costs arising from the time and effort diverted from governing, devising policies or attacking opposing parties while the party is engaged in a leadership ejection and/or election. Decision costs are especially high for parties in government because a lengthy leadership election may distract the government from pressing economic or international problems.[26] There are also *financial costs* in running a contest to replace the evicted incumbent. Usually, these are not a major consideration, although all-member ballots can be expensive for financially constrained parties. Party costs are an inevitable feature of leadership contests, and although they are unavoidable in contests for vacant posts, they may be seen as an unnecessary infliction on the party when there is an incumbent who wants to remain in post. Consequently, MPs and other intra-party actors are harder to mobilise for evictions than they are in contests for vacant posts.

A final type of cost worth considering is 'legitimacy costs'. Leaders who have been elected enjoy legitimacy from that very fact and it is stronger the nearer in time the contest was. Incumbent leaders can appeal to this source of legitimacy in order to shore up their positions: Duncan Smith repeatedly made such appeals when he was under pressure from his MPs in 2002 and 2003. Some commentators have argued that membership ballots, by endowing leaders with greater legitimacy, offer them enhanced protection from internal challenges.[27]

The scale of the risks and costs involved in a leadership challenge or putsch frequently ensure that revolts against an incumbent leader stall or do not progress beyond grumbling. Whether it is because of the difficulties of mobilising opposition or the uncertainty of who will replace an ejected leader, party actors regularly calculate that they would be better off sticking with the incumbent, for all his faults. Nevertheless, parties do sometimes attempt to remove leaders who have outstayed their welcome. The following section applies the cost-benefit schema sketched above to different types of leader-eviction methods.

Leader-eviction methods

Methods of ejecting party leaders can be divided into two main types: institutional and non-institutional. The former entail the use of parties' formal leadership-eviction rules. The precise methods by which leaders can be institutionally evicted vary between parties, but certain generic mechanisms are commonly found. Table 1.2 shows the main eviction institutions currently in use in the major British parties. The two main institutions are formal leadership challenges and confidence votes. Non-institutional methods of eviction entail intra-party actors, usually MPs, withdrawing their support from the leader and forcing his resignation.

Leadership challenges

Formal leadership challenges entail a rival candidate putting his name forward and running in a competitive leadership election against the incumbent leader. Usually, certain nomination thresholds must be passed and it is common for other conditions to be set. In the Labour Party, challengers must be publicly nominated by 20 percent of the Parliamentary Labour Party (PLP). The '20 percent rule' was introduced in 1988 to prevent left-wingers making frivolous but damaging challenges to Kinnock: previously, the threshold was only 5 percent. Contests must occur annually when Labour is in opposition, although full contests take place only if a rival candidate is willing to put his name forward and

Table 1.2   Institutional Mechanisms for Removing Leaders in British Parties

	Labour	Conservative	Liberal Democrat
Method	Leadership challenge	Confidence vote	Leadership challenge and/or confidence vote
Trigger	Challenger collects nominations of 20% of Labour MPs (identities revealed)	Vote called for by leader or by 15% of Tory MPs (identities concealed) in writing to chairman of 1922 committee	Contest takes place if: leader calls one; 75 local parties write to president calling for one; no contest held within a year of last general election (unless Lib Dems in govt); or leader loses confidence motion by majority of all Lib Dem MPs
Timing	Annual vote by electoral college at autumn party conference (subject to majority vote by conference to affirm principle of a contest when Labour in govt)	Can take place at any time but if leader wins vote, s/he cannot face another vote for at least a year	Any time, but at least once per parliament (except when Lib Dems in govt)
Eviction requirement	Majority of votes for challenger in electoral college (alternative vote)	Leader evicted by majority of those voting in secret confidence ballot. S/he cannot stand in subsequent leadership election	Majority of votes for challenger in OMOV ballot (alternative vote)

secure sufficient nominations, otherwise the incumbent is re-elected unopposed. In government, contests take place only if requested by a majority on a card vote at Labour's annual conference, and again, a full contest occurs only if there is a rival candidate who has accepted the nomination and passed the threshold.[28]

In the Conservative Party, direct challenges to incumbents are no longer possible, with confidence votes used instead. However, under their old system of parliamentary ballots, the Conservatives had provisions for leadership challenges between 1975 and 1998. Contests took place annually, provided a candidate secured the nominations of two MPs, although between 1991 and 1998, a contest was triggered only if 10 percent of Tory MPs demanded one by writing to the chairman of the backbench 1922 committee.[29] Thatcher forced Heath's resignation after one such challenge in 1975, while Thatcher herself resigned after she was challenged by Michael Heseltine in 1990.

The Liberal Democrats do not enable their MPs to instigate a leadership challenge to an incumbent. However, there are various means by which a contest can be started, including the incumbent himself calling one, the incumbent losing a confidence vote among Liberal Democrat MPs, or 75 local parties writing to the president of the party to demand a contest. A contest must also take place within a year of the previous general election when the party is in opposition. Once a contest has been triggered, any MP can enter it provided that he secures the nominations of 10 percent of Liberal Democrat MPs (raised from two MPs in 2005).

One of the striking things about formal party leadership challenges in Britain is their rarity. Between 1960 and 2010, 88 candidacies were launched by 67 individual politicians in elections for the position of party leader in the Labour, Conservative, Liberal, SDP and Liberal Democrat parties (Table 1.3). Only eight of these candidacies were direct challenges to incumbents: three in the Labour Party (Wilson in 1960, Greenwood in 1961 and Benn in 1988), and five in the Conservative Party (Thatcher and Fraser in 1975, Meyer in 1989, Heseltine in 1990 and Redwood in 1995[30]). (Full details of these leadership elections are in Appendices A–C.) None of the Labour challengers was successful. Of the Conservatives, only Thatcher was successful, although Heseltine achieved the second-order goal of removing the incumbent while failing to win himself. The historical record does not offer much encouragement to politicians eager to seize the crown through regicide.

It is also noteworthy that only 13 politicians who had failed in earlier leadership bids tried again in later contests: six Labourites, four Conservatives, two Liberal Democrats, and one Social Democrat.[31] Only five were successful second time around: three in the Labour Party (Wilson, Callaghan and Foot), one in the Conservative Party (Howard) and one in the SDP (Owen). The latter two won their respective contests unchallenged. Of these five first-time losers who achieved later success, four had initially lost in contests for vacant positions. Only Wilson won after an unsuccessful earlier *challenge* to an incumbent leader and even in his case, Stark reports Wilson's political secretary, Marcia Falkender, as saying that he never expected to get a second chance.[32] Very few politicians directly challenge incumbents, and few manage to come back after a defeat,

Table 1.3 Leadership Candidacies and Challenges in UK Parties 1960–2010

	Candidacies			Challengers		Successful challengers	
Labour	34	1960: 2 1961: 2 1963: 3 1976: 6 1980: 4 1983: 4	1988: 2 1992: 2 1994: 3 2007: 1 2010: 5	3	1960: 1 1961: 1 1988: 1	0	
Conservative	33	1965: 3 1975: 7 1989: 2 1990: 4 1995: 2	1997: 5 2001: 5 2003: 1 2005: 4	5	1975: 2 1989: 1 1990: 1 1995: 1	1	1975: 1
Liberal Democrat	12	1988: 2 1999: 5	2006: 3 2007: 2	0		0	
Liberal	5	1967: 3	1976: 2	0		0	
SDP	4	1982: 2 1983: 1	1987: 1	0		0	
Total	88			8		1	

Notes: Conservative candidacies in the 'magic circle' in 1963 excluded. Figures include those who stood as the only candidate (SDP 1983 and 1987, Conservatives 2003 and Labour 2007) but exclude interim leaders and unchallenged incumbents facing annual re-election.

even in contests for vacancies. It is not much of an endorsement in a leadership contest if a candidate has lost in the past.[33] This point stands in contrast to the widespread view that candidates can 'lay down markers' in contests they do not expect to win in order to boost their credentials in the future. In reality, the decision to run for the leadership of a political party is very risky and the decision to challenge an incumbent is riskier still.

Challenges are rare because the benefits for challengers are uncertain and the costs of mobilising potential allies very high. Although great rewards of 'power, prestige and income' are available if a challenger wins a contest, the probability of doing so is significantly lowered when the incumbent leader participates. First, there is always likely to be residual loyalty to a party leader. Each loyal vote for the incumbent is a vote that is not available to a challenger. Second, politicians who directly challenge incumbents may come to be seen as disloyal and divisive figures, ill-placed to demand loyalty from others and thereby less likely to deliver party unity. Heseltine suffered from this perception when he challenged Thatcher in 1990.[34] Third, a candidate's credibility would be greatly enhanced if he could secure the backing of his senior colleagues. However, that backing would be less likely to be forthcoming in a challenge to an incumbent, not least because potential supporters would fear the consequences of backing an unsuccessful challenge, including the potential termination of their own frontbench careers. If the party were in government, the convention of collective responsibility would normally require senior politicians to resign their frontbench positions before backing a challenger. Furthermore, challengers always risk letting one of their rivals take the prize: one of the reasons Wilson was never challenged in the late-1960s was that Roy Jenkins and James Callaghan were each worried they might let in the other. For these reasons, an incumbent's rivals for the leadership usually prefer not to make direct challenges.

The costs of organising challenges are increased by high nomination thresholds to instigate a contest. Labour's 20 percent nomination rule has prevented any formal challenges from occurring since the adoption of the rule (there was one leadership challenge under the previous 5 percent threshold). Mobilisation costs are also increased by restrictions on the timing of leadership elections: if there is only one point in the calendar when a challenge is permitted, as in the Labour Party and as was the case in the Conservative Party before 1998, the leader's opponents must mobilise at that particular moment, which might not necessarily be the ideal time.

Leadership challenges fuse together two separate processes: evicting the incumbent and choosing his successor. That can increase mobilisation costs for potential candidates: loyalty to the incumbent and the risks in being seen to rally to a rival make it harder for a challenger to win support. Moreover, the challenger himself, by playing the role of 'assassin', can come to appear as deceitful and untrustworthy, a perception that will make it more difficult for him to secure support. Would-be leaders can reduce these risks if a 'stalking-horse' candidate first challenges the incumbent in order to force his resignation. If that attempt is successful, then other candidates can enter the contest for the now vacant post free of accusations of disloyalty. That will reduce the costs of winning round potential supporters. The Conservatives' system of parliamentary ballots before 1998 enabled such manoeuvres by requiring the incumbent to win a super-majority in the first ballot and by enabling the entry of new candidates in the second ballot. This system effectively separated the processes of leader eviction (first ballot) and replacement (second and third ballots). In contrast, Labour's parliamentary ballots required all candidates to enter in the first round, although it was possible for a stalking horse to damage the incumbent.

Party costs in membership ballots can be dissuasive factors in removing a leader. Decision costs are high: OMOV contests usually take two or three months to complete, during which time the party is distracted from the process of governing or opposing the government. The leader's opponents may need to look for ways of speeding up the process, such as agreeing on a single candidate and thereby obviating the need for a ballot, as the Tories did in 2003 (see Chapter 4). If a contest is bitter, disunity costs will be high and persist over a long period. Financial costs can also be a problem in OMOV systems for financially-constrained parties.

Confidence votes

Some parties make provisions for formal *confidence votes* in the leader, with voting rights usually restricted to MPs. In the Conservative Party, the leader can call a confidence vote or one can be instigated by a formal written request to the chairman of the backbench 1922 committee by 15 percent of Tory MPs (whose names are not publicly revealed). If a vote is triggered, the leader needs to achieve a bare majority in a secret ballot of Tory MPs. If he loses, a leadership election is triggered, and the defeated leader is not permitted to participate.[35] The Liberal Democrats also make provisions for confidence votes: if a majority of all Liberal Democrat MPs passes a motion of no confidence in the leader, a leadership election is triggered.[36] The defeated leader is permitted to stand for re-election, although there would probably be serious doubts about his participation. Labour does not make provisions for confidence votes in its leader.

Where a confidence-vote mechanism does exist, the incumbents' opponents do not immediately need to identify a replacement leader or challenger. Eviction and election of a new leader are sequentially separate stages. The absence of the need to name a challenger reduces the risks for potential replacement leaders because they do not have to play the role of assassin. It is also possible for rival factions to collude in a confidence vote to remove the incumbent before backing their own candidates to replace him in the next stage. On the other hand, if there are deep divisions over who should take over, some opponents of the incumbent may prefer to keep him in post for fear of getting someone even worse.

A key issue is the threshold for instigating a confidence vote. The 15 percent threshold in the Conservative Party is easier to achieve than

Labour's 20 percent rule for nominations, partly because it is 5 percent lower but also because Labour's threshold applies to each individual candidate who wishes to enter a contest rather than to the principle of a vote. Also important is whether those demanding a vote can retain their anonymity: the Conservative process promises anonymity although presumably some MPs would remain worried that their names might leak out. In contrast, those nominating a challenger in the Labour Party have their identities revealed. That can be a strongly dissuasive factor for many would-be rebels and consequently it increases the costs to the plotters of mobilising wider opposition.

Frontbench coups

A further means of leader eviction relies not on institutions, but on political pressure on the incumbent to go. In these cases, the intention of those moving against the leader is to force his resignation rather than instigate a formal challenge or a confidence vote. In some cases, eviction institutions might not even exist, making other means necessary. Leadership challenges were not possible in the Conservative Party until 1975 and Labour had no provisions for challenges to prime ministers until the formation of the electoral college in 1981. There are two general ways in which parties can seek to remove incumbent leaders against their will when eviction institutions are either not available or hard to set in motion: frontbench coups and backbench rebellions.[37] Each involves a show of strength from the leader's opponents and a threat publicly to withdraw their confidence unless he voluntarily stands aside.

Frontbench coups involve a delegation of 'men in grey suits' visiting the leader and informing him that he must go. Without the confidence of his senior colleagues, particularly his (shadow) cabinet members, a leader's authority is badly damaged and it becomes extremely difficult for him to continue. Occasionally, junior frontbenchers, perhaps acting in collusion with more senior colleagues, might take the lead: in 2006, a parliamentary under-secretary of state and seven private parliamentary secretaries resigned from the Labour government and called on Blair to depart in what the deputy prime minister, John Prescott, reportedly called a 'corporals' coup'.[38] However, there are significant obstacles to front-bench coups, in particular, the difficulty of organising collective action among career-conscious frontbenchers and the incumbent leader's power of patronage. To see the advantage that an incumbent leader enjoys in relation to other senior politicians, consider three different distributions of power inside the (shadow) cabinet.

First, there is the case of the *dominant leader* with no obvious rivals for his or her position, such as Thatcher for much of her time as prime minister.[39] The greatest power a leader possesses is that of patronage, which he can use to manoeuvre ideological allies into the key positions within the (shadow) cabinet. There may be some 'big beasts' whose political abilities or ideological following in the wider party demand inclusion at the top table. However, these can usually be constrained if they are surrounded by loyalists.

A second scenario is that the (shadow) cabinet contains a clear *heir apparent*, a leader-in-waiting who has no rivals to replace the incumbent when the latter finally goes. The heir apparent may be the accepted successor of the incumbent, as Eden was of Churchill, or the incumbent may be less enthusiastic about him, as Blair seemingly was of Brown. Either way, the presence of an heir apparent can be advantageous for the incumbent. An heir apparent may be more prepared to bide his time, knowing that the prize is almost certain to come his way regardless. The alternative is to try to grab power more quickly but at the risk of losing the crown altogether in a rash and petulant coup attempt that leaves him looking disloyal. Leaders can also use reshuffles to break up alliances that currently favour the heir apparent and promote loyalists to check his power.[40]

A third situation is the existence in the (shadow) cabinet of *rival 'crown princes'*. These are powerful figures who vie with each other to succeed the incumbent. The Wilson government in the 1960s contained several crown princes at different times: George Brown versus James Callaghan, and later Roy Jenkins versus James Callaghan. Anthony Crosland and Denis Healey were also potential leaders. Wilson believed that the existence of rival crown princes was advantageous to him because their clashing ambitions ensured that they held each other in check.[41] A crown prince sees higher office and policy benefits from his own leadership than from the incumbent's, but he also usually prefers life under the incumbent than under a rival crown prince should the latter become leader. A crown prince who is defeated for the leadership by another crown prince will probably assume that his chances of ever taking the top job have been killed off. Consequently, there is usually a low probability that they will join forces to overthrow the incumbent in a coup.

Collective-action problems among (shadow) cabinet members thus help to protect the incumbent leader. Rival crown princes are afraid of handing the prize to each other, while more junior figures may prefer to let others take the risks in confronting the leader. As David Miliband reportedly complained to Peter Mandelson during one of Gordon Brown's leadership crises, '[t]here's a lot of "After you, Claude" going on'.[42] The alternative to collective action is individual action in the form of resignations from the frontbench. These resignations can normally, although not always, be shrugged off.[43] Brown was able to survive the resignation of James Purnell after poor local-election results in 2009. On the other hand, Thatcher was badly wounded by Geoffrey Howe's resignation in 1990, an event that eventually led to her own downfall.

It is frequently argued that, for a frontbench coup to be successful, it requires unanimity among senior (shadow) cabinet members on who should replace the incumbent.[44] Wilson's internal enemies believed that the main reason they failed to remove him was that there were rival claims to succeed him and none of these crown princes would support each other, whereas had they combined forces, it would have been impossible for Wilson to survive.[45] Perhaps the best chance for a frontbench coup to succeed is for all but one of these senior figures to have no leadership ambitions of their own, and therefore no clashing ambitions to take into account. However, it is rarely the case that most of the senior figures are unambitious for the top job and those that are may find short-term loyalty expedient. Enoch Powell's verdict on Harold Macmillan's premiership is of more general applicability:

> You lose the public, you lose the press, you lose the party in the House, but the men whose heads you can cut off before breakfast you lose last. The most difficult operation there is is for a Cabinet itself to depose a Prime Minister.[46]

Backbench revolts

Whereas frontbench coups rely on the *quality* of their personnel, backbench rebellions rest on the *quantity* of their participants. They entail backbenchers demonstrating the breadth of opposition to the incumbent in the hope of forcing his resignation. If a leader is seen not to be able to carry a large section of his own party, then his authority will be badly damaged. The principal question for the plotters, therefore, concerns how to demonstrate the breadth of opposition. Over the years, a number of methods have been used. At the lower end of the scale are grumbles by individual MPs to journalists, rising to more important forms, such as hostile speeches and individual calls for the leader to resign. More important still are rebellious votes in parliament, particularly if they involve large numbers of MPs. However, by far the most dangerous development for an under-pressure leader is when groups of critical backbenchers coalesce to demand that the leader steps down. If there are no formal mechanisms to instigate votes or there are mechanisms but they are difficult to set in motion, backbenchers must find other ways to advertise their numbers. One is to organise round-robin letters, as happened in the Labour Party against Attlee in 1947 and Wilson in 1968 and 1969.[47] A round-robin might just be designed as a show of strength but in the case of Wilson in 1969, it was the prelude to an attempt to call a party meeting to discuss the leadership issue and – the rebels hoped – end in a confidence vote.

Mobilising the incumbent's opponents in sufficient numbers presents a rival coalition with a significant collective-action problem but some MPs may be more likely plotters than others. Many backbenchers may hold out hope of one day being promoted to the frontbench. They will normally be wary of causing trouble for the leader lest it damage their chances of promotion. However, there are other backbenchers for whom promotion is less of an issue. In their analysis of backbench legislative revolts, Giacomo Benedetto and Simon Hix identify three types of potential backbench rebel: 'the rejected, the ejected and the dejected'.[48] The 'ejected' are former ministers; the 'rejected' are backbenchers who have given up all hope of being promoted to the frontbench; and the 'dejected' are normally ideological radicals who never expected to be promoted. In all three cases, office incentives are weak and therefore rebellious behaviour against the leadership more likely to occur, other things being equal, because it is harder or unpalatable to buy them off with future job offers. Some might still be swayed by the possibility of elevation to the House of Lords, but many would not be. The risks are lower for those with less to lose. That is not to say there are no risks: there remains the possibility of being deselected by their local parties, but the denial of promotion undoubtedly weakens the leader's ability to use his patronage powers to influence his critics.

One of the problems with backbench rebellions is that they often lack organisation. That was evident in the plots against Brown and the ones against Duncan Smith in the Conservative Party. It is hard for disparate rebels to coordinate their actions. One way in which this task can be made easier is by having some form of leadership, to bring order and direction to the attempted eviction. If the rebellion consists of a leadership challenge to the incumbent, then the leader of the plot will be the challenger himself. If, however, the plot consists of an attempt to instigate a confidence vote or to put pressure on the incumbent to force his resignation, there might not be an obvious plot leader. The major parties usually have certain important figures sitting on their backbenches, such as former ministers. The most senior of these may have the authority to offer such leadership. Alternatively, backbench plots can be assisted by the presence of former whips within their ranks. Whips learn the importance of collecting information in order to head off trouble for the leader. Former whips working against the leader can use these skills in reverse, discovering and organising rebels while frustrating attempts by the leader's allies to obtain information about the plotters.[49] Wherever leadership comes from, it can assist unorganised plotters in reducing their mobilisation costs. Without leadership, those costs are higher.

Conclusion

The reform of selection and eviction rules in the major British parties offers a chance to gauge the effects of institutions on the recruitment and survival of party leaders. There are two key ways in which institutions may matter: (1) the potential for individual members to use different selection criteria than MPs use; (2) the effect of eviction rules on leaders' security of tenure. The fact that political parties periodically revise their selection systems and even replace them altogether suggests that many politicians believe that institutions do matter. It is the purpose of this study to assess the evidence from recent OMOV contests to establish whether institutional change has been important. The answers will be provisional: there are a limited number of cases to examine and there is always a risk in drawing general conclusions from what might turn out to be unusual events. Nevertheless, the analysis of Stark demonstrated that a simple hierarchy of selection criteria went a long way to explaining outcomes in contests between 1963 and 1995. Those sections of this book that examine selection contests are in many respects an extension of Stark's study.

The remaining sections on leadership eviction are part of the different but equally important question of whether institutions are significant in the saving or dispatching of under-pressure leaders. It may be the case that the most important thing for a leader is to retain the confidence of his parliamentary colleagues, with institutional rules of secondary significance.[50] However, the fact, once again, that all three major parties have tightened their rules on challenging incumbents indicates that leaders believe that institutions have at least some effect on their security of tenure. This book explores this vital question and looks at what happens when institutional eviction is either unfeasible or impossible. Before turning to the various forms of membership participation, it is necessary to examine briefly the previous dominant type of system in British parties, in which MPs selected and ejected leaders.

2
Selection and Ejection by the Parliamentary Party

The use of parliamentary ballots to select, and sometimes to evict, party leaders had a long history in British parties, although not quite as long as commonly supposed. Labour used parliamentary ballots to select its leaders from the party's formation in 1900, although until 1922 leaders were called chairmen and typically served for only a year or two. The system remained in place until the formation of the electoral college in 1981. The Conservatives did not adopt parliamentary ballots for leadership selection until 1965, before which Tory leaders 'emerged' during confidential discussions among party elites. The party switched to a hybrid parliamentary-membership ballot system in 1998. The Liberal Party used a variety of means to choose its leaders but only once, in 1967, was a parliamentary ballot used in a contested election. In 1976, the party adopted a form of one member-one vote (OMOV). The Liberal Democrats have never used parliamentary ballots.

This chapter examines the use of parliamentary ballots to select and remove leaders in British parties. Such ballots are not the main focus of this book but they were the system used in all the parties before the adoption of membership ballots. It is, therefore, worthwhile exploring their operation and consequences in relation to the two main areas of interest in this study: the election of leaders (and the criteria by which they are chosen) and the removal of leaders who have outstayed their welcome.

The chapter begins by setting out the main rules that governed contests in the different parties and describes their use in leadership contests over the years. The following section undertakes a case study of the 1997 Conservative leadership election to illustrate the nature of contests in parliamentary-ballot systems and to illustrate the criteria that MPs used to choose their leaders. It will be recalled that Stark argued that candidates' acceptability, electability and competence were foremost in selectors' minds and this case study offers support to that view.

The final part of the chapter examines leader-ejection by MPs. The most famous instance of a leader being removed by MPs is Margaret Thatcher in 1990 and this case is analysed. It is argued that the nature of the Conservatives' eviction institutions was a major factor in Thatcher's demise, a point made by comparing her case with that of Harold Wilson, who survived similar threats and traumas in the Labour Party in 1968–69, partly because there were no institutions available to his opponents to remove him. This discussion is an important reference point for the remainder of the book because, despite the subsequent shift to various forms of OMOV, all of the parties largely left leader-eviction in the hands of their MPs.

Leader selection and ejection by MPs

The shift to membership ballots and electoral colleges for leadership elections in British parties was usually opposed by some in those parties on the basis that parliamentary ballots were a superior system. Supporters of selection by MPs have pointed to a number of advantages of the system. First, MPs are more likely than party members and voters to know the candidates well, given that the latter are themselves MPs. In theory, that should give MPs better insights into the candidates' characters and leadership qualities. Most Conservative MPs wanted to return to parliamentary ballots when the OMOV system was being reassessed in 2005 in order to prevent individual members imposing another poor-quality leader on them.[1] Second, following the 'law of curvilinear disparity', it is sometimes suggested that MPs are more likely than members to choose ideologically 'moderate' leaders because MPs are more mindful of electoral success. That was the feeling among centrist Labour MPs in the 1980s.[2] However, it was Labour MPs who chose the left-wing Foot over the centrist Healey in 1980 and Tory MPs preferred the right-wing Thatcher in 1975. Conversely, individual Labour members joined trade unionists and MPs in choosing their party's most centrist leader, Blair, in 1994.

A third advantage often claimed for selection by MPs is procedural. Parliamentary ballots are quick, cheap and easy to organise, compared with membership ballots, which are necessarily time-consuming, expensive and logistically complicated. Parliamentary ballots can thus entail lower 'party costs' than membership ballots. A consultation paper issued by the Conservative Party's management board in 2005 recommended replacing the OMOV system because it was 'expensive and protracted, causing maximum uncertainty and disruption'. To overcome these problems, the board wanted a return to parliamentary ballots.[3]

There are many different ways of running parliamentary ballots, with systems varying over such factors as nomination thresholds, secret or non-secret ballots, categorical or preferential voting, simple- or super-majorities, first- or later-ballot entry of new candidates, and the existence or otherwise of provisions to challenge incumbents. These differences, and their consequences, can be gleaned by looking at each of the main parties in turn.

Labour Party

Labour's system of parliamentary ballots for leadership elections was relatively simple. When the party was in opposition, there would be a leadership contest every year in the autumn, provided that a candidate came forward to challenge the incumbent. That was rarely the case: challenges occurred in 1922, 1960 and 1961. There were no provisions for leadership contests when the party was in government, because of the need for governmental stability. However, when Wilson resigned as prime minister and Labour leader in 1976, the party had to organise a leadership contest and used the same rules that it deployed in opposition. Each candidate, who had to be an MP, required a proposer and a seconder, who also had to be MPs and whose identities were made public. All properly nominated candidates entered a series of eliminative secret ballots among Labour MPs. Selectors could vote for one candidate only and the winner needed to secure a majority of votes cast. If no one managed to achieve a majority, the candidate with the fewest votes was eliminated, with the other candidates going through to the next round. If the last two candidates' combined votes were less than the third-to-last candidate, both would be eliminated. The process continued until one candidate secured a majority. Candidates could withdraw at any moment but all had to join the contest from the start, with no provisions for new candidates to enter later ballots.[4]

Labour first used parliamentary ballots to select its leaders, or chairmen as they were initially called, in 1906, when it increased its number of MPs from two to 29. The fact that the party had chairmen rather than leaders was largely a reflection of the suspicion of socialists and trade unionists of the entire notion of leadership. However in 1922, Labour overtook the divided Liberals and became the second major party in British politics. In the process, Labour formed the official opposition to the Conservative government and was required to choose a leader of the opposition. In a ballot of Labour MPs, the existing chairman, J. R. Clynes, was defeated by Ramsay MacDonald, who mobilised support among the large intake of new Labour MPs to become the party's first formal leader.[5]

Although Labour formed two minority governments in the 1920s, it was not until after the Second World War that it became a major contender for government. The party's first leadership election in the post-war era was held in 1955 when the former prime minister, Clement Attlee retired. Hugh Gaitskell won the contest to succeed him, convincingly defeating Aneurin Bevan and Herbert Morrison. Gaitskell's time as leader was marked by division and controversy, with factional conflict between his own centre-right 'Gaitskellite' grouping and the left-wing 'Bevanites'. Gaitskell openly refused to accept a decision by Labour's annual conference in 1960 to commit the party to a policy of unilateral nuclear disarmament.[6] His actions prompted Anthony Greenwood to resign from the shadow cabinet to challenge Gaitskell, but he stood aside after Harold Wilson announced that he would run for the leadership. Gaitskell won convincingly but party divisions were not healed (Greenwood challenged him in 1961, though again, Gaitskell won easily). Wilson could have damaged his chances of ever becoming leader, but Gaitskell's death in 1963 offered him the chance to present himself as someone who could unite the party's left and right factions.[7] Wilson won the contest, defeating George Brown and James Callaghan, becoming the first and still the only British politician from a major party to have lost a formal leadership challenge to a sitting leader and returned at a later date to win the prize.

Wilson led Labour for 13 years and won four general elections, although only one with a convincing parliamentary majority. He served as prime minister twice, from 1964–70 and 1974–76. The later years of his first spell were marked by seemingly incessant plots by his colleagues to unseat him, as his government grappled with Britain's economic problems (see below). His second spell ended in 1976 when he unexpectedly announced his resignation. As noted earlier, there were no official rules for leadership contests when Labour was in government. However, at a PLP meeting, Labour MPs decided to stick with the system of exhaustive parliamentary ballots, despite some criticism from the left. A large field of six candidates, all cabinet ministers, representing left and right battled for the leadership and the premiership. An inconclusive first ballot saw the centre-left Michael Foot and the centre-right Callaghan finish far ahead of the other four candidates. Subsequently, the left-leaning Tony Benn and the centre-right Tony Crosland and Roy Jenkins all withdrew from the contest. Foot and Callaghan were joined in the second ballot by Denis Healey. Healey was then eliminated and Callaghan overtook Foot to top the second ballot before winning the final ballot by 176 votes to 137.[8]

The final contest in which Labour MPs had the exclusive right to choose their leader took place in 1980. The previous year, Labour under Callaghan had lost the general election and gone into opposition. The activist left, assisted by allies in the trade unions, were in the process of introducing reforms to Labour's constitution to bring MPs under the control of the party outside of parliament. A decision had been reached at the party conference in September 1980 to create an electoral college, but a special conference was called for January 1981 to determine the precise weightings between the different sections (see Chapter 3). Callaghan resigned in this period between the two conferences, ensuring that the leadership election would take place under the old system of parliamentary ballots, much to the anger of the left.[9]

The left's standard bearer, Benn, refused to contest the election, claiming it was illegitimate. However, the centre-left Foot decided to enter and he was joined by Peter Shore and John Silken, two other figures from the centre-left of the party. The only candidate from Labour's centre-right was Healey. Opinion polls indicated that Labour voters preferred Healey, whereas activists largely supported Foot. The first ballot saw Healey come top with 112 votes out of 265 cast, with Foot second on 83. Both Silkin (38) and Shore (32) were eliminated and each encouraged his supporters to switch to Foot in the second ballot. This appeal was successful, as Foot came from behind to beat Healey by 139 votes to 129.[10]

Conservative Party

Before their adoption of parliamentary ballots in 1965, the Conservatives had no codified procedures for choosing their leaders. This state of affairs was in part a reflection of the party having no *de jure* party leader: there were distinct leaderships in the House of Commons and the House of Lords, although it was usually the leader in the Commons who assumed the role of party leader. It was also in part a reflection of the tendency for leadership successions to occur when the party was in government. As it is the monarch's constitutional duty to appoint the British prime minister, the Conservative practice was traditionally to undertake a series of confidential discussions among party elites, known as 'the magic circle', to settle on a name to recommend to the monarch. Once this individual was appointed as prime minister, he was then usually acclaimed as leader. Balfour, Baldwin, Neville Chamberlain, Eden, Macmillan and Douglas-Home all became leader in this way.[11] When the Conservatives returned to opposition, the former prime minister usually continued to be regarded as party leader. If he retired, was forced out or died in office, a new figure would be selected as the leader of Conservative MPs.

The 'magic circle' came into disrepute after Alec Douglas-Home was surprisingly chosen to replace Macmillan as Tory leader and prime minister in 1963.[12] Douglas-Home's aristocratic image and the lack of transparency in his selection jarred with a more modern and less deferential age. When the Conservatives lost the 1964 general election, Douglas-Home asked the party chairman to look into ways of reforming the selection system. It was agreed by the committee examining reforms that any new system should give a predominant voice to Conservative MPs, be quick to operate and produce a definitive winner.[13]

The committee eventually recommended, and the party accepted, a system of parliamentary ballots. However, it differed from Labour's system in a number of ways. Although it was envisaged that the winner would emerge from a series of ballots, different rules applied to victory thresholds, instigation of, and entry into, a contest in different rounds of voting. In the first ballot, a candidate needed to win a majority of those voting and hold a 15 percent lead over his nearest rival. One intention was to determine whether a candidate could command broad support in the party. If no candidate could attain this margin, a second ballot would be called, in which the winner would need only a majority of votes cast. However, unusually, all candidates from the first ballot could participate and they could be joined by new candidates. The rationale was that it would be possible for compromise candidates to emerge. If a third ballot were needed, it would be confined to the top three candidates, with no new candidates permitted to enter. Although it was not formally specified that voting was by secret ballot, that is how the first contest in the system was run and the practice was formalised in 1975.[14] Crucially, the original rules did not make provisions for regular elections, with contests occurring whenever a leadership vacancy arose through the resignation, incapacity or death of the incumbent.[15]

The first contest to be conducted under the new rules was in 1965, when Edward Heath defeated Reginald Maudling and Enoch Powell. Heath led Maudling by 150 votes to 133 in the first ballot, with Powell a long way behind on 15. Heath did not enjoy a 15 percent lead but Maudling and Powell both withdrew and no new candidates entered. A second ballot was not required. Heath would serve as Conservative leader for almost ten years, winning one general election but losing three, including two in 1974. Those latter defeats weakened his position in the party. His critics successfully pushed for a reform of the selection system in 1975 to enable challenges to incumbent leaders.[16] Provided that a challenger came forward, there would be an annual election, which would take place in the first four weeks of a new session of parliament or the first six months of a new parliament. Annual elections applied whether the party was in government or opposition. Candidates would require the nominations of two MPs, whose identities would not be revealed. It was also decided that candidates' vote shares would be calculated on the basis of eligible voters rather than votes cast. This move was widely interpreted as an attempt by Heath's opponents to make his re-election more difficult, as abstentions would effectively be votes against him in the first ballot and thus a hindrance to achieving a 15 percent lead.[17] Formal provisions were also made for MPs to consult with, but not to be mandated by, their local associations.

The '15 percent rule' ensured that the function of the first ballot was to determine whether the incumbent enjoyed the confidence of MPs. If he did not, then he would be expected (although not compelled) to resign because his authority would be badly damaged.[18] His senior colleagues could then enter the second ballot. Indeed, it was possible for candidates to sit out the first ballot, professing loyalty to the leader in public, but being ready to enter should he not secure a 15 percent lead. Candidates could encourage their supporters to vote for any challenger in the first ballot in order to force the incumbent's resignation.[19]

That same year, Margaret Thatcher, who had been education secretary under Heath, declared that she would contest the leadership. It was a major surprise and few observers gave her much of a chance of winning. Her intention had been to draw in other candidates to challenge Heath.[20] She was joined in the first ballot by Hugh Fraser, a backbencher. The result was sensational. Thatcher led Heath by 11 votes but fell short of a 15 percent lead. Heath announced he would not contest the second ballot. Fraser also withdrew but several new candidates entered the second ballot, the most important being William Whitelaw. He was an ally of Heath who chose not to challenge his leader out of loyalty. Had he entered the first ballot, he would likely have started as the favourite but he had left himself too much ground to make up. Thatcher won the second ballot, taking 53 percent of the vote. There were important ideological undercurrents, with the right supporting Thatcher and the Tory left voting first for Heath and then for Whitelaw.[21]

According to Stark, Thatcher's victory in 1975 was the main exception to the argument that a candidate who is seen as best on acceptability, electability and competence will win the contest. Whitelaw was stronger than Thatcher on all these criteria. Stark explained the discrepancy in terms of the idiosyncrasies of the selection system. The requirement for a super-majority in the first ballot and the provision for the entry of new candidates in the second ballot encouraged some MPs to support her in order to remove Heath, after which they could support other candidates in the second ballot. However, Thatcher's strong performance in the first ballot enabled her to establish momentum and push on for victory.[22]

Thatcher went on to become the Conservatives' most electorally successful post-war leader, winning three general elections. However, her leadership style and right-wing policies made her a divisive figure in the country and in her party. In 1989, she was formally challenged by a little-known backbencher, Sir Anthony Meyer. Thatcher won easily but 60 MPs declined to support her. A year later, she faced a much more serious challenge from the former cabinet minister, Michael Heseltine. Despite leading the first ballot, Thatcher failed to secure a 15 percent lead over Heseltine and she was persuaded to retire from the contest so that other cabinet colleagues could enter and stop Heseltine. John Major eventually emerged as the unity candidate and beat Heseltine and Douglas Hurd. Thatcher's eviction is examined in more detail later in this chapter.

These contests brought renewed scrutiny of the selection system. In 1990, a rule change required the names of the MPs nominating candidates to be made public. A year later, annual contests were made contingent on 10 percent of Tory MPs writing to the chairman of the backbench 1922 committee to demand an election (their names would not be revealed).[23] In the event, this procedure was never activated in the system's remaining years in use. In 1995, Major called a leadership election to draw out his Eurosceptic enemies, but in doing so, the requirement for 10 percent of MPs to request a contest was redundant. Major was challenged by his cabinet colleague, John Redwood, but managed to secure a first-ballot victory by 218 votes to 89.

Liberal Party

In the late-nineteenth and early-twentieth centuries, when the Liberal Party was regularly in government, its choice of leader was bound up with the appointment of prime ministers by the monarch. In 1894, Queen Victoria appointed Lord Rosebery as prime minister and he became Liberal leader largely by default. Given the greater balance in power between the House of Commons and the House of Lords, it was not always clear whether the party's leader in the Commons or its leader in the Lords was its overall leader. There was an absence of a clear mechanism for choosing a leader in each house. In 1899, Campbell-Bannerman became leader in the Commons after discussions among the leading contenders and he was then formally and unanimously elected by Liberal MPs. He was succeeded as leader (and by then, as prime minister) by Asquith in 1908 after a joint meeting of Liberal peers and MPs. The following 25 years were often confusing in terms of who was the party leader. The party split during the First World War and split again in the 1930s. In 1916, Asquith remained Liberal leader but was replaced as prime minister by fellow Liberal, Lloyd George. In the 1920s, after Asquith had lost his parliamentary seat, Lloyd George was chosen as chairman of the party in the Commons but was not regarded as the overall leader of the party.[24]

After the Second World War, the Liberal Party went into decline. Its parliamentary representation fell to 12 MPs in 1945 and six in 1955. Leaders were generally chosen after discussions among MPs, as Clement Davies was in 1945. He served for 11 years before yielding to grassroots pressure after disappointing election results. He was replaced in 1956 by Jo Grimond, who helped revive the party in the 1960s. He stood down in 1967 and in the search for a replacement, the Liberals held a ballot of MPs to choose their new leader. Jeremy Thorpe defeated two other candidates, winning six of the 12 available votes. The other two candidates each won three votes, preventing a reallocation of votes under the alternative-vote system that was used, but both agreed to withdraw from the contest.[25] That was the last succession to be decided by MPs and in 1976, when Thorpe resigned, the new leader, David Steel, was elected by individual party members.

The Conservative Party leadership election of 1997

A case study can illustrate the various elements of leadership selection by MPs. The most recent instance of the selection of a leader in a parliamentary ballot was during the Conservative leadership contest of 1997. It was made necessary by the resignation of Major after the Conservatives' landslide defeat in that year's general election. The two principal names that had been floated before the election as likely candidates were unable or unwilling to stand. Michael Portillo, the standard-bearer of the Eurosceptic right, had lost his parliamentary seat.

Two days after the election, Heseltine, the major pro-European in the party, was taken to hospital suffering from heart problems. He subsequently declared he would not participate in the leadership contest.[26]

There was no shortage of candidates, however. The former chancellor of the exchequer, and prominent pro-European, Kenneth Clarke, declared his intention to stand less than two hours after Major resigned on 2 May.[27] He was followed in the next few days by former cabinet ministers Redwood, Peter Lilley, Michael Howard, William Hague and Stephen Dorrell. The first three were Thatcherite Eurosceptics who were largely competing for the votes that Portillo would have targeted had he been able to stand. Dorrell was from the pro-European left of the party, although he had tried, not always successfully, to sound more Eurosceptical. He quickly realised he had little support among MPs and dropped out. At 36, Hague was the youngest and least experienced of the candidates. His candidacy attracted controversy because he was alleged to have agreed a deal to back Howard in return for becoming deputy leader and party chairman, a deal he reneged on after calculating that Howard could not win, but that he, Hague, could.[28]

The Conservatives continued to be badly divided by the issue of European integration and, in particular, whether Britain should join the single European currency. Europe, and not the reasons why the party lost the general election, would be the key issue in the leadership contest.[29] The parliamentary party was even more Eurosceptical after the 1997 general election, a fact that complicated matters for Clarke.[30] His main hope was that, as the Tories' most popular politician, he would appeal to MPs who wanted to boost the party's standing with the electorate. On the other hand, the presence of three Eurosceptic candidates threatened to split the Eurosceptic vote. It was in this context that Hague realised that he could come through the middle and win.[31]

When nominations closed in early June, Clarke, Hague, Howard, Lilley and Redwood made it onto the ballot paper. Clarke secured the support of most of the remaining shadow-cabinet members who were not contesting the election. Hague secured backing from the newer members of the parliamentary party.[32] The candidates of the right faced differing problems. Lilley was regarded as bright but uncharismatic. Redwood suffered from perceptions that he had been disloyal in challenging Major in 1995. Meanwhile, Howard was subjected to a devastating attack by Ann Widdecombe, a former minister, over his record as home secretary, in which she memorably said that there was 'something of the night' about his character.[33]

In the first ballot on 10 June, Clarke topped the poll with 49 votes, which was not enough to win on the first ballot. Indeed, his total was just eight more than Hague and he was left looking vulnerable (Table 2.1). Redwood squeezed out Lilley and Howard for third place, leading the latter two to drop out of the contest. Both endorsed Hague, who was seen as most likely to block the pro-European Clarke.[34] Although he finished second, Hague was now the favourite because he was more likely to collect the votes of the right-wing candidates in a run-off with Clarke.[35] No further candidates entered the contest. In the second ballot a week later, no candidate secured victory but Hague managed to cut Clarke's lead to two votes. Redwood trailed in third place and by the rules applicable for the second ballot was eliminated.

Two days separated the second and third ballots, but they saw extraordinary manoeuvres. Clarke and Redwood agreed to a pact in which Redwood urged his supporters to back Clarke. In return, Redwood would become shadow chancellor and on the vexed issue of the single European currency, a free vote of the parliamentary party was promised should the issue be brought before parliament.[36] The pact was partly motivated, for Redwood, by concerns that Hague had adopted an opportunistic position on Europe. Hague had ruled out membership of the single currency for two parliaments and had demanded that all members of a Hague-led shadow cabinet would have to sign up to this policy. However, Redwood suggested that if Hague were sincere, he would have ruled out membership on principle.[37]

The intention of Clarke and Redwood was to unite the party by arranging a peace deal between the pro-European and Eurosceptic

Table 2.1 Conservative Party Leadership Election 1997

	First ballot	Second ballot	Third ballot
William Hague	41	62	92
Kenneth Clarke	49	64	70
John Redwood	27	38	–
Peter Lilley	24	–	–
Michael Howard	23	–	–
Abstentions/spoilt	0	0	(2)
TOTAL	164	164	164

Notes: All figures refer to number of MPs. To win on first ballot, candidate needed to secure majority of eligible votes and 15% lead over nearest rival. To win on second ballot, candidate needed majority of eligible voters. To win on third ballot candidate needed majority of those voting. See also Appendix B.

factions. In fact, it helped to secure victory for Hague. The pact led to cries of 'betrayal' by some Eurosceptics and prompted Lady Thatcher to endorse Hague. Some MPs who had supported Clarke defected to Hague, so that although Redwood brought 10–12 of his supporters with him in the third ballot, Clarke's vote went up by only six. Other Redwood backers, including Iain Duncan Smith, switched to Hague, who scored a decisive 92–70 victory.[38]

Selection criteria

To understand why Hague won, it is important to consider the three selection criteria identified by Stark: acceptability, electability and competence. On the criterion of competence, Clarke had the edge over his rivals. In terms of parliamentary and governmental experience, he had enjoyed greater longevity than the other candidates. At the time of the 1997 leadership contest, Clarke had spent 27 years as an MP, compared with Howard and Lilley's 14 years, Redwood's ten years and Hague's eight years. More important, he had been a cabinet minister for longer than his rivals and held higher posts: he had served a total of 12 years in cabinet, with Lilley and Howard each serving seven years, while Redwood and Hague both served two years. Moreover, Clarke had held two of the three great offices of state: he had been home secretary for one year and a successful chancellor of the exchequer for four years. Howard had been a controversial home secretary for four years, and held other lower portfolios. Lilley had not occupied any of the great offices of state. Redwood and Hague had each held only one cabinet position, and in both cases it was secretary of state for Wales, one of the most junior positions.[39]

   Clarke was also the strongest candidate on electability. An ICM poll for the *Guardian* in June 1997 asked voters who they would like to see as the new Tory leader. The largest category was the 39 percent that replied, 'don't know'. Among the candidates themselves, Clarke was far ahead with 31 percent, followed by Redwood and Hague, each on 9 percent, Howard on 7 percent and Lilley on 6 percent. That reflected the received wisdom that Clarke had far more electoral appeal than any other candidate, partly because of his record and partly because of his down-to-earth personality.[40] However, although he left his rivals in the shadows on electability, he was far from being an irresistible force, securing the backing of less than one-third of the electorate, most of whom presumably had little interest in the Conservative contest after the party's eviction from office. The other candidates were in much worse positions, however. Redwood had never been able to live down his other-worldly persona, while there were serious concerns among MPs about Lilley's electoral appeal.[41] Howard had image problems, as highlighted by Widdecombe, and Hague had a low public profile.

Clarke thus enjoyed significant advantages over his opponents on both electability and competence, but his failure to win the Tory leadership election in 1997 was down to his ideological unacceptability to most Conservative MPs. Clarke's pro-European politics put him at odds with most of his colleagues, although on economic and social questions, he was also in a minority. That much is clear from Timothy Heppell and Michael Hill's database of ideological positions of Conservative MPs during the 1997 leadership contest. Heppell and Hill categorised MPs on three-point scales on questions of morality, economics and Europe. On morality, MPs could be liberal, conservative or agnostic; on economics, they could be 'wet' (statist), 'dry' (neo-liberal) or agnostic; and on Europe, they could be Europhile, Eurosceptic or agnostic. The ratings for individual MPs were based on indicators that included parliamentary division lists, early day motions, membership of party groups, and public comments.[42] Among the leadership contenders, Clarke was the only pro-European, the only economic wet and the only social liberal, standard positions of the traditional Tory left. The other four candidates all represented the Thatcherite wing of the party, being Eurosceptic free-marketeers who took conservative positions on morality.[43] In practice, there was some variation among them, with, for example, Hague's Euroscepticism usually being seen as 'softer' than that of Redwood, Howard or Lilley, although he hardened his position during the campaign.[44]

Clarke had no competitor for the votes of the traditional Tory left, but this group was small in the parliamentary party. During the Thatcher years, the party had become increasingly Eurosceptic and economically 'dry', but the 1997 general election, in which the Conservatives lost half of their parliamentary seats, accentuated this shift. On the key issue of Europe, 80 percent of Conservative MPs were now Eurosceptics.[45] That helped to explain why four of the five candidates were Eurosceptics, although that led to a splintering of the Thatcherite vote. The three most Thatcherite candidates, Howard, Lilley and Redwood, filled the final three places in the first ballot. Some observers have claimed that, had there been one Thatcherite candidate instead of three, he – whoever it was – could have topped the first ballot and even won the contest.[46]

Hague, however, was able to come through the middle. With the eclipse of the 'hard' Thatcherites, he could present himself as the 'unity' candidate.[47] He was able to do that partly because he was seen as ideologically inoffensive to most sections of the party: certainly, there was no bloc of hostility to him in the way that there was to Clarke and Redwood. Yet there was not much enthusiastic support either and most of the 41 votes he received in the first ballot would likely have gone to Portillo had the latter been eligible to stand.[48] Hague was also the preferred candidate of those who thought the party should 'skip a generation' in order to match Blair's youthful appeal.[49] Doing so could draw a line under the past and enable the party to unite behind a leader untainted by the infighting of the Major years.

Hague's victory over Clarke in the final ballot rested principally on his greater ideological acceptability to Tory MPs.[50] Heppell and Hill concluded that 'the defeat of Clarke... was a victory for ideological dogmatism over traditional conservative statecraft, that is, pragmatism in the pursuit of power'.[51] However, probably a fairer appraisal is that Clarke was simply deemed too divisive to be Conservative leader at a time when the party was still convulsed by infighting over Europe. It was unrealistic to expect a Eurosceptic party to unite behind a leader who disagreed with it on the issue closest to its collective heart. Major had failed to balance the factions when the pro-Europeans were stronger. It is inconceivable that Clarke could have done better in less hospitable circumstances. The Conservative leadership election of 1997 thus offers support to Stark's argument that, in divided parties, the unity candidate normally wins.

Ejecting leaders

In the era of parliamentary ballots, British parties did not always have codified eviction methods, but when they did, they were normally through means of formal challenges to incumbent leaders. In the Labour Party, leadership elections, and thus challenges, could take place annually when the party was in opposition, but there were no formal provisions for contests when Labour was in government until the formation of the electoral college in 1981. When the Conservative Party adopted its parliamentary-ballot selection system in 1965, there was initially no means for instigating a challenge to the incumbent. That changed in 1975 when the party adopted annual leadership elections and enabled challengers to enter provided they were nominated by two MPs.

The question of leader eviction is not a purely theoretical one because in 1990 Conservative MPs removed their leader and the country's prime minister. The 1991 reforms to the selection system (see above) were motivated by a widespread feeling in the party that it was too easy to instigate a challenge. That suggested that Tory MPs believed that the party's institutions had played *some* role in Margaret Thatcher's eviction. In the remainder of this section, a closer examination of Thatcher's removal is provided in order to establish the importance of eviction institutions. They were not the only, or even the main, factor in her defenestration but they were a component of the explanation. To illustrate this point, the section concludes with a comparison of Thatcher and another under-pressure prime minister from the era when MPs chose party leaders, Harold Wilson. Labour MPs tried and failed to evict Wilson in 1968 and 1969. One factor in that failure was the absence of a formal eviction mechanism.

The removal of Thatcher

The downfall of Thatcher as Conservative leader and prime minister was one of the seminal events of post-war British political history. For 11 years, she had been one of the most domineering prime ministers of the twentieth century and the most electorally successful. Her removal would plunge her party into a decade of factional infighting over the issue of European integration. However, in 1990, most Conservative MPs were looking no further than the next election, and there were clear incentives for them to evict Thatcher amid increasing concerns that she had become an electoral liability and a divisive figure.

After the Conservatives' election victory in 1987, the Thatcher government appeared to assume an increasingly arrogant tone in the eyes of many inside and outside the party. The most obvious expression was the implementation of the community charge, or 'poll tax' as it became known, a new system of local-government taxation. Thatcher hailed the charge as a flagship policy, but it rapidly looked more like an iceberg that threatened to wreck the party's electoral prospects.[52] The tax was a flat rate in each locality, independent of ability to pay. This regressive element caused popular discontent.

A second contentious issue was that of European integration. In her pronouncements on Europe, especially in her speech to the College of Europe in Bruges in 1988, Thatcher had adopted an increasingly Eurosceptic tone.[53] Although this stance delighted the anti-Europeans in the Conservative Party, it appalled the sizeable group of pro-Europeans, both in government and on the backbenches. Thatcher's reluctance to take Britain into the European Monetary System's Exchange Rate Mechanism had pushed her into conflict with her chancellor, Nigel Lawson, who favoured British entry. Lawson eventually resigned from government in 1989, citing the influence of Thatcher's Eurosceptic economic advisor, Sir Alan Walters. Lawson believed that Walters was making his, Lawson's, job impossible.[54] A year later, Thatcher denounced the federalist vision of the European Commission's president, Jacques Delors, in strident tones in parliament. This intervention prompted the resignation of another senior member of the government, the deputy prime minister, Sir Geoffrey Howe.[55]

Internal divisions over Europe and opposition to the poll tax caused considerable damage to the poll ratings of both the Conservative Party and the prime minister. Figure 2.1 shows the Tories' opinion-poll lead over Labour from the 1987 election up to Thatcher's downfall, as well as Thatcher's own net satisfaction ratings. Both showed a slow decline from 1987 to 1989 and then a steep drop in the first half of 1989, after the local elections and the European parliamentary elections. Dismay over Thatcher's hostility to Europe and the fear that she was an electoral liability led to a leadership challenge in November 1989. The challenger was Sir Anthony Meyer, a pro-European backbencher who had never held ministerial office and no longer expected to do so. Meyer offered himself up as a 'stalking horse' whose sole purpose was to mobilise opposition to the prime minister and, he hoped, to draw in a more serious challenger. Meyer's preference was Michael Heseltine, a pro-European who had resigned from the cabinet in 1986 in protest at Thatcher's style of government during the Westland affair.[56] Meyer failed to dislodge Thatcher but he did inflict some damage: he secured 33 votes, to Thatcher's 314, while another 27 MPs abstained, thus depriving the prime minister of one-sixth of the parliamentary party's support. The most significant aspect of Meyer's move was that it broke the taboo on challenging an incumbent prime minister, as it was something that had never previously been attempted, at least not through a formal eviction process. It made a later challenge easier to envisage and indeed expected, as Heseltine's challenge the following year would be.

Events took a turn for the worse for Thatcher in early 1990. Anger at the poll tax culminated in a riot in Trafalgar Square in March. In the same month, the Conservatives lost a safe seat to Labour in the Mid-Staffordshire by-election. The Tories found themselves trailing Labour by 24 points in the national opinion polls, while Thatcher's net satisfaction rating stood at –56. The pressures eased on Thatcher after local-election results in May were not as bad as first feared. The Conservatives' poll standing improved, as did Thatcher's satisfaction ratings (Figure 2.1), though they remained low. The turnaround was sufficient to leave Thatcher's internal opponents, including Heseltine, feeling pessimistic about challenging her later that year.[57] It would take the extraordinary circumstances of Howe's resignation in the autumn, when he criticised her European

Figure 2.1 Conservatives' Poll Lead and Thatcher's Net Satisfaction Rating 1987–90

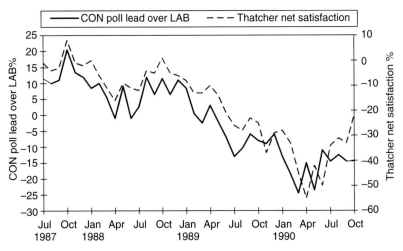

Source: A. King (ed.), *British Political Opinion 1937–2000: The Gallup Polls* (London: Politico's, 2001), pp. 16–17, 194–5.

Notes: Q1. 'If there were a general election tomorrow, which party would you vote for?' [CON poll lead over LAB = % Conservative minus % Labour] Q2. 'Are you satisfied or dissatisfied with Mrs Thatcher as prime minister?' [Thatcher net satisfaction = % satisfied minus % dissatisfied]

policy, to re-create the circumstances for a possible eviction.[58] Howe's resignation speech to parliament was the catalyst for Thatcher's downfall.

The timing of Howe's resignation was propitious in the sense that it occurred immediately before the Conservatives were due to conduct their annual leadership contest in November. Heseltine would have preferred Tory MPs to have forced Thatcher out without his intervention, because he feared that '[h]e who wields the knife never wears the crown'.[59] However, Howe's speech, in which he called on 'others to consider their own response to the tragic conflict of loyalties with which I have myself wrestled for perhaps too long', left Heseltine with little option but to challenge the prime minister or lose his credibility as a potential leader.[60] He duly announced that he would stand for the leadership.

It is not the purpose of this discussion to go into detail about the events of the contest, as these are well-documented elsewhere.[61] However, after a brief campaign, the contest saw Thatcher win 204 votes to Heseltine's 152, narrowly failing to reach the required 15 percent margin of victory.

Thatcher's immediate response was to declare her determination to carry on, as was her right, to fight the second ballot, in which only a bare majority of eligible voters was needed for victory. However, in the frantic two days between the first ballot and the close of nominations for the second ballot, Thatcher was prevailed upon by senior colleagues to stand aside and allow others to enter the contest. She met members of the cabinet individually on the eve of the deadline for nominations for the second ballot. Most told her that, while they supported her, they did not think she could beat Heseltine.[62]

John Major and Douglas Hurd subsequently joined the contest. Major was able to appeal both to Thatcherites who had remained loyal to the leader in the first ballot, as well as to some MPs who had supported Heseltine in order to remove the prime minister, by presenting himself as the candidate best placed to deliver party unity.[63] Major led the second ballot with 185 votes to Heseltine's 131 and Hurd's 56. That was not officially enough to claim victory outright – Major missed a majority of those entitled to vote by two votes – but both Hurd and Heseltine announced their intention to support him in the third ballot, which was thereby rendered unnecessary (see Appendix B). Heseltine had effectively played the role of 'stalking horse' for Major, forcing Thatcher's resignation but evoking fierce opposition from her right-wing supporters. That ensured that he would be considered too divisive to be leader, as he had feared.[64] Major secured victory with the support of Eurosceptics, who could not countenance voting for Heseltine.[65]

It is a commonplace in the literature on leadership elections that Thatcher was forced out of the contest because of a loss of support among her cabinet colleagues. For example, George Jones writes that 'neither the parliamentary party nor the party in the country delivered the final blow. The cabinet killed her'.[66] Similarly, Alderman and Carter claim that '[t]he cabinet was the crucial body'.[67] Even Thatcher herself appears to hold to this position.[68] In fact, although, ministerial support had indeed evaporated by the time Thatcher spoke with cabinet ministers individually the night after the first ballot, ministers were responding to the collapse in her support throughout the day on the backbenches, including among many who had voted for her in the first ballot.[69] Their message to Thatcher was not that they wanted her to go but that they did not think she could win, precisely because they were aware of these wider developments.[70] *Pace* Jones, it was Tory backbenchers who delivered the mortal blow.[71]

On becoming leader, Major moved to tighten the rules for removing leaders. Henceforth, 10 percent of MPs would need to demand a contest before one took place (restrictions on timing remained in place and indeed were shortened). It was a clear indication that influential people in the party believed that the eviction rules had played an important role in Thatcher's downfall: if they had not, there would have been no reason to change them so swiftly.

Some observers, such as the former Conservative leader, Michael Howard, have argued that eviction institutions did not matter in Thatcher's downfall because Heseltine's candidacy was a serious one that would have been able to overcome higher entry barriers to start a contest.[72] There is no way of determining whether that is true. However, there are strong reasons for supposing that institutions mattered.

First, Heseltine required only two nominations to enter the ballot. The costs of mobilising two MPs to endorse him were very low. In contrast, it is fair to ask whether Heseltine would have been able to surmount a 20 percent nomination threshold, as used in the Labour Party. At the time, that would have required 74 other Conservative MPs *publicly* to support his challenge. Many fewer MPs than that openly supported Heseltine. It is, perhaps, more likely that, under a 20 percent threshold, any move by Tory MPs against Thatcher would have assumed a different form. There is a fair chance that it might never have happened at all.

Second, the secret ballot enabled MPs, including members of the government, to vote against Thatcher without sanction. That made it easier to mobilise opposition to her and again stands in contrast to the Labour Party, where votes in the MPs section of the electoral college are publicly recorded.

Third, the provision allowing new candidates to enter the second ballot separated the eviction of Thatcher from the election of her successor. Those MPs looking for a change of leader were not compelled to vote for the assassin, except strategically in the first ballot. Thus, when Major entered the Thatcher-less second ballot, the contest was now for a vacancy and the costs of mobilising supporters was significantly lower than it was for Heseltine in the first ballot, as these allies were now free of demands for loyalty to the incumbent leader.

Fourth, 'party costs' were low because the entire contest was conducted cheaply and inside two weeks at Westminster. Later chapters show that all-member ballots operate very differently. Overall, the institutional impact of the Conservatives' system of parliamentary ballots on the costs of evicting leaders was very low. This system serves as a comparator for other systems examined in this book.

Comparing Thatcher and Wilson

It is impossible to say with certainty what Thatcher's fate would have been under different institutions. However, it is worth comparing the situation facing her in 1989–90 with that confronting Harold Wilson in 1968–69 because in some respects the circumstances were similar. The selection institutions, however, were different: no formal mechanisms existed in the Labour Party at the time to challenge a prime minister. The only options for Wilson's opponents were non-institutional methods, such as a putsch by the cabinet or a backbench rebellion, but neither was forthcoming, despite a strong desire for change by important figures in the party.

Having been elected to office with a majority of just four seats in 1964, the Wilson-led Labour Party was returned with a bigger majority, of 96 seats, in 1966. For a year after the 1966 election, Labour largely maintained its lead over the Conservatives in the opinion polls and Wilson's own net satisfaction rating remained positive (Figure 2.2). Events then began to take over. In particular, Labour was to suffer badly in the areas of economic management and industrial relations. Britain's economy was suffering from a persistent balance-of-payments deficit but the

Figure 2.2   Labour's Poll Lead and Wilson's Net Satisfaction Rating 1966–70

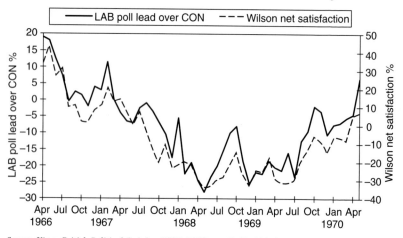

Source: King, *British Political Opinion 1937–2000*, pp. 9–10, 188–9.

Notes: Q1. 'If there were a general election tomorrow, which party would you vote for?' [LAB poll lead over CON = % Labour minus % Conservative] Q2. 'Are you satisfied or dissatisfied with Mr Wilson as prime minister?' [Wilson net satisfaction = % satisfied minus % dissatisfied]

government had resisted calls for devaluation, fearful of the consequences for Labour's reputation for economic competence. Instead, taxes went up and a wage and price freeze was implemented. Attacks by currency speculators led the government to devalue the pound in November 1967. The government also implemented spending cuts and introduced some charges in the health service.[73]

Compounding these economic problems were tensions with the trade unions. In 1969, the government proposed reforms of labour laws, including plans to fine strikers who took unofficial industrial action, in a white paper entitled *In Place of Strife*. Although the proposals were popular with the public, they were bitterly opposed by the unions and many inside the Labour Party. Most significant of all, they were opposed within the cabinet, not least by the home secretary, James Callaghan, who made public his dissent. Eventually, the proposals were diluted and sanctions on strikers dropped, but not before the party had been badly split and a backbench revolt against the prime minister aborted.[74]

The electoral effect of these crises was a sharp drop in Labour's poll rating: for much of 1968–69, Labour trailed the Conservatives by more than 20 points in the opinion polls, while Wilson's net satisfaction rating hovered between –20 and –30 (Figure 2.2). The government suffered a series of catastrophic by-election defeats, including three on a single day in March 1968.[75] Morale in the party collapsed and it became common currency to predict a defeat at the next election on the scale of the 1931 catastrophe when Labour was reduced to a rump.[76] In the event, the party did indeed lose the 1970 general election, but not by much.

There are some parallels in the electoral crises facing the Wilson government in 1968–69 and the Thatcher government in 1989–90. Both trailed the major opposition party by 20 percentage points in the opinion polls, although in the case of the Thatcher government, the gap had narrowed to 14 percent by the autumn of 1990; if anything, Wilson's government was facing a worse electoral predicament than Thatcher's. On the other hand, Wilson's net satisfaction ratings were not quite as bad as Thatcher's, the latter's falling into the –40 to –50 range in the spring of 1990 at the height of anger over the poll tax, although later they improved slightly. Both Thatcher and Wilson evoked considerable dismay from cabinet colleagues over their styles of government. While Thatcher was considered by many to be arrogant, Wilson was regarded as high-handed, autocratic, and even 'presidential'. He was accused of taking decisions by fiat by the foreign secretary, George Brown, who ostensibly resigned over the issue in 1968.[77]

It is not surprising that the leadership plots that were a feature of 1989–90 had their echoes in 1968–69. The major threat to Wilson's position from within the cabinet in 1968 came from Roy Jenkins, the chancellor of the exchequer and a figure on the party's social-democratic right. A year later, the principal threat appeared to come from another figure from the right, but one closer to its working-class traditions, the home secretary, James Callaghan. Supporters of both men plotted against Wilson during 1968–69 and only a mutual fear by Jenkins and Callaghan of each other taking over stopped a putsch against the prime minister.[78] There were also two attempts made by backbenchers to organise round-robin letters calling for Wilson to stand aside.[79] In 1969, backbench supporters of Jenkins and Callaghan combined to attempt a revolt against Wilson during the debate over *In Place of Strife*, but it was called off when the Callaghanites split at the last minute after their man alienated some with an abrasive performance at a joint meeting of the cabinet and Labour's ruling national executive.[80] At any rate, the chairman of the Parliamentary Labour Party (PLP), Douglas Houghton, insisted that he would permit a discussion of the leadership at a PLP meeting only if the rebels could secure the signatures of 120 MPs (one-third of the PLP) in support of such a demand. There was no constitutional basis for this threshold but Houghton was reportedly prepared to allow a vote only if it were absolutely certain to succeed. His own priority, like that of many Labour MPs, was to defeat *In Place of Strife*; he did not want Wilson to win a vote and use it as a mandate to push ahead with the bill. This very high threshold, together with the requirement that the names of those signing a motion be made public, vastly increased the mobilisation costs of Wilson's opponents. Sixty MPs were ready to go public with a call for Wilson to go, but an estimated 40 MPs, including 20 frontbenchers, who were prepared to vote against Wilson in a secret ballot, would not go public.[81]

Despite the febrile atmosphere, Wilson survived and a challenge never materialised. A crucial reason, according to Wilson's biographer, Pimlott, was the absence of an eviction mechanism:

> [T]he rules of the Labour Party, unlike those of the Conservatives after the introduction of elections to the Party Leadership, contained no constitutional method for disposing of a prime minister in office. This meant that for any assault, to succeed, [it] needed overwhelming support from ministers and back-benchers; it also meant, since the outcome of any attempt was uncertain and the

price of failure high, that there were always good reasons for postponement.[82]

The presence in the cabinet of rival credible contenders in Jenkins and Callaghan, together with other potential candidates in Healey and Crosland, ensured that there was no consensus over who should replace Wilson.[83] That was usually sufficient to scupper the various plots. Had a mechanism existed whereby a leadership contest could have been instigated as easily as it was in the Conservative Party in 1989 and 1990, it is quite possible that it would have happened. Indeed, some MPs floated the possibility of a stalking-horse challenger to Wilson in 1968. However, it would have first required the question of the leadership to be brought before a PLP meeting, but not enough MPs were prepared to break cover and demand it.[84] In contrast, Thatcher's demise began with Meyer's challenge in 1989, a move that required just two other MPs to propose and second his candidacy (and their names were not made public). The following year, the much more serious challenge of Heseltine would destroy her.

Pimlott concluded of Wilson's travails in 1968 that, 'a prime minister with little support in the country, the press or the Government... survived only because of the inertia of his party, and the lack of a mechanism for getting rid of him'.[85] The 'inertia' was largely explained by the costs of collective action for backbenchers and rival crown princes in the cabinet. The absence of a formal eviction mechanism protected the incumbent and something similar would have been helpful to Thatcher in 1989–90. Indeed, Thatcher would later complain – quite wrongly – that the Tories' eviction mechanism was, by 'unwritten convention', to be used only when the party was in opposition.[86]

Wilson faced no overt challenge despite polling figures that were as bad as, or worse, than Thatcher's, and despite a host of other problems that also afflicted Thatcher, including criticisms of his style of government and divisive policies. An important reason is that he enjoyed greater institutional security of tenure, enough to leave his enemies scratching around for ruses to mobilise MPs against him but always failing to do so. That in turn increased their costs of mobilising opponents in the PLP, whereas an easily-instigated secret ballot would have dramatically reduced these costs, as it did in the Conservative Party in 1989–90. Consequently, backbench discontent with Wilson needed to find expression in the cabinet if it were to be effective. In the absence of formal procedures, much of the initiative remained with the prime minister, who was able to outwit his opponents.[87]

Institutions are thus important. However, their effect should not be overstated. The Conservative government of John Major trailed Labour by 20 to 30 percentage points after the fiasco of Black Wednesday, when the pound was forced out of the European Exchange Rate Mechanism by currency speculators in September 1992. Major's own net satisfaction ratings fell into the –50 to –60 range throughout 1994. The parliamentary party was extremely divided over the issue of European integration, with the Eurosceptic right highly critical of Major for signing the Maastricht Treaty, which paved the way for further integration. After persistent speculation of leadership challenges, Major decided on the high-risk strategy of calling a leadership contest in July 1995 to lance the boil and catch his critics off-guard.[88]

Redwood resigned from the cabinet and announced that he would challenge Major. However, Portillo, who had been seen as the leading figure on the Eurosceptic right, decided to sit out the first ballot, as did Heseltine, the doyen of the pro-European left. There were predictions that supporters of both men would vote strategically for Redwood in order to force Major's resignation and open up the contest. In the event, Major won by 218 votes to 89, enough for victory in the first ballot. It appeared that the supporters of Heseltine in particular were worried about losing to Portillo if the contest went to a second ballot.[89]

Major won because his opponents in the parliamentary party were divided factionally and by preferred successor. For that reason, he clung on despite his low net satisfaction ratings and the party's poor opinion-poll ratings. Institutions were less significant in his survival, despite the fact that a contest was granted by the leader himself and that there was a provision for the entry of new candidates in the second ballot. Heseltine and Portillo could have allowed Redwood to play the role of assassin, but each wanted to be the beneficiary and that could not be guaranteed. Many MPs on right and left considered Major to be more palatable than a leader from the respective opposing faction. This case is a reminder that eviction institutions are only *one* factor, albeit a very important one, when considering the security of tenure of leaders.

It is possible that, had a leadership contest taken place in the Labour Party during 1968–69, Wilson might have won for the same reason that Major did, namely, that his opponents were divided among themselves. However, there was at least one major difference. Wilson's principal rivals were all on the right of the Labour Party, while Wilson was considered to be on the left. There would have been fewer ideological barriers to the followers of the right's crown princes joining forces for an eviction than there were for the supporters of Portillo and Heseltine in 1995, despite

Callaghan and Jenkins adopting different positions on *In Place of Strife*. Indeed, scores of supporters of Callaghan and Jenkins were prepared to join a putsch in 1969 and had Houghton's informal threshold for a ballot at the PLP been lower, they might have been successful. Consequently, there are good reasons for supposing that the absence of eviction institutions was an important factor – although not the only factor – explaining Wilson's survival.

Conclusion

This chapter provided a brief overview of the use of parliamentary ballots to select and eject party leaders in Britain. Such systems are easy and quick to operate, virtues that have not always been associated with membership ballots. However, despite their popularity with many MPs, the exclusive use of parliamentary ballots to choose leaders increasingly sat uneasily in a more participatory and democratic age.

Most of the parliamentary ballots Stark analysed saw victories for the candidates who were the deemed the strongest on the highest-order selection criterion that was relevant in their respective contests. The only exception was the victory of Thatcher in 1975. The present chapter showed that Hague's victory in 1997 also fit Stark's explanatory approach. The Tory leadership election of 1997 was but one case study but it did illustrate many of the important considerations that come into play. It was a useful case to examine because of the widespread feeling that Clarke was the more electable candidate. Despite the franchise being restricted to MPs, the latter did not choose the most electorally popular candidate. On the other hand, Tory MPs were not blind ideologues but understood the great dangers of choosing a leader who could not easily unite his party because of his divisive views on European integration.

Leader-eviction rules did not always exist in parties, even when they had formal systems for choosing new leaders. However, where such rules did exist, eviction was usually by means of a leadership challenge. For the most part, 'party costs' – the collective costs to the party of conducting a contest, such as time, money and disunity – were fairly low because the ballots were cheap and quick to organise. In the case of the Labour Party, where all candidates had to enter the contest in the first round of voting, the processes of ejection and selection were fused into one. In the Conservative Party, the provision for second-ballot entry effectively separated these processes. That enabled 'stalking horses' to damage incumbents, or, in the case of Heseltine, for a serious challenger to provide unintentional cover for other candidates to seize the crown. This point is explored further in later chapters. It was also shown that the absence of formal rules frustrated Wilson's opponents in the Labour Party. In the next chapter, it is argued that having eviction rules that are hard to operationalise is little different from having no eviction rules at all.

3
The Labour Party: The Electoral College

The Labour Party made its first moves towards extending leadership selection beyond MPs in 1981 with the formation of an electoral college. The tripartite college gave votes to all of the major stakeholders in the party, including MPs, trade unions and constituency parties. Initially, balloting was limited and many votes were cast as blocks by organisations but successive reforms of the college enfranchised more individuals. Almost a million individual votes were cast in the 1994 leadership contest. However, the operation of the electoral college has been controversial since its inception, with most attention focused on the role of the trade unions. At first, unions cast large block votes that appeared to determine the trajectory of leadership contests. With the abolition of block voting in 1993, it was thought that the role of the unions would become less contentious. However, the 2010 leadership election led to renewed criticism about the power of the unions.

This chapter examines the electoral college. It begins by describing the formation of the institution in 1981. It then provides an overview of leadership contests between 1983 and 2007 before embarking on a detailed account of the 2010 leadership election. The contest is analysed in terms of the three principal selection criteria of acceptability, electability and competence. It is shown that this contest was one of only a few in which the precise selection rules had a decisive effect on the outcome.

The electoral college has also been important in recent attempted ejections of Labour leaders. It is argued that the high thresholds for instigating leadership challenges have usually compelled opponents of Labour leaders to search for different means of ejecting them. The attempts to remove Tony Blair are briefly recounted before the chapter turns to Gordon Brown and his survival of three coup attempts. It is shown that institutions were a major factor in the plotters' failure to remove Brown from office.

The electoral college

The creation of Labour's electoral college in 1981 was the culmination of a decade-long campaign by left-wing activists to extend the franchise in leadership elections from MPs to the wider party.[1] Throughout the 1970s, resolutions were put to successive Labour conferences to change the method of electing the leader and support gradually built up. It was given a boost in 1976 when the Parliamentary Labour Party (PLP) chose Callaghan, a stalwart of the Labour right, to succeed Wilson as prime minister and party leader at a time when the left was growing in strength in the Constituency Labour Parties (CLPs) and the trade unions. That year, the National Executive Committee (NEC) established a working party to formalise the position that the PLP leader should be the leader of the entire party (a change adopted in 1978). It also mooted the possibility of an electoral college representing all sections of the party in 1977. That proposal was defeated at the 1978 conference, as was a similar one in 1979, by which time Labour was back in opposition.

In 1980, an electoral college was back on the agenda after it was recommended by a commission of enquiry that had been set up by the NEC but which was dominated by the major trade unions. Although the precise division of votes it proposed was rejected, the principle of an electoral college to replace PLP ballots was now broadly, though not unanimously, accepted. The 1980 party conference voted in favour of the principle of extending the selectorate but again could not agree on the division of votes. A special conference at Wembley was called for January 1981, when different options would be put to a vote. The three-month adjournment till the special conference was engulfed in controversy when Callaghan decided to resign as leader, paving the way for a leadership contest held under the old selection rules of a PLP ballot. Tony Benn, the leader of the left, refused to participate, claiming that it was an illegitimate ballot. However, Michael Foot did contest the election and eventually defeated three other candidates, including Denis Healey, to win the leadership (see Chapter 2).

The left took its revenge at the Wembley special conference. It took advantage of divisions on the right to secure a distribution of votes that put the PLP and CLPs on an equal footing while giving the greatest power to the unions. The right wanted to maximise the PLP's share of the votes and started to coalesce behind a 50-25-25 formula (henceforth, the first number refers to the percentage of votes for the PLP, the second for CLPs and the third for affiliated organisations – mainly unions but also small socialist societies). The left had initially wanted an equal split between the PLP, CLPs and the unions, but shifted to 30-30-40. This formula had been proposed by the Union of Shop, Distributive and Allied Workers (USDAW), whose leaders were now looking to extricate themselves from supporting it in order to vote for 50-25-25. The left realised that it needed USDAW's large block vote and mobilised behind 30-30-40, which eventually won. Even then, victory was possible only because the Amalgamated Union of Engineering Workers (AUEW) had mandated its delegates not to support any proposal that failed to give the PLP an absolute majority of the votes, i.e. 50 percent plus one. That 'purity' ensured that the AUEW had to abstain once its own preferred option of 75 percent for the PLP had been defeated.[2]

The effect of the vote was dramatic. The following day a group of right-leaning Labour MPs announced the formation of the Council for Social Democracy, which became the Social Democratic Party two months later. In their founding 'Limehouse Declaration', they lamented that '[a] handful of trade union leaders can now dictate the choice of a future Prime Minister'.[3] The rest of the right vowed to overturn the decision. Partly to forestall such a move, Benn decided to use the new procedures quickly. Rather than challenging Foot for the leadership, a move that would have split the left, he challenged Healey for the deputy leadership. Benn lost by just 1 percent but succeeded in entrenching the college, which was reluctantly accepted by the right as the price for ensuring party unity.[4]

Features of the electoral college

The electoral college contained a number of specific features in addition to the new distribution of voting rights.[5] First, eligibility to participate as a candidate was restricted to MPs, largely for reasons of practicality. Second, each candidate would need to be publicly nominated by a minimum proportion of Labour MPs. Initially, this hurdle was set at 5 percent. Third, leadership contests would take place annually when Labour was in opposition, provided that a rival candidate came forward. Contests would take place at the party conference, with nominations due at the beginning of the summer. If Labour were in government, a contest would take place only if a majority vote at the party conference supported the principle of an election. This rule was designed to prevent destabilising challenges to Labour prime ministers. Fourth, all candidates would be required to join a leadership contest in the first ballot, rather than being permitted to join in later rounds. Fifth, a system of exhaustive ballots would be used. The winner would need to achieve a majority of votes cast and failing that on the first ballot, the lowest-ranked candidate would drop out and another vote would take place. The process would continue until one candidate passed the 50 percent threshold. The votes would be cast by MPs and delegates representing the CLPs, unions and socialist societies at the party conference (or at a special leadership conference if a vacancy arose and it was impractical to wait for the annual conference). Initially, it was left to CLPs and affiliates to determine how to choose a candidate to support, with postal and branch ballots permissible. In practice, most CLPs left the decision to their activist-led (and often left-wing) general committees. Similarly, trade unions had the option of balloting their members, letting their executives decide or leaving the decision to their conference delegates.

In the years following the formation of the electoral college, there were a number of changes to it. In the wake of Benn's unsuccessful challenge to Neil Kinnock in 1988, the nomination threshold for leadership candidates was increased from 5 percent of the PLP to 20 percent in order to prevent frivolous challenges.[6] This reform increased the institutional security of tenure of Labour leaders.[7] After Bryan Gould, the only serious rival to John Smith, struggled to surmount the 20 percent hurdle in the 1992 contest, a new 12.5 percent threshold was introduced for contests for vacancies, but 20 percent remained the rule for challenges.[8]

With each successive use of the electoral college, greater numbers of CLPs balloted their members rather than leaving the mandating decision to general committees. The leadership contests of 1983 and 1988 demonstrated that when balloting was used, the votes tended to favour centre-left and centre-right candidates rather than the far left.[9] In 1989, local balloting was made compulsory in the CLP section, but CLPs continued to cast their votes in the electoral college on a winner-takes-all basis (i.e. block voting). A further reform came in 1991, when Labour Members of the European Parliament (MEPs) were enfranchised and permitted to vote in the PLP section, participating for the first time in the 1992 contest.[10]

An important factor in electoral-college contests was the role played by the trade unions. Although they controlled less than 40 percent of the votes, the unions' power was magnified by the concentration of their votes in undivided blocks.[11] In 1988, the Transport and General Workers' Union (TGWU) alone controlled 8 percent of the entire electoral college, equivalent to about 160 CLPs or 60 MPs. The effect was to encourage candidates to seek early backing from the big unions, first in the form of a nomination and later as votes. It also led to accusations that the unions were king-makers in leadership contests, particularly in 1983 and 1992 when the major unions quickly offered their support to Kinnock and Smith respectively.[12]

Following Labour's fourth consecutive election defeat, in 1992, a debate between what came to be known as 'modernisers' and 'traditionalists' took place over trade-union influence in the party. The modernisers, associated with Tony Blair and Gordon Brown, argued that the union link had damaged Labour in the election.[13] The traditionalists, among whose ranks were the left and most of the major union leaders, disputed this claim and sought to defend union influence. The NEC established a review group, dominated by traditionalists, to examine the party-union link.[14] Its primary focus was on parliamentary-candidate selection, but leadership elections also came in its sights. The new leader, Smith, agreed with the modernisers in wanting the unions removed completely and replaced by a new 50:50 college comprising MPs and individual party members. However, traditionalists were not prepared to go that far, preferring a reweighted tripartite college, in which each section had one-third of the votes. Smith eventually agreed to retain union votes in a one-third-one-third-one-third college as the price for winning union support for the more crucial shift to one member-one vote (OMOV) in candidate selection. At the 1993 party conference, the proposed reforms of the electoral college were overwhelmingly accepted.[15] Details of the electoral college as it is currently composed are set out in Box 3.1.

Full OMOV was confirmed in the members section but now it would take place in a national ballot of party members, rather than in local ballots to determine each individual CLP's block vote, as previously. It was no longer practical to use exhaustive ballots, as that could entail expensive multiple ballots and so the alternative vote (AV) system was adopted for all sections of the college, with the winner needing to pass the 50 percent mark on first or later preferences.[16] In the affiliates section, block voting was abolished at Smith's insistence and individual union members who paid the political levy, a small sum in addition to union dues, were given votes, provided that they confirmed that they supported the Labour Party. Again, the votes would be cast in a national ballot of all the unions' levy-payers, rather than members voting to decide which candidate their own individual unions would support. Union executives could send recommendations to their members on how to vote.[17] Finally, MPs and MEPs would vote in the parliamentary section.

Box 3.1   Labour Party Leadership Election Rules

- Leadership elections take place annually at party conference in September, provided candidates come forward. Otherwise, incumbent leader considered re-elected
- When Labour is in government, annual leadership contests take place only if party conference votes by a majority on a card vote to approve principle of a contest. No such requirement when Labour is in opposition
- If vacancy arises due to death, incapacitation or resignation of incumbent, special conference may be called if waiting for annual conference is impractical
- Candidates must be MPs
- In the case of a vacancy, candidates must secure nominations of 12.5 percent of Labour MPs. In the case of a challenge, candidates must be nominated by 20 percent of Labour MPs. Nominations failing to pass these thresholds declared null and void
- Supporting nominations by MEPs, CLPs, unions and socialist societies also permitted but no thresholds specified
- Electoral college has three sections, each accounting for one-third of total votes:

  Section 1: Labour MPs and MEPs, who vote in a non-secret ballot

  Section 2: Individual party members of good standing, who vote in a secret postal ballot on an aggregated and national basis

  Section 3: Individual members of affiliated organisations (trade unions and socialist societies), who vote in a secret postal ballot on an aggregated and national basis. Voters must confirm on their ballots they are not members or supporters of other parties otherwise their ballots are considered spoilt
- Vote totals aggregated across the three sections for each candidate. All sections use alternative-vote system. If no candidate secures overall majority of votes cast in first count, candidate with fewest votes eliminated and his votes redistributed to other candidates. Process continues until a candidate passes 50 percent mark.

Source: *Labour Party Rule Book 2008*, Chapter 4, Clause B.2.

Leadership contests in the electoral college, 1983–2007

Three leadership and four deputy-leadership contests took place in the electoral college before the 1993 reforms. All but one of these contests resulted in overwhelming victories for the respective winners. The 1981 deputy-leadership contest, in which Healey defeated Benn by less than 1 percentage point, took place amid the extraordinary circumstances of intense factional warfare inside the Labour Party. However, all of the leadership elections, which are the principal concern here, saw landslide victories for, respectively, Kinnock in 1983 (in which he secured 71.3 percent of the college votes), Kinnock again in 1988 (securing 88.6 percent) and Smith in 1992 (who won 91.0 percent).

Kinnock's success in a four-candidate race in 1983 came despite facing Roy Hattersley, who had a better claim to electoral appeal and governmental competence. However, he was on the Labour right and Kinnock, as a centre-leftist, was deemed better able to unite the party after the trauma of the 1983 general-election defeat.[18] In 1988, Kinnock faced a challenge from Benn in a doomed attempt by the hard left to halt the modernisation drive. Kinnock was stronger than Benn on all three selection criteria.[19] When Kinnock resigned after Labour's defeat in the 1992 general election, Smith easily defeated Gould and was the superior candidate on all three selection criteria.[20] In each of these contests, the victorious candidate won in all three sections of the electoral college (see Appendix A). In 1983, Kinnock won overwhelming majorities in the CLP and affiliates sections and a 49.3 percent plurality in the PLP section. In 1988, he won huge majorities in all three sections, as did Smith in 1992.[21]

The 1994 leadership and deputy leadership elections were the first to be organised under the post-1993 rules. The contests came about through the death of Smith from a heart attack in May 1994. His deputy, Margaret Beckett, took over as interim leader until a new leader could be chosen in July. Party rules stipulated that any deputy-leadership contest should take place at the party conference, as there was no vacancy. However, Beckett decided to bring forward that contest to coincide with the leadership election. Furthermore, she announced that she would run for the leadership herself, as well as standing in the deputy-leadership election.[22] John Prescott from the 'traditionalist' wing of the party also entered both contests. They were joined in the leadership election by Tony Blair, a youthful moderniser who had enhanced his reputation in the preceding years. It was claimed that Blair persuaded Gordon Brown not to enter the contest, as doing so would split

the modernisers' support. This incident would ultimately poison relations between the two men throughout Labour's period in government
after 1997.[23] A maverick left-winger, Denzil Davies, also tried to enter
the contest, but he received insufficient nominations.

Blair was quickly established as the frontrunner, securing significant
support from the PLP. He was also popular among Labour members,
who were ready for a change of direction after four general-election
defeats. More surprisingly, he appealed to trade-union members, who
were assumed to be more centrist than union leaders and officials. Blair
ultimately triumphed, securing an overall majority on the first count
in all three sections of the electoral college. He won 60.5 percent of
the parliamentary section, 58.2 percent of the members section and
52.3 percent of the affiliates section to give him 57.0 percent of the
college overall. Prescott came second, winning 24.1 percent of the college
and Beckett was third, with 18.9 percent. In the deputy-leadership
contest, Prescott defeated Beckett by 56.5 percent to 43.5 percent.[24]
According to Stark, Blair was the leading candidate on all three selection criteria. In particular, polls indicated that he was the most electorally appealing candidate.[25] Despite his centrist stance, Labour was
far less divided than it had been a decade earlier and so party unity was
not a major issue in the contest.

Brown finally got his chance to become Labour leader 13 years later.
He had plotted to secure the position for many years and his allies
destabilised Blair's leadership (see below). When Blair finally announced
that he would stand down in 2007, Brown fought hard to ensure that he
would seize the prize unchallenged. His allies denigrated the chances of
potential rivals. They also set about accumulating nominations from MPs
until Brown reached a figure that ensured no other candidate would be
able to enter the contest. A Blairite challenger failed to materialise and
two left-wingers, John McDonnell and Michael Meacher, each failed to
secure the requisite 45 nominations (12.5 percent of the PLP), even after
Meacher stood aside to give McDonnell a clear run. McDonnell eventually received only 29 nominations to Brown's 313.[26] However, there was
a six-candidate contest for the deputy leadership, which was narrowly
won by Harriet Harman.[27]

The Labour Party leadership election of 2010

The operation of Labour's leadership-selection rules can be illustrated by
an in-depth examination of the 2010 leadership election, which commenced after the general election in May. The election had resulted in a

hung parliament with the Conservatives emerging as the largest party. As the different parties looked for ways to form a coalition government, it became clear that Brown was a major obstacle to Labour's chances of doing a deal with the Liberal Democrats.[28] To increase the chances of an agreement, Brown resigned as Labour leader and announced a leadership contest. Harman took over as acting leader. Ultimately, Brown's move was to no avail, as the Conservatives and Liberal Democrats formed a coalition government and Labour was back in opposition. The leadership contest was therefore destined to become a post-mortem of the Labour government.

The candidates

Some of the candidates who entered the contest were predicted to do so but there were also some surprises. As expected, the former foreign secretary, David Miliband, announced his candidacy two days after Brown's resignation. He was a centrist and quickly installed as the favourite. Three days later, his younger brother, Ed, the former climate change minister, unexpectedly announced that he would also run, presenting himself as a left-leaning alternative. Ed Miliband had rarely been spoken of as a potential candidate in the past. Two other members of the previous cabinet, Ed Balls, the former children, schools and families secretary, and Andy Burnham, formerly the health secretary, announced that they would stand. Balls was a confidant of Brown and seen by many as a factional figure, whereas Burnham extolled his loyalty to both Blair and Brown. Finally, two left-wingers, McDonnell and Diane Abbott, declared their candidacies.

Not only was Abbott the only woman to enter the contest, she was also the first black candidate to run for the leadership of a major British political party. At 56, she was the oldest of the candidates and had spent her 23 years in parliament on the back benches. Her candidacy was a surprise, but McDonnell's was not. He was also a backbencher who had not served in government but he had attempted to run against Brown in 2007. The other four candidates were all in their forties, had been in parliament for less than a decade, had served in the cabinet and were former special advisors.

Among the prominent figures not to enter the contest were Alistair Darling, the former chancellor, as well as Alan Johnson, the former home secretary and Jack Straw, another former foreign secretary. Johnson immediately endorsed David Miliband. Jon Cruddas, an influential figure on the left with strong union connections, announced that he would not stand. Yvette Cooper, another former cabinet minister, decided not to stand but instead endorsed her husband, Ed Balls.

The party decided to hold a long campaign over the summer, rather than a quick contest. The major reason was that it would be cheaper to organise the electoral college at the party conference in September. This decision was also seen as disadvantageous to David Miliband, who was deprived of the chance to exploit his early position as favourite. It gave his opponents, especially his brother, the chance to spend the summer catching up.

The nomination period was initially very brief but it was extended by two weeks to 9 June after complaints that there was insufficient time. Each candidate had to secure the nominations of 12.5 percent of the PLP. As there were 257 Labour MPs, candidates needed 33 nominations (candidates could also nominate themselves). Each MP could nominate only one candidate. Balls and the Miliband brothers quickly passed the threshold, but the other candidates had more problems. Burnham eventually reached the threshold on deadline day. McDonnell agreed to withdraw in order to increase Abbott's chances of gaining enough nominations. She finally secured her place on the ballot paper after senior figures, including David Miliband, Harman and Straw, agreed to nominate her. Many felt that it was important that there should be at least one female candidate, although Abbott's nominators were not bound to vote for her in the selection ballot. David Miliband secured 81 nominations, followed by his brother on 63, while Balls, Burnham and Abbott each received 33. Fourteen MPs, including Gordon Brown, did not use their nominations (Table 3.1).

Most of the party's leading figures eventually endorsed David Miliband. Eleven shadow-cabinet members, including Darling, Straw and Johnson sent a letter to party members endorsing him.[29] He was also endorsed by the former home secretary, David Blunkett (as his second choice after Burnham). Neither Blair nor Mandelson publicly endorsed any candidate, but each offered coded support to David Miliband. Most MPs

Table 3.1   Nominations of Labour Leadership Candidates 2010

	MPs	MEPs	CLPs	Trade unions	Socialist societies
D. Miliband	81	6	165	2	1
E. Miliband	63	6	151	6	3
Abbott	33	0	20	2	1
Balls	33	0	17	1	0
Burnham	33	1	44	0	1

Source: Labour Party, 'Leadership 2010', available at <http://www.labour.org.uk>.

identified as Blairites supported him but so too did Cruddas and the veteran leftist, Dennis Skinner. Ed Miliband was endorsed by the former leader, Lord Kinnock.

Supporting nominations were permitted from other sections of the party, although these were not required (Table 3.1). The party's 13 MEPs divided six apiece for the Milibands and one for Burnham. The CLPs narrowly favoured David over Ed Miliband, although over a third did not nominate anyone. Six socialist societies nominated a candidate, with three going for Ed Miliband. Finally, 11 trade unions nominated candidates, with Ed Miliband securing six, including the 'big three' of Unite, UNISON and GMB.

The campaign

The selection system required different forms of campaigning among the candidates. Campaigning for support among MPs could be done at Westminster but winning the votes of party and union members required the candidates to speak directly to them. During the summer, the candidates undertook a punishing round of about 40 hustings. Four of these were special television events but most were organised by trade unions and CLPs, lasting about two hours and being generally well-attended. There were few direct attacks on each other by the candidates, though there were coded criticisms relating to the Blair-Brown divisions, the Iraq War and the size of the state.[30]

The need to win support from individual party and union members required the candidates to give clear and public indications of the direction in which they wanted to take party policy. Abbott, Balls and Ed Miliband took positions clearly to the left of David Miliband, with Burnham occupying a centrist position. Balls criticised the plan of the previous Labour chancellor, Alistair Darling, to halve the budget deficit within one parliament and argued for a clearer focus on economic growth. Ed Miliband said that Darling's plan should be merely a 'starting point'.[31] Abbott also criticised cuts to public services but said that the Trident nuclear missile programme should be cut. David Miliband accepted Darling's plan, but in a tack to the left, he advocated a 'mansion tax' on properties worth over £2 million. Other candidates also called for targeted tax rises. Abbott and Ed Miliband wanted the temporary 50 percent top rate of tax introduced by Darling to become permanent, while Balls wanted it to apply to incomes of £100,000 rather than the prevailing level of £150,000. Abbott also called for higher taxes on the banks and the financial sector. Burnham advocated a 10 percent tax on people's estates after their deaths to pay for a national care service for elderly people free at the point of delivery. However, he said that spending cuts in the National Health Service (NHS) might be necessary.[32]

New Labour's public-service reforms were criticised by Abbott, Balls, Burnham and Ed Miliband, who all decried marketisation in the public sector. Ed Miliband also criticised the way the largely public-sector trade unions had been left out in the cold by New Labour. The policy of university tuition fees came under attack, with both Balls and Ed Miliband arguing for a graduate tax. In contrast, David Miliband generally sought to defend the record of the Blair government on public services.

Ed Miliband reinforced his left-leaning credentials by calling for a 'living wage' set above the level of the minimum wage and for a fair-pay review to look at salaries in the public and private sectors. Most controversially, he criticised the Iraq War, a divisive issue in the party, claiming that he had opposed it at the time. However, he had not been an MP in 2003 and so did not have to vote on the conflict. Rival candidates expressed incredulity at his claim but he made it repeatedly and in doing so exploited his brother's support for the war.[33]

The issue of immigration also emerged during the contest. Balls in particular was critical of the Labour government's policy of permitting large-scale immigration, which, he said, had the effects of depressing wage levels for low-earners and putting pressure on housing and public services. Balls' intervention was interpreted as an appeal to disenchanted working-class Labour supporters and to union leaders concerned about cheap immigrant labour undercutting their members' wages.[34]

The long campaign compelled candidates to undertake fundraising. The Electoral Commission, which regulates political finance in Britain, reported that David Miliband's campaign secured cash and non-cash donations worth £623,000 (See Appendix L). These included cumulative donations worth over £180,000 from Lord Sainsbury, the supermarket entrepreneur and former Labour minister. Ed Miliband's campaign secured over £336,000, including £100,000 from the union, Unite. Balls attracted £158,000, of which £126,000 came from the author, Ken Follett. Burnham secured less than £50,000 while the Electoral Commission listed £13,000 in donations to Abbott's campaign. Together the rival campaigns raised nearly £1.2 million for the contest. The party set a spending limit of £156,000 by each candidate, representing £1 for each individual party member registered on 31 December 2009. However, this limit did not apply to spending on staff.[35]

The contest was slow to take off but it came alive in the final four weeks. Sensing that his lead was slipping, David Miliband warned the party not to slip back into its old-Labour 'comfort zone'. That prompted Ed Miliband to retort that the bigger danger was remaining in a 'New Labour comfort zone'. Meanwhile, Mandelson spoke of his fears that the Brownites would lead Labour into an 'electoral cul-de-sac'.[36] Ballot papers were sent out in early September and in the same week, Blair's memoirs were published. In a television interview, Blair justified the Iraq War and also laid bare the divisions between himself and Brown. He said that the party under Brown should not have moved 'a millimetre' from New Labour's strategy and he offered a coded endorsement of David Miliband.[37] (It was later revealed that Blair made a donation worth £27,000 to David's campaign.[38]) The interventions by Blair and Mandelson sharpened divisions over New Labour's legacy. All of the candidates acknowledged the need to move beyond the New Labour era. However, David Miliband was in the awkward position of being widely seen as the Blairite candidate. He was reluctant to disavow the record of the government in which he had served whereas the other candidates were more open in their criticisms.

During the campaign, the pollsters, YouGov, carried out two major surveys of Labour Party members and trade unionists who belonged to Labour-affiliated unions and supported the party. The leading centre-left website, *Left Foot Forward*, maintained a list of endorsements by MPs, a list that was used by YouGov to provide an estimate of support in the PLP section of the electoral college. The results of these surveys are presented in Table 3.2.

Both polls gave David Miliband a clear lead on first preferences in the electoral college, with Ed in second place and the other candidates out of the race. However, the expectation was that, under the AV voting system, a majority of those supporting Abbott, Balls and Burnham would transfer their votes to Ed Miliband as the more left-leaning candidate. These polls supported that belief. However, there was a shift in support for the two leading candidates as the campaign progressed. In July, David Miliband enjoyed a clear lead of 8 points overall in the two-candidate preferred vote over his brother. Among union members, his lead was 12 points. By September, however, Ed Miliband had taken a narrow lead in the electoral college, with the biggest shift among union members. The latter now preferred Ed to David by 14 points.

Part of this shift within the unions followed communication between union leaders and their members. The unions were entitled to include voting recommendations along with ballot papers to their members,

Table 3.2 Polling of Labour Leadership Election 2010

	July Poll				September Poll			
	MPs/ MEPs	Party members	Union members	Total	MPs/ MEPs	Party members	Union members	Total
First preferences								
D. Miliband	39	38	34	**37**	41	38	29	**36**
E. Miliband	30	32	26	**29**	29	31	36	**32**
Burnham	12	10	13	**12**	11	10	14	**12**
Abbott	5	13	17	**12**	4	11	12	**9**
Balls	14	7	11	**11**	14	9	9	**11**
Run-off								
D. Miliband	55	50	56	**54**	56	48	43	**49**
E. Miliband	45	50	44	**46**	44	52	57	**51**

Source: YouGov, 'Labour leaders (summary)', poll for the *Sunday Times*, 12 September 2010, available at <http://www.yougov.co.uk>. Data on MPs'/MEPs' preferences from *Left Foot Forward*, available at <http://www.leftfootforward.org>. In run-off, MPs/MEPs supporting Abbott, Balls and Burnham assumed to divide equally between Milibands.
Notes: All figures are percentages. Labour Party members: N = 1,184 (July), N = 1,011 (September). Trade-union members: N = 1,102 (July), N = 718 (September)

provided that the recommendations were put in a separate envelope inside the larger envelope containing voting and campaign materials (sending separate envelopes in the mail would be more expensive). Controversy surrounded the actions of GMB and Unite, which were both accused of breaking the spirit, if not the letter, of the rules. Unite's recommendation was in a transparent envelope, while GMB's large outer envelope had a picture of Ed Miliband on the front and an endorsement of him.[39]

Voting closed for union members on 21 September and the following day for party members, MPs and MEPs. Labour's annual conference assembled on 25 September and the result was announced (Table 3.3). As expected, David Miliband led after the first count with 37.8 percent, but with his brother close behind on 34.3 percent. The other three candidates each won between 7 and 12 percent. Abbott was the first candidate to be eliminated, followed by Burnham and then Balls. The reallocation of Balls' votes was decisive. Given that he was seen as occupying the same centre-left territory as Ed Miliband, it was not surprising that most of his supporters' votes transferred to the latter in the final round. Indeed, the left-wing vote in general was split between Abbot, Balls and Ed Miliband in the early rounds of voting but transferred to Ed Miliband as the count proceeded. It was enough to deliver him victory by just 1.3 percent, the closest ever result in a Labour leadership election. However, David Miliband won majorities in both the parliamentary and members sections. In the former, he won 134 MPs to his brother's 115 in the final round of counting, although MEPs split

Table 3.3   Labour Party Leadership Election 2010

Electoral College (1/3, 1/3, 1/3)	First count (%)	Second count (%)	Third count (%)	Fourth count (%)
Ed Miliband	34.3	37.5	41.3	50.7
David Miliband	37.8	38.9	42.7	49.4
Ed Balls	11.8	13.2	16.0	–
Andy Burnham	8.7	10.4	–	–
Diane Abbott	7.4	–	–	–

Source: Labour Party, 'Summary of voting by round', available at <http://www.labour.org.uk>.
Notes: Parliamentary section: 253 MPs and 13 MEPs (a further four MPs did not vote), turnout 98.5%; Members section: 127,331 votes, 457 spoilt ballots, turnout 71.7%; Affiliates section: trade-unions members (96.3%) and socialist societies (3.7%), 247,339 votes, 36,105 spoilt ballots, turnout 9.0%. Alternative-vote electoral system. Full details of result in Appendix A.

7-6 for Ed. In the members section, David's majority was 8.8 percent in the final round of counting; he secured a plurality of first preferences in no fewer than 97 percent of CLPs. However, these leads were wiped out by his brother's victory in the affiliates section by 59.8 percent to 40.2 percent, a lead of 19.6 percent. Ed Miliband became the first winner of a Labour leadership contest since the electoral college was formed not to have won majorities or pluralities in all three sections. Indeed, he won a majority in only one section.

Selection criteria in 2010

The division of the electoral college into three sections created the possibility that different stakeholders in the party could prefer different candidates. YouGov's polls of party members and trade unionists carried questions on leadership qualities. (There was no similar polling of MPs.) In a poll two weeks before the result was announced, David Miliband was seen as the strongest candidate by party and union members on the criteria of electability and competence. The results are set out in Table 3.4. Fully 55 percent of party members believed he was the candidate most likely to lead Labour to victory at the next general election, while 42 percent of trade unionists thought the same. His nearest rival was Ed Miliband, deemed the most electable candidate by 25 percent of party members and 24 percent of trade unionists, with the other three candidates in single figures.

Voters also preferred Miliband senior, although there was a lot of uncertainty about the candidates. A YouGov poll of all voters found that 19 percent regarded David Miliband as the best potential leader, while 36 percent of Labour supporters agreed. The other candidates were far behind, with Ed Miliband preferred by 8 percent of all voters and 13 percent of Labour supporters. Abbott was seen by both groups as the worst candidate.[40]

David Miliband was seen as the most competent candidate. He had been in government longer than the other candidates and, as foreign secretary, had held the highest position. Asked which candidate would make the best prime minister, 45 percent of Labour members and 33 percent of trade unionists believed it was David Miliband, while 28 percent of both members and trade unionists thought it was his brother. Similarly, 44 percent of members and 31 percent of trade unionists thought David most likely to be effective in holding the government to account, while 21 percent of members and 23 percent of union members thought Ed would.

Table 3.4 Labour Party and Trade Union Members' Views of Candidates' Qualities (September 2010)

Candidate qualities	Labour party members					Labour-affiliated trade unionists				
	Abbott	Balls	Burnham	D. Miliband	E. Miliband	Abbott	Balls	Burnham	D. Miliband	E. Miliband
Most effective, as leader of the opposition, at holding present government to account [competence]	6	19	5	44	21	6	16	7	31	23
Most likeable	12	8	20	25	27	11	8	17	21	22
Most shares your political views	17	10	12	24	29	14	9	14	16	24
Most in touch with lives of ordinary voters	16	11	27	16	16	15	9	21	12	15
Most likely to lead Labour to victory at next general election [electability]	3	5	3	55	25	2	6	4	42	24
Would make best Prime Minister [competence]	4	7	4	45	28	4	7	6	33	28

Sources: YouGov, 'Labour leaders (Labour members)' and 'Labour leaders (trade unionists)', polls for the *Sunday Times*, 12 September 2010, available at <http://www.yougov.co.uk>.

Notes: Q. 'Which of the candidates, if any, do you think...?' [Respondents could name only one candidate for each criterion] All figures are percentages. Respondents replying 'none'/'don't know' excluded from table. Labour Party members: N = 1,011; Trade-union members: N = 718

If David Miliband was regarded as the most electable and most competent candidate, but still lost the leadership contest, one conclusion was that he must have trailed his brother on the criterion of acceptability. The poll did not ask respondents which candidate would be best able to unite the Labour Party. However, acceptability is closely linked to ideology, on which the polls contained a number of questions. In

Figure 3.1   Labour Party Members' Ideological Positions and Perceptions of Candidates (September 2010)

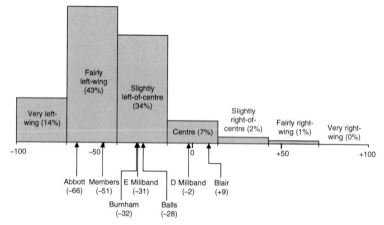

Figure 3.2   Labour-affiliated Trade Unionists' Ideological Positions and Perceptions of Candidates (September 2010)

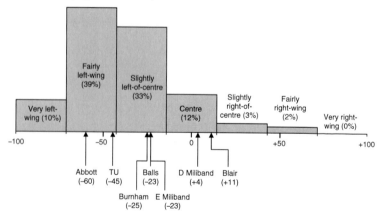

Sources (both figures): YouGov, 'Labour leaders (Labour members)'; 'Labour leaders (trade unionists)', polls for the *Sunday Times*, 12 September 2010, available at <http://www.yougov.co.uk>. *Notes*: Q. 'As you probably know, the Labour Party is holding an election to decide its next leader. Where would you place each of the candidates/yourself on this scale?' Percentages recalculated to exclude respondents replying 'don't know'. Labour Party members: N = 1,011; Trade-union members: N = 718

Table 3.4, Ed Miliband was regarded as the candidate who most shared the political views of members, although differences between the candidates were fairly small. A more detailed snapshot of ideology was provided by questions asking respondents to position themselves and the candidates on the traditional left-right scale. The results are displayed in Figures 3.1 and 3.2. Party members and Labour-supporting trade unionists had similar aggregate ideological distributions, with each group skewed towards the left. Fully 77 percent of members and 72 percent of trade unionists classified themselves as either fairly left-wing or slightly left-of-centre. On a scale where −100 was very left-wing, +100 was very right-wing and 0 was in the centre, the average member was positioned at −51 and the average trade unionist (TU) at −45. Very few members of either group positioned themselves in the centre or on the right.

There was also agreement among party and union members over where the candidates were ideologically situated. Both groups regarded Abbott as the most left-wing and David Miliband as the most centrist, with party members positioning him on average at −2 while union members put him at +4 (close to where they positioned Blair, who is included for the purpose of comparison). They agreed that Balls, Burnham and Ed Miliband were ideologically close, in the 'slightly left-of-centre' category.

If party and union members had voted purely on ideological proximity, Abbott would have won a majority among both groups and David Miliband would have struggled. In fact, Abbott eventually came fifth among party members with just 7.3 percent of the votes and third among affiliates with 12.3 percent. David Miliband would ultimately be the choice of party members. Thus, ideology did not operate in a simplistic way in the leadership contest; the candidates' other qualities also mattered.

Ideology was, nevertheless, an undercurrent to the campaign. There was a contrast in the support garnered by the two leading candidates. The average left-right position of party members supporting David Miliband was −41 while for those supporting Ed Miliband, it was −61. Similarly, trade-union supporters of David were, on average, positioned at −34, while those supporting his brother were at −53. David's support came from party and union members who were slightly left-of-centre, centre and right-of-centre. Ed's supporters were more likely to be very or fairly left-wing.

The question is whether these ideological differences in support reflected deep divisions over policy and strategy. The most contentious issue during the campaign was the New Labour legacy. All of the candidates to varying degrees advocated moving on from the New Labour era, including David Miliband and, to a greater extent, Burnham. However, Ed Miliband, as well as Balls and Abbott, each sought to define themselves in opposition to New Labour. That involved trenchant criticisms of Blair, the Iraq War and public-sector reform. David Miliband had first been spoken of seriously as a potential leader when Blairites urged him to run against Brown in 2007. From then on, he was seen as a leader-in-waiting, an impression reinforced by his aborted challenge to Brown in 2008 (see below). These incidents ensured that he would come to be seen, not entirely accurately, as the Blairite candidate in 2010.[41] That risked making him appear divisive to a party that wanted to move on from the past. In the final month of the campaign, he sought to counter this impression by presenting himself as the 'unity candidate'.[42]

Divisions over Blair and New Labour emerged very clearly in YouGov's polls of party and union members. Table 3.5 shows differing perceptions of Blair between the Miliband brothers' supporters. On balance, David's supporters viewed Blair as an asset to the Labour Party. In contrast, large majorities of Ed's party supporters saw Blair as a liability.

Table 3.5 Attitudes to Tony Blair among Labour Party and Trade Union Members 2010

	Blair asset	Blair liability	Blair net asset
Party members			
All party members	34	58	−24
D. Miliband supporters	47	43	+4
E. Miliband supporters	21	74	−53
Trade unionists			
All trade unionists	38	50	−12
D. Miliband supporters	55	36	+19
E. Miliband supporters	27	65	−38

Sources: YouGov, 'Labour leaders (Labour members)' and 'Labour leaders (trade unionists)', polls for the *Sunday Times*, 12 September 2010, available at <http://www.yougov.co.uk>.
Notes: Q. 'Do you think [Tony Blair] is an asset or liability to the Labour Party these days?' All figures are percentages. Don't knows excluded. D. Miliband and E. Miliband 'supporters' defined as respondents who selected each in a two-candidate run-off. Labour Party members: N = 1,011; Trade-union members: N = 718

These divisions were replicated in relation to party strategy (Table 3.6). Around 70 percent of David Miliband's party and union supporters thought Blair was right that Labour should not 'move a millimetre' from the New Labour strategy and only a quarter thought he was wrong. In contrast, most of Ed's party and union supporters believed Blair was wrong, while about a third considered him right.

Table 3.6 Attitudes to New Labour Strategy among Labour Party and Trade Union Members 2010

	Wholly/largely right	Wholly/largely wrong	Net right
Party members			
All party members	51	47	+4
D. Miliband supporters	73	25	+48
E. Miliband supporters	31	69	−38
Trade unionists			
All trade unionists	49	44	+5
D. Miliband supporters	69	26	+43
E. Miliband supporters	36	62	−26

Sources: YouGov, 'Labour leaders (Labour members)' and 'Labour leaders (trade unionists)', polls for the *Sunday Times*, 12 September 2010, available at <http://www.yougov.co.uk>. *Notes*: Q. 'Tony Blair has said recently that Labour should not "move a millimetre" from his New Labour approach to politics and government. Do you think Mr Blair is wholly right/largely right/largely wrong/wholly wrong?' All figures are percentages. Don't knows excluded. D. Miliband and E. Miliband 'supporters' defined as respondents who selected each in a two-candidate run-off. Labour Party members: N = 1,011; Trade-union members: N = 718

There were also divisions over the Iraq War. Although most party and union members rejected the view that the next leader should declare the war illegal, David Miliband's supporters were much stronger in their rejection. Only 14 percent of David supporters among party members believed that the next leader should declare the war illegal (74 percent disagreed), while 35 percent of Ed's supporters did (49 percent disagreed). Although Ed Miliband never went that far, he did raise the issue of Iraq repeatedly during the campaign and condemned Blair's decision to go to war. It played well with the left of the party.[43]

One issue on which there appeared to be slightly more of a consensus among selectors, perhaps surprisingly, was on the coalition government's programme of spending cuts to reduce the budget deficit. Fully 56 percent of party members and 48 percent of union members thought Labour should accept the principle of cuts but oppose their size, detail and timing as being too extreme. A minority of both groups – 25 percent of party members and 26 percent of union members – wanted the party to oppose all cuts in principle. Among David Miliband's party supporters, this proportion was 19 percent, but among Ed Miliband's, it was 30 percent.[44]

It is clear that there were genuine divisions within the Labour Party over attitudes towards Blair and New Labour. These divisions deepened during the course of the leadership contest, as Ed Miliband and the three 'minor' candidates criticised New Labour in increasingly strident terms. As the candidate most closely associated with New Labour, David Miliband frequently found himself on the defensive.

It is tempting to conclude that Ed Miliband won the leadership because he was seen as the candidate best able to unite the Labour Party. From this perspective, he successfully managed to avoid being identified as either the Brownite candidate, as Ed Balls was, or the Blairite candidate, as David Miliband was. He ran as the candidate of the soft left. As Jonathan Freedland put it, '[a]lmost uniquely in the war between the Blair and Brown camps, Ed Miliband somehow emerged unscathed'.[45] Indeed, his candidacy was initially regarded by the Brownites as a strike at the ambitions of their favoured candidate, Balls.[46]

The problem with this analysis is that it tells only part of the story. David Miliband undoubtedly suffered from the attempts by his opponents to depict him as a Blairite. Despite being described as the favourite, he was never able to pull away from the field, though it might have been much easier to do so had his brother not entered the contest. Nevertheless, if he really were so divisive, it is difficult to see how he could have won majorities of MPs and party members. These groups saw him as ideologically acceptable. Indeed, David's breadth of support was wider than his brother's, ranging from Skinner and Cruddas on the left to the Blairites on the right. Ed Miliband's support was concentrated on the soft left of the party, with lower-preference votes from the hard left.

The role of the trade unions

David Miliband lost the leadership contest in the affiliates section of the electoral college. In the final round of counting, he secured only 40.2 percent of votes in this section, to his brother's 59.8 percent. The leaders of the three major trade unions each endorsed Ed Miliband for the leadership. Most of the unions had shifted decisively to the left during the New Labour years. They elected a new generation of left-wing leaders in Derek Simpson, Tony Woodley (both Unite), Dave Prentis (UNISON) and Paul Kenny (GMB). The unions were more prepared to take on the government, signalling their discontent by reducing funds to Labour in 2002–03.[47] Overall, there was much greater ideological uniformity in the union movement in 2010 than there had been a generation earlier. In the 1970s and 1980s, Labour-affiliated unions were split between left and right, with votes often on a knife-edge at the party conference. Unions such as the electricians and later the engineers were firmly on the right of the labour movement.

In 2010, the trade-union right had all but disappeared. That would ultimately deprive David Miliband of victory.

It is true that unions could not cast block votes and that union members voted as individuals. However, the leaders and executives of most of the major unions nominated a candidate for the Labour leadership election and sent out recommendations to their members to support that candidate in the leadership contest. It is possible to gauge the effect of these endorsements by examining the voting behaviour of members of each individual union. Table 3.7 provides the breakdown of first-preference votes within each trade union. Overall, Ed Miliband won 41.5 percent of first preferences, followed by 27.5 percent for his brother, with the other three candidates winning 8–12 percent each. However, these overall figures conceal considerable variations between individual unions. Ed Miliband was nominated by the big three unions of Unite, UNISON and GMB, and he won clear pluralities in all of them, leading by 12.6 percent in UNISON, 22.8 percent in GMB and 27.0 percent in Unite. He was also nominated by the construction workers' union (UCATT), whose members voted for him even more heavily, giving him a lead of 49.8 percent over his nearest rival. Ed Miliband did not win a plurality of first preferences in any union whose leadership did not endorse him.

David Miliband was nominated by two unions (Community and USDAW) and in both cases he won overwhelming majorities. Balls was nominated by one union, the postal workers (CWU), and again it gave him a healthy plurality, the only union to do so: indeed, in no other union did he secure more than 12.7 percent of first preferences. Abbott was nominated by two transport unions, ASLEF and TSSA. Among ASLEF members, she collected over half of first-preference votes, the only union in which she managed this feat. In TSSA, she narrowly came second to David Miliband. Burnham was not nominated by any union and he failed to win more than 12.8 percent of first preferences in any union. Candidates who were nominated by unions secured about 30 percent more first-preference votes among those unions' members than among the members of unions that did not nominate them (Table 3.8). Union nominations and endorsements mattered hugely in the leadership contest. Of the nine unions that nominated a candidate and sent out ballot papers, the nominee won a plurality or majority of the respective union's members in eight.

One further issue in the affiliates section was the extremely low turnout. In 1994, union turnout was 19 percent, but in 2010 it was less than half that figure, at just 9 percent (compared to a turnout of 71.7 percent

Table 3.7 Trade Union Members' Votes in Affiliates Section 2010

Union	Nominee	First preferences					Two-candidate run-off*		Turnout[†]	Share of section[‡]
		Abbott	Balls	Burnham	D. Miliband	E. Miliband	D. Miliband	E. Miliband		
ASLEF	Abbott	50.4	6.4	6.9	17.6	18.7	43.7	56.3	25.2	1.7
BECTU	None	24.5	8.1	8.7	29.7	29.0	46.6	53.4	10.6	1.1
BFAWU	None	14.8	12.7	12.8	40.4	19.3	56.9	43.1	7.7	0.6
Community	D. Miliband	9.5	8.5	7.0	59.7	15.3	70.0	30.1	11.8	1.0
CWU	Balls	11.4	45.2	9.0	21.4	13.0	48.3	51.7	10.9	7.4
GMB	E. Miliband	8.7	6.9	8.5	26.5	49.3	36.4	63.6	7.8	17.4
MU	None	30.6	7.3	6.9	26.6	28.6	45.0	55.0	12.4	1.4
TSSA	Abbott	30.5	9.7	10.0	31.3	18.5	51.9	48.1	15.3	1.4
UCATT	E. Miliband	4.8	5.0	6.2	17.1	66.9	23.7	76.3	10.5	1.7
UNISON	E. Miliband	12.3	9.0	9.9	28.1	40.7	40.9	59.1	6.7	11.2
Unite	E. Miliband	11.7	7.3	8.4	22.8	49.8	34.0	66.0	10.5	45.1
USDAW	D. Miliband	9.9	6.1	6.8	64.2	12.9	73.6	26.5	4.3	6.1
Total		12.3	10.2	8.5	27.5	41.5	40.2	59.8	9.0	100.0

Source: Labour Party, 'Votes by affiliated members', available at <http://www.labour.org.uk>.

Notes: All figures are percentages. Two unions, Unity and the National Union of Mineworkers, nominated Ed Miliband but did not participate in the ballot.

* Estimation of two-candidate preferences (official figures not released). Votes from Abbott, Balls and Burnham redistributed to Milibands in ratio of 41.0:59.0 (DM:EM) for each union (figure based on average proportions in which votes were redistributed in entire affiliates section).

[†] Turnout rates based on *total* votes cast (incl. spoilt ballots).

[‡] Each union's % share of votes in affiliates section based on *valid* votes cast. Total of 100.0% includes socialist societies, whose members cast 3.7% of valid votes in the section (not listed in table).

Table 3.8 Difference in Support for Candidates in Nominating and
Non-nominating Unions

	Abbott	Balls	Burnham	D. Miliband	E. Miliband
Nominating unions average %	40.5	45.2	n/a	62.0	51.7
Non-nominating unions average %	13.8	7.9	8.5	26.2	19.4
Nomination boost %	+26.6	+37.3	–	+35.8	+32.3

Source: Labour Party, 'Votes by affiliated members', available at
<http://www.labour.org.uk>.
Notes: Figures are averages of first-preference percentages won in nominating and
non-nominating unions.

in the CLP section). Of 2.75 million union and socialist-society
members eligible to vote, only 247,339 did so. Of these, 36,105 'spoilt'
their ballots, primarily because they failed to tick a box confirming
that they supported the policies and principles of the Labour Party.[48]
That left 211,234 valid votes, a valid turnout of only 7.7 percent. In
UNISON and GMB, turnout was 6.7 percent and 7.8 percent respectively. In USDAW, it was only 4.3 percent. An above-average turnout of
10.5 percent in Unite gave that union a proportionately larger share of
the affiliates section than it would have secured on a uniform turnout
among the affiliates' members – 45 percent instead of 33 percent.

The alternative explanation to proactive union influence is that
union leaders' endorsements merely reflected the views that their
members already held. However, that argument sits uneasily with what
is known about how the unions decided their endorsements. Unite's
leadership initially considered supporting Balls, but as David Miliband
moved into an early lead, the union decided to support his brother as
the centre-left candidate best placed to defeat him. After talks between
the leaderships of Unite, UNISON, GMB and the CWU, the first three
endorsed Ed Miliband, while only the CWU supported Balls.[49] The 'big
three' unions chose Ed Miliband, not because of any great groundswell
of support among grassroots union members but because their leaders
identified David Miliband as the candidate least likely to further union
interests and as he was the frontrunner, they required a plan to stop
him.[50] The campaign in Unite was run by its political officer, Charlie
Whelan, a former special advisor to Gordon Brown. The union did not
merely send out a recommendation to its members but set up phone

banks and sent text messages and emails to members. Whelan also claimed to have persuaded six MPs supporting Balls to switch their second preferences from David to Ed Miliband.[51]

Both David and Ed Miliband would have been broadly acceptable to the PLP and party members. However, David was not acceptable to the leaders of the major trade unions. Polls of Labour-affiliated and Labour-supporting trade unionists in July 2010 appeared to show few significant differences between them and party members in their preferences, but by mid-September, Ed Miliband was the clear choice of union members (see Table 3.2 above). Among members of the biggest union, Unite, Ed led David 66-34 head-to-head. By then, union members had already received campaign literature from their unions and seen their leaders' endorsements.

It is incontrovertible that union participation in the electoral college decisively influenced the outcome of the leadership election. David Miliband would have won both a parliamentary ballot and a straight OMOV ballot of party members. Ed Miliband would have won a much more resounding victory had block voting still been used in the electoral college. Nevertheless, the 2010 Labour leadership election is the clearest example since Thatcher's victory in the Conservative Party in 1975 of a candidate being denied the leadership by the selection system.

Seeking to eject Labour leaders I: Tony Blair

Having examined the operation of the electoral college in leadership elections, the focus now turns to the question of how the college affects leaders' security of tenure. Labour leaders can be removed in formal leadership challenges that activate the electoral college. One such challenge occurred in 1988 but the nomination threshold for starting a contest then was only 5 percent of the PLP. It was subsequently increased to 20 percent and since then, there have been no formal challenges. However, both Blair and in particular Brown faced serious efforts to remove them from power. This section and the next assess the effect of Labour's institutions in saving them from direct challenges.

During the final few years of his premiership, Blair endured almost constant speculation about his position. In itself, that was unremarkable but what was unique was the circumstances in which the rumours occurred. Blair's period as Labour leader and prime minister was highly unusual in terms of his relationship with Brown, the chancellor of the exchequer and heir apparent. Never before had such a powerful chancellor frustrated the prime minister's plans while waiting impatiently to take his job. This rivalry went back to the Labour leadership election of 1994 when Brown reluctantly agreed to stand aside for Blair. In return, Brown allegedly demanded sweeping powers in a future Labour government and a promise that Blair would hand over power to Brown at some point, although the details of the story have been disputed. A semi-permanent war of attrition between the allies of both men continued over the course of the Labour government.[52] Once Blair's position weakened during Labour's second term in office, most of the speculation about when he would step aside was couched in terms of his rivalry with Brown.

In March 2003, Blair might have resigned had he not secured majority support among Labour MPs in a parliamentary vote on military action in Iraq. Despite two cabinet resignations and the biggest backbench revolt by a governing party's MPs for over 150 years, Blair survived because the rest of the cabinet, including Brown, stood by him, although Brown remained silent on the subject for a long time.[53] In January 2004, Labour rebels, led by Nick Brown, a close ally of the chancellor, threatened to defeat the government in a parliamentary vote on tuition fees. The chancellor intervened at the last moment to try to persuade the rebels to vote with the government and Blair narrowly won the vote. This about-turn was seen by some as evidence of Brown's fear that he would be blamed by the party for the subsequent resignation of Blair.[54] The following day, Blair escaped censure in the Hutton report on the death of David Kelly, a weapons inspector, who had committed suicide after criticising the government over Iraq to a journalist and was then exposed. Many observers agreed that the Hutton report and the tuition-fees vote both had the potential to topple Blair.[55]

Brown's apparent preference was that Blair should voluntarily step aside and allow him to take over. However, Blair was determined to hold on and in September 2004 he announced that he would fight the next general election and serve a full third term if elected. That would always prove difficult because the knowledge of his imminent departure risked diminishing his authority. In 2006, poor local-election results, a party-funding scandal in which he became the first serving prime minister to be interviewed (as a witness) by police in a criminal investigation, and Blair's reluctance to call for a ceasefire during Israeli military action in Lebanon combined to weaken his position.

In September, a group of backbench MPs and low-ranking members of the government attempted a putsch against the prime minister.[56] It transpired that the plotters had met at a curry-house in Wolverhampton to plan the coup. The MPs, mainly Brownites together with a few previously-loyal Blairites, circulated a letter calling on Blair to stand down immediately. It contained 17 signatures, one of which belonged to a junior minister: Tom Watson, a close ally of Brown. It was later discovered that, shortly before the coup, Watson had travelled to Scotland to visit Brown at his home. When this visit was revealed, Watson insisted it was a purely social call but this claim was ridiculed by Blair's supporters. They implied that Brown had authorised the coup. Watson resigned, as did seven unpaid parliamentary private secretaries, each calling for Blair to go. Although his allies successfully organised a counter-putsch, Blair bowed to pressure and signalled that he would depart in 2007.

Why did Brown not challenge Blair?

The first point to note about Blair's security of tenure as Labour leader is that he faced neither a general cabinet revolt nor a general backbench revolt. Only in September 2006 did he face a serious threat, led by junior members of the government. A major reason is that, unlike Labour under Brown between 2008 and 2010 (see below), Labour under Wilson during 1968–69, or the Conservatives under Thatcher during 1989–90, there was no catastrophic slump in Labour's poll rating under Blair.

Figure 3.3 shows Labour's poll lead over the Conservatives between 2003 and 2007. For much of this period, Labour led the Tories. It was only from the spring of 2006 that Labour fell consistently behind in the polls but always by less than 10 points. Blair's own net satisfaction ratings were poorer, usually falling in the –20 to –35 range during 2003–05 and in the –30 to –40 range during 2006–07. However, the effect was muted by the fact that Conservative leaders usually had ratings that were as bad or worse, particularly Hague and Duncan Smith. In short, there was no general collapse in Labour's electoral strength.

Instead of polling weaknesses, there were two reasons for the periodic threats to Blair's position: Labour divisions over policy and the constant agitating of Brown for the leadership. The major policy divisions under Blair were over the Iraq War and public-sector reform, such as tuition fees. Brown could almost certainly have engineered defeats for Blair over Iraq or tuition fees, but pulled back. He was reportedly worried about the Heseltine precedent of wielding the knife but never wearing the crown.[57] It would do him no good if he appeared overtly disloyal or inherited a disunited party that was headed for electoral defeat. Brown's position as heir apparent carried advantages and disadvantages (see

Figure 3.3   Labour's Poll Lead and Blair's Net Satisfaction Rating 2003–07

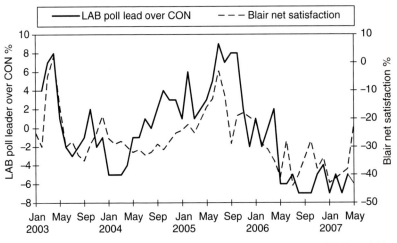

Sources: YouGov, 'Political trackers 2003–2005' and 'Political trackers 2005–2007', available at <www.yougov.co.uk>; Ipsos-MORI, 'Political monitor: satisfaction ratings 1997–present', available at <www.ipsos-mori.com>.
Notes: Q1. 'If there were a general election tomorrow, which party would you vote for?' [LAB poll lead over CON = % Labour minus % Conservative] Q2. 'Are you satisfied or dissatisfied with the way Mr Blair is doing his job as Prime Minister?' [Blair net satisfaction = % satisfied minus % dissatisfied]

Chapter 1). The main advantage was that he was widely, although not universally, seen as the only credible candidate. However, the disadvantage of this position was that it always made caution seem the attractive option, particularly to a naturally cautious politician such as Brown. A premature move risked destroying his chances of taking over and so he usually held back. Brown could never be sure that the party would tolerate him bringing down its most electorally successful leader. An ICM poll of Labour Party members in February 2004 found that, in the event of an immediate leadership election, 55 percent would vote for Blair and only 30 percent for Brown, with 15 percent undecided. It was a similar story with voters: in the aftermath of the coup attempt in September 2006, 61 percent of Labour supporters preferred Blair, while only 29 percent preferred Brown.[58]

Blair largely retained support among his senior colleagues during the coup. The cabinet was mainly staffed by Blair's allies or dependable figures.[59] (Key Brown allies such as Ed Balls and Ed Miliband were not yet in the cabinet.) Crucially, the deputy prime minister, Prescott, remained supportive of Blair throughout the coup.[60] This elite support ensured that the demand for a timetable for departure did not become a demand for an immediate departure. It also ensured that the coup attempt was left to junior figures and backbenchers.

Brown was not really frustrated by Labour's eviction institutions. If he had wanted to challenge Blair, he would almost certainly have been able to surmount the 20 percent nomination hurdle. Nevertheless, it would be premature to say that institutions were irrelevant. A lower nomination threshold in Labour leadership elections might have enabled the far left to field a stalking horse against Blair at key moments of weakness. It should be recalled that a similar challenge to Thatcher in 1989 paved the way for her ouster a year later.

Seeking to eject Labour leaders II: Gordon Brown

Brown's three years as prime minister between 2007 and 2010 offer a good example of a Labour leader who lost the voters and much of his party but who managed to cling on to power because his opponents found it difficult to remove him. The absence of an easily-operable eviction mechanism left his enemies trying to organise coups on at least three occasions. However, the clash of ambitions among potential successors and the requirement for leadership challengers to be nominated by 20 percent of the PLP combined to protect Brown until he led his party to electoral defeat.

Brown's tenure as prime minister was tumultuous. After a brief 'honeymoon' period on assuming the post in June 2007, he squandered it by allowing fevered speculation to mount that he would call an early election in the autumn to capitalise on Labour's popularity. A late shift in the polls to the Conservatives persuaded Brown to announce that there would be no early election.[61] The 'election that never was' severely dented his credibility, as did a farcical attempt to deny that unfavourable polls had played any role in his decision not to call an election. Labour's poll rating and Brown's personal ratings nosedived (Figure 3.4). The damage was compounded by a series of mishaps, including the abolition of the 10 percent starting rate of income tax in April 2008, a move that hit lower-income earners hardest. Labour MPs were accosted in their surgeries by angry voters and a large-scale rebellion, led by the backbencher, Frank Field, started brewing in the PLP. After initially resisting demands to change policy, Brown caved in.[62]

Poor local-election results in 2008 and devastating by-election defeats in Crewe & Nantwich and Glasgow East left Labour trailing the Conservatives by 20 points in the opinion polls, while Brown's personal net satis-

Figure 3.4   Labour's Poll Lead and Brown's Net Satisfaction Rating 2007–10

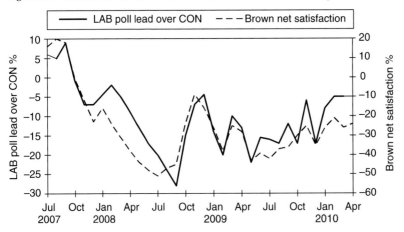

Source: Ipsos-MORI, 'Voting intention in Great Britain: Recent trends' and 'Political monitor: Satisfaction ratings 1997–present', available at <http://www.ipsos-mori.com>.
Notes: Q1. 'How would you vote if there were a general election tomorrow?' [LAB poll lead over CON = % Labour minus % Conservative] Q2. 'Are you satisfied or dissatisfied with the way Mr Brown is doing his job as Prime Minister?' [Brown net satisfaction = % satisfied minus % dissatisfied]

faction rating stood at –51 in July. Temporary respite was afforded by Brown's strong response to the financial crash in September 2008. He enjoyed a 'bounce' in the polls, although it was short-lived. By June 2009, Labour was back to nearly 20 points behind the Conservatives. That gap narrowed as the general election approached in 2010 but Labour never looked like catching up with the Tories. The party subsequently polled its second-lowest share of the vote since 1918.

Three non-challenges

Throughout the 2008–10 period, the impending sense of electoral oblivion focused minds in the cabinet and on the backbenches on the leadership issue. The first threat to Brown's position came just over a year after he took over. The poor local-election and by-election results of 2008 had already prompted some backbenchers, allegedly allies of Jack Straw, the justice secretary, to call for Brown's departure.[63] In July, the foreign secretary, David Miliband, wrote an article in the *Guardian* setting out what Labour needed to do to reconnect with voters.[64] The article was framed as a critique of the Conservatives, but criticised traits associated with Brown, such as not having a clear vision and exaggerating achievements. It failed to mention Brown by name, which was implied to mean that if Labour were to enter 'a radical new phase', it would do so without Brown at the helm.[65] It was widely interpreted as a signal that Miliband would be prepared to run for the leadership.[66]

The effect was explosive. Two backbench MPs, Bob Marshall-Andrews and Geraldine Smith, called for Miliband to be sacked.[67] Brown's spin doctors briefed against the foreign secretary, accusing him of being 'disloyal... self-serving and lacking judgement and maturity'.[68] However, senior cabinet ministers were slow to come to Brown's defence. Brown was fortunate, nevertheless, in that there did not appear to be much coordination between cabinet ministers during Miliband's challenge to the prime minister's authority and no senior figures came out in active support of him.

In September, a small-scale insurrection erupted in the PLP. The former home secretary, Charles Clarke, a long-standing critic of Brown since returning to the backbenches, said that Labour was heading for 'utter destruction' under Brown, but that he and others would 'not permit that to happen'.[69] It emerged that 12 MPs had written to Labour HQ requesting nomination papers for a leadership ballot, a request that was denied.[70] One was Siobhain McDonagh, an assistant whip who was then dismissed from the government. McDonagh had long felt frustrated that Brown had not competed in a proper leadership election and believed that he ought to do so, even if belatedly. In her opinion, 'a whole contrivance put a guy in a job that just wasn't for him and we had had no say'.[71] This complaint was a frequent one among Brown's PLP critics, as they believed it deprived him of legitimacy and a proper mandate.[72] McDonagh was joined in her calls for a contest by Joan Ryan, a party vice-chair, and several ex-frontbenchers, most of whom had been supporters of Blair.[73] Days later, David Cairns, a junior Scottish office minister, resigned and called for a debate on the leadership.[74]

Brown survived not because the cabinet rallied round – support was lukewarm – but because the rebels' timing was poor. Just as it looked as though momentum for a coup was building, the world economy was convulsed by one of the biggest financial crashes in history.[75] Suddenly, Labour plotting looked parochial and trivial, especially as Brown commanded international respect for his response to the crisis. By the time of the Labour Party conference at the end of September, Brown could tell delegates that, with the stakes so high, it was 'no time for a novice'. Ostensibly a criticism of the Tory leader, David Cameron, it was widely interpreted as a swipe at Miliband.[76] Brown buttressed his position by bringing Mandelson back into government, in the process hoping to neutralise further Blairite attacks.[77]

The second attempt to remove Brown came nine months later in June 2009. The political world was in turmoil as a scandal over parliamentary expenses claimed by MPs took hold in May.[78] All parties were harmed but Labour, as the governing party, suffered particular damage, with several ministers deciding to leave the government. Days later, Labour took a drubbing in the local and European parliamentary elections, finishing third in both. The results increased fears among Labour MPs that their parliamentary seats were at risk under Brown's continued leadership.

News had already emerged of a 'Hotmail plot' by backbenchers, who were seeking to mobilise opposition to Brown by encouraging MPs to email their support for a letter calling for him to go. Potential rebels were assured that the letter would not be published until it had the support of 50 MPs.[79] As the polls closed on election night, the work and pensions secretary, James Purnell, announced his resignation from the government. In his resignation letter, released to the media, Purnell wrote: 'I now believe your [Brown's] continued leadership makes a Conservative victory more, not less likely... I am therefore calling on you to stand aside to give our Party a fighting chance of winning. As such I am resigning from Government.'[80] Purnell's resignation reignited the 'peasants' revolt' of backbenchers that had been simmering for days, with several demanding that Brown should go.[81]

Crucially, no other cabinet minister followed Purnell's assault on the prime minister. David Miliband might have been able to bring down Brown had he resigned with Purnell, but decided against it. Straw, Harman and Johnson each continued to support Brown, as did Mandelson who crucially rallied to him.[82] There were several resignations from the government, but they were not coordinated and most were muted because they were retirements (with the prospect of future peerages) or related to the expenses scandal. That diminished their effectiveness, which would have been much greater had they been choreographed.[83] On the backbenches, Blairites continued to call for Brown's resignation and Barry Sheerman, a select-committee chairman, called for a secret ballot of Labour MPs to decide whether Brown should continue. However, the far left, including Marshall-Andrews, Michael Meacher and the Campaign Group of MPs, rallied to Brown and condemned the rebels, largely because they feared that any replacement would be a Blairite.[84]

The final attempt to remove Brown before the general election came on 6 January 2010. Two former cabinet ministers, Geoff Hoon and Patricia Hewitt, emailed a letter to Labour MPs on the issue of the leadership. The letter demanded that there should be a confidence vote in Brown, by secret ballot, among members of the PLP.[85] Labour's constitution does not make provision for confidence votes in the leader. It would be up to the PLP chairman, Tony Lloyd, to decide whether to allow such a vote. However, that was unlikely, given his reputation as a Brown loyalist and it was impossible without considerable backing from Labour MPs.[86] That support was not forthcoming, with the exception of some isolated 'usual suspects' on the back benches.

The plotters invested more hope in a frontbench coup. Rawnsley quotes Hoon as saying that he was assured that 'sufficient numbers of senior members of the Cabinet would act if we raised the flag'. Harman and Straw, who were expected to confront Brown and call for him to resign, pulled back at the last moment, with Straw reportedly saying, '[r]egicide is not the answer'.[87] However, cabinet ministers were very slow to offer public support for Brown. According to one veteran plotter, one of the characteristics of the modern media is that, 'people are literally asked within seconds of anything happening, "are you loyal or are you disloyal?", and if you say anything less than "I am loyal", you're basically gone'.[88] Consequently, the ground was prepared by the plotters to ensure that cabinet ministers remained out of sight during the coup and did not answer their telephones. It was several hours after the Hoon-Hewitt email was sent before Harman, Straw, Johnson or Miliband offered their support to Brown and only then when it was clear that the putsch had failed.[89]

Why was Brown not removed?

On the face of it, there appeared to be a strong electoral incentive for Labour MPs to remove Brown before the general election. Labour looked to be heading for a heavy defeat, with ministers becoming shadow ministers shorn of government salaries and numerous MPs losing their seats. One problem for Brown's opponents was that removing him was not guaranteed to improve matters. In September 2008, shortly after the first backbench uprising, a YouGov poll for the *Daily Telegraph* asked respondents to say which party they would support in a general election if Labour were under different leadership. Under Brown, Labour trailed the Conservatives by 20 points but under Miliband, the gap closed only slightly to 19 points, while under Straw, it was 17 points.[90] Without evidence that they would do better, there was less chance of Miliband or others mobilising support. That problem was acute because it was widely believed that, if Brown were removed as leader, there would need to be a general election shortly afterwards.[91]

A second factor that helped Brown survive was that there was no consensus within the cabinet over who should replace him. Straw reportedly backed away from challenging Brown in 2008 partly because he feared opening the way for someone else.[92] Johnson did not have a reputation as a plotter and if Brown were removed, he could have presented himself as the person best able to unite the party.[93] However, during the Hoon-Hewitt coup, he reportedly declined to become involved after being sounded out by Straw and Harman.[94] Miliband would also have been a potential candidate but after finding little cabinet support for his *Guardian* article in 2008, he feared appearing divisive.[95] Mandelson claimed that Miliband could have brought down Brown had he resigned with Purnell but would have ended up like Heseltine in 1990, in that he would have 'wielded the knife, but failed to reap the benefit'.[96] Miliband, like Harman, was considered by leading plotters to be unlikely to move against Brown unless he was sure that he would become leader.[97] Moreover, it is possible that, had there been a leadership election, a previously unfancied candidate, such as Purnell before his resignation, might have been able to establish him/herself during the contest, in much the way that Ed Miliband and Ed Balls did in 2010.[98] That too would have been considered by the major contenders. Although it is not impossible for cabinet ministers to bring down a prime minister, it is difficult because of the clash of ambitions and the risks of collective action.

A further point in relation to the costs of plotting that appeared particularly important in this case was the fear of frontbenchers and backbenchers alike of Brown's methods of dealing with dissent. After his non-challenge in 2008, Miliband was subjected to a fierce briefing operation, allegedly by Brown's lieutenants, Balls and Damian McBride.[99] A junior minister, Ivan Lewis, had details of an incident allegedly involving over-familiar text messages to a female civil servant leaked to the press shortly after he criticised Brown.[100] These tactics also made it risky for cabinet ministers to voice criticisms of Brown among themselves because word might get back to him. Consequently, communication among senior figures who wanted to remove Brown was often difficult.[101] Brown's critics also accused him of using patronage to retain the loyalty of those around him. Most of the leading figures in the 'curry-house coup' against Blair in 2006 were given government jobs by Brown.[102]

The third principal factor that enabled Brown to survive was the protection afforded to him by Labour's eviction institutions. Rules on timing stipulated that electoral-college votes would be declared at the annual conference in the event of a formal challenge (too late for the 2010 plotters). Mobilisation costs were very high: it was difficult for a potential challenger to persuade 20 percent of the PLP, or 71 MPs, to sign his or her nomination papers for a leadership challenge. Clarke believed that he might have been able to secure enough nominations in the event of a challenge but the worry remained that the cabinet would rally round Brown.[103] Unlike in the Conservative Party, votes cast by Labour MPs in leadership elections are not secret and so cabinet ministers would not be able to support Brown in public but vote against him in private. A major fear of the plotters was that a challenge to Brown would be defeated, leaving him ensconced in power and invulnerable.[104] If, however, Labour had the system used to evict Thatcher in 1990, whereby a challenger needed to be nominated by only two MPs before participating in a secret ballot of the parliamentary party, it is highly likely that Brown would have faced a stalking-horse challenge at the very least: Clarke stated that he would have challenged Brown under such a system, although not as a stalking horse but as a serious candidate.[105] Frank Field claimed that he would either have signed Clarke's nomination papers or they would both have signed another challenger's had Labour used this system.[106]

It was precisely because Labour's eviction institutions were difficult to set in motion that the plotters resorted to other means. They hoped for a cabinet coup, but that was hard to organise. Most of the overt manoeuvring was left to backbenchers, particularly, but not exclusively, ex-ministers. Chief among these was Clarke, but others included Hoon, Hewitt and Stephen Byers, as well as more junior figures.[107] One Blairite who did not pursue Brown was Mandelson. He might have been receptive to a coup in 2008 but then Brown brought him back into government. That move ultimately helped to divide Blairite opposition to Brown after Purnell's resignation in 2009.[108]

Some of these figures had an ideological incentive to oppose Brown, perhaps further motivated by personal pique. They also had weaker office incentives to remain loyal because they had already left the government. However, they still faced major problems mobilising the considerable banks of opposition to Brown within the PLP. Many MPs might have desired a change of leader but most preferred others to take the risks in bringing it about. The rebels understood this point. The 'Hotmail plot' sought to enable MPs to email their support for a coup while concealing their names from the whips.[109] The demand for nomination papers to be sent out to all Labour MPs in 2008 was another attempt to reduce mobilisation costs. Once MPs had the nomination papers in their hands, they would be forced to say definitively whether or not they still supported Brown. The tactic of demanding nomination papers was decided upon because the rebels had grown frustrated waiting for the cabinet to provide leadership in a move against Brown. Field said, '[g]iven we haven't got a cabinet stuffed with people who would win political VCs, this strategy is forced upon MPs because the cabinet has so far failed to carry out one of its key roles'. Brown's allies feared that distributing nomination papers to the entire PLP would be like handing a 'loaded gun' to the rebels and so the NEC refused to do so.[110]

The most effective way for malcontent MPs to overcome their collective-action problem would have been through a confidence vote by secret ballot. Brown's opponents could vote against him free from the fear of retribution. That would be particularly important for those MPs who held government jobs. Precisely such a demand was made by Sheerman after Purnell's resignation and by Hoon and Hewitt in their joint letter in 2010. In the absence of such institutional facilitation of a coup, the plotters had to resort to other methods of mobilising opponents. None was ultimately successful because too many MPs were not prepared to break cover unless they saw clear evidence that others were doing so. A secret ballot would have overcome that problem, but party managers forestalled it.

One of the great virtues of a secret confidence vote, from the plotters' point of view, was that it would have separated the tasks of removing Brown and finding a replacement. Indeed, Clarke has argued that 'there's a case for having a process of some kind that doesn't require someone to wield the dagger in quite that way', even though ultimately, 'an actual live politician has to summon up the courage'.[111] The problem, as Field observed, was that 'members of the cabinet lacked the courage to act against Brown' and so he survived.[112]

The plotters considered the 'legitimacy costs' of removing Brown to be low because Brown had not come to power in a proper leadership election. However, they were concerned that 'party costs', in particular, disunity and decision costs, would be more of a problem. Many opponents of Brown feared that an attempt to remove him would inevitably be bloody because he would refuse to go unless formally compelled to do so. If he participated in a leadership election, it too would be vicious and these high disunity costs dissuaded some from moving against him.[113] Others believed that the party had reached such a nadir that it was worth the risk.[114] Similarly, decision costs were assumed to be high because of the widespread belief that any leadership election would inevitably be lengthy. Again, Clarke sought to tackle this concern. Most MPs thought a contest would take two to three months, a prospect regarded as 'horrific'. Clarke produced a plan to curtail a leadership election to just three weeks from the moment of Brown's resignation to the election of his successor, but many remained unconvinced.[115] Thus, unlike the situation in the

Conservative Party in 2003 when an OMOV ballot was avoided, Labour's rebels were unable to reduce the decision and disunity costs of a leadership contest and that made it harder to mobilise Brown's opponents for a putsch.

The electoral college makes it very difficult to unseat Labour leaders. The 20 percent nomination threshold imposes very high mobilisation costs on challengers and effectively rules out stalking horses. Non-secret voting in the parliamentary section also increases plotters' mobilisation costs because MPs know they cannot hide their opposition to the leader in the ballot box. Labour's system fuses leader ejection and selection: it requires a serious challenger to come forward to play the role of assassin. As noted in Chapter 1, only one challenger has defeated a sitting leader in a British party since 1945 and that was in the Conservative Party. In a party such as Labour, which is often thought to be unwilling to dispatch its leaders, assassins may be even more unlikely to succeed. Finally, OMOV entails high party costs and there was scepticism about the prospects of shortening a contest to reduce them. In combination, these factors offer considerable institutional protection to Labour leaders.

Conclusion: The distribution of power in the electoral college

Where does power reside in the electoral college? It was assumed that the abolition of block voting and the diminution of the unions' vote share in 1993 had shifted power away from union leaders to the parliamentary section. The period between 2007 and 2010 provided some confirmation of that view but also some reasons for believing it was overstated.

The high nomination thresholds in the electoral college ensure that the PLP has considerable control over the instigation of contests and the emergence of candidates. 'The PLP' is not a completely unified body, however, and high thresholds serve the additional function of ensuring that leadership candidates must usually enjoy broad support among MPs to enter a contest. In contests for vacancies, the 12.5 percent threshold was too high for the left-wingers, McDonnell and Meacher, to surmount in 2007. In 2010, Abbott would not have been able to enter the contest had she not 'borrowed' the nominations of MPs who had no intention of voting for her. Indeed, only seven MPs subsequently voted for her as their first preference.

At the selection stage, the votes of MPs and MEPs are worth significantly more than those of party and union members. In the 2010 contest, 266 valid votes were cast in the parliamentary section, 126,874 in the members section and 211,234 in the affiliates section. Thus, the vote of each MP or MEP was worth that of 477 party members or 794 affiliate members. That is why it is so important for candidates to build up a strong base of support among MPs early in the contest, as doing so can create unstoppable momentum. One of David Miliband's problems in 2010 was that, although he quickly acquired solid support among MPs, his lead was never big enough to make his victory appear inevitable despite being the favourite.

In the members section, a strong turnout in 2010 was testament to the interest that the leadership contest sparked among party members. However, unlike in the affiliates section, there are no organisational leaders who can seek to mobilise large numbers of members' votes behind one candidate. Party members are more dependent on mailings from each of the candidates and coverage in the media. It was noticeable that there was only a small shift in support for the Miliband brothers among party members in the two YouGov polls of July and September 2010. In contrast, there was a big shift in the affiliates section after the leaders of the big unions had urged their members to support Ed Miliband.

The most controversial aspect of the electoral college has always been the role played in it by the trade unions. Originally, the contentious issue was block voting, which enabled unions to sew-up contests early on. The shift to individual voting and Blair's victory in 1994 appeared to have taken the sting out of the issue. However, the 2010 contest showed that determined campaigns inside the unions could sway votes. A combination of union mergers, ideological uniformity and one-sided campaigning increased their influence.[116] It was exaggerated further by very low turnouts, leaving union activists to cast most of the votes and usually follow the recommendations of their leaders. A higher turnout would presumably have seen greater numbers of inactive union members participating.

Defenders of the system described the contest in 2010 as a 'national primary' and sought to express the result in terms of the absolute number of votes cast for each candidate. On this basis, Ed Miliband defeated his brother by 175,000 votes to 147,000.[117] However, this format is precisely the way in which electoral-college votes *cannot* be expressed. The college has three sections with different-sized constituencies. The affiliates section potentially has an extremely large number of selectors, standing at 2.7 million in 2010. The parliamentary section had only 270 potential selectors that year, the same absolute number of selectors as a small socialist society. However, the recognised importance of MPs ensures that their votes are weighted much more heavily. If all individual votes in Labour leadership elections were worth the same, there would be no need for an electoral college. Similarly, union members' votes were not worth the same as those of party members. A pure OMOV system would not enfranchise all levy-payers but only those who joined the party.

The electoral college of 2010 did not concentrate as much power in union leaders' hands as it did in 1981–93, as many union members ignored their leaders' recommendations on how to vote. Nevertheless, they still had a significant amount of power and tipped the outcome in Ed Miliband's favour. The latter's failure to carry a majority of MPs or party members, however, left a question mark over his legitimacy: in the opinion of one critic, he had 'less of a mandate than [Iain Duncan Smith]', who managed to win a majority of Tory members if not Tory MPs.[118] Charles Clarke, while not disputing the outcome, described the affiliates section as 'totally corrupt', claiming that 'it doesn't work in any kind of democratic or fair way'.[119] It remains to be seen whether the 2010 contest will lead to a fundamental rethink over union involvement in Labour leadership elections.

The electoral-college rules were also significant in the failure of Labour MPs to remove Brown as prime minister and party leader during the 2008–10 period. One of the most important factors was the requirement for challengers to secure the nominations of 20 percent of the PLP. This barrier ruled out a stalking horse and compelled Brown's critics to use other means to undermine him, such as resignations and demands for confidence votes. Leader eviction remains in the hands of MPs and so there is less of an issue over the distribution of power between party stakeholders. Nevertheless, the rules were controversial and although they helped to preserve Brown, they did not put a stop to the plotting and speculation about the leadership. In some ways, Brown's position was similar to John Major's in the 1990s: the failure of his opponents to find an assassin ensured that the leadership issue continued to fester. Major eventually lanced the boil by calling a leadership election himself. Brown was never likely to do that. However, his survival in office and the drag he appeared to exert on Labour's popularity ensured that, when he was finally compelled to face the voters, Labour's defeat was heavier than it might have been. Eviction institutions that serve the interests of under-pressure leaders need not necessarily serve the interests of their parties if they prevent those parties from tackling leadership weaknesses head on.

4
The Conservative Party: Enfranchising the Members

The Conservative Party was the last of the major British parties to extend voting rights in leadership elections from MPs to individual members, which it did in 1998. The first election to be conducted under the new system provoked enormous controversy and sparked a debate about where the balance should lie between the rights of MPs and members. The first eviction of a leader just two years later was scarcely less controversial and would lead to an unsuccessful campaign to abolish the system and revert to the *status quo ante*. This chapter analyses these events in detail. It looks at the reasons for the change of system and assesses whether party members have proved to be the unthinking ideologues that critics of the system feared they would be. It is argued that some of the criticisms of the new system are misplaced and that the much-maligned members, far from being unconcerned with their party's prospects when choosing leaders, made understandable choices given the candidates on offer.

The chapter begins by recounting the formation of the new system in 1998. It then looks in detail at the 2001 and 2005 leadership contests, examining the criteria by which party members selected Iain Duncan Smith and David Cameron respectively. The next section addresses key issues concerning the relative power of MPs and party members that arise from the system's operation to date. The final substantive section turns back chronologically to examine the role of the post-1998 rules in Duncan Smith's ejection by MPs in 2003.

Reforming the Conservatives' selection system

After their landslide defeat in the 1997 general election John Major resigned the Tory leadership and William Hague was elected as his replacement.[1] Responding to disquiet among Conservative activists about their subordinate role in the party, Hague announced his intention to reform the party's organisation. These reform plans, set out in a consultation document, included proposals to change the rules on leadership selection.[2] One motive in proposing change was to undertake 'democratisation' of the Conservative Party in response to increasing demands from party activists for a greater say in decision-making. A further motive was to increase the incumbent leader's security of tenure.[3]

Pressure for membership involvement in leadership elections had been building up steadily for some years. On becoming leader, Hague indicated his willingness to see members participate in future leadership contests. However, he also wanted MPs to retain their leading role. Hague's new party chairman, Sir Archie Norman, insisted that MPs' votes should continue to predominate. That set the scene for some form of electoral college, with reports suggesting that the members would take about 20 percent of the votes – more than before but still greatly subordinate to the MPs, who would take the rest.[4] The prospects of this reform materialising were destroyed at the 1997 Tory conference, a stormy affair at which activists denounced the behaviour of MPs during the Major government and expressed anger at the meagre votes they were being offered in leadership elections.[5] If there were to be an electoral college, activists wanted the members' share to be nearer to 40 percent.[6] In response to the rancour at the conference, a decision over leadership elections was postponed.

Towards the end of 1997, opinion within the parliamentary party began to shift in response to the grassroots revolt. However, there were fears that, although an electoral college might start off with a low share of votes for activists, it could easily be ratcheted up in the future.[7] Support began to grow among some MPs for a form of one member-one vote (OMOV). Instead of separate sections in an electoral college for MPs and party members, there could be a two-stage leadership-selection process in which MPs would first decide on two candidates to put forward to the members and the latter would then decide between them. The system avoided the messiness of weighted votes in an electoral college and appeared to address the fears of those MPs who were worried that the members might impose an unacceptable candidate on the parliamentary party. Candidates reaching the OMOV ballot would require considerable support from MPs.[8]

The absence of consensus among Conservative MPs over selection rules led the backbench 1922 committee to announce a series of ballots of Tory MPs in January 1998 to establish which system to adopt, rather than seeking a decision by acclamation, as it usually did.[9] MPs voted strongly in favour of moving to a hybrid system in which the top two candidates in a series of eliminative ballots among MPs would go through to a ballot of party members. This option was preferred to both an electoral college and the maintenance of the *status quo*.[10] MPs also decided to adopt a new eviction mechanism. When he resigned temporarily as party leader in 1995, Major triggered a leadership contest that was effectively a confidence vote. Hague wanted to create a proper confidence-vote procedure, which would obviate the need for such ruses, as well as others, such as 'stalking-horse' challenges to incumbent leaders. It would also rule out the need for annual leadership contests, which was thought to have been a factor in destabilising Thatcher and Major.[11] Contests would take place only if the leader resigned, died or became incapacitated, or if he lost a confidence vote. MPs voted in favour of this mechanism.[12] It was also agreed that, to win a confidence vote, the leader would need only a bare majority and if he won, he would be safe from another such vote for 12 months.

The only controversy concerned the threshold at which a confidence vote could be called. Under the old system, a leadership contest would take place only if 10 percent of Conservative MPs requested one in writing to the chairman of the 1922 committee. Hague wanted the confidence-vote trigger to be significantly higher.[13] Tory MPs were divided over what the threshold should be, but when the 1922 committee tried to impose a 20 percent level, there was a revolt. The following day, a 15 percent threshold was agreed by acclamation.[14] The leader would also have the right to call a confidence vote (Box 4.1).

The new system appeared to make it harder for Tory MPs to evict their leader; it should be recalled that even the previous threshold of 10 percent had never been reached. However, some of the changes looked to be disadvantageous for incumbent leaders. The confidence-vote rule ensured that rebel MPs would not need a stalking-horse challenger, but would instead merely need to mobilise enough MPs to reach the 15 percent threshold. Moreover, votes in the confidence ballot would be secret and the writers of letters requesting a confidence vote would be promised anonymity. The fact that a confidence vote could be called at any time in the calendar was also disadvantageous to the incumbent. Under the old system, there were tight time constraints on when contests could be called, and these had possibly saved Thatcher from a challenge during the Westland crisis in 1986.[15] On the other hand, the provision ruling out further confidence votes for a year

Box 4.1   Conservative Party Leadership Election and Eviction Rules

Contests (arising from incumbent's death, resignation or defeat in confidence vote)

(1) Contestants announce candidacies by agreed deadline and require nominations, in writing, of two Conservative MPs, whose names are made public. No further nominations permitted after this point
   - If only one nominee, he is announced elected (unless party board decides to ask individual party members to ratify candidate in a ballot within one month)
   - If only two nominees, contest progresses immediately to postal ballot of individual party members (see (3) below)

(2) If more than two nominees, series of eliminative parliamentary ballots to reduce field to two candidates
   - In each ballot, each MP votes for one candidate. Candidate with fewest votes eliminated. If tie for last place, ballot re-run. If tie for last place in re-run ballot, both candidates eliminated, unless only three candidates, whereby ballot re-run
   - Successive ballots held (beginning on Tuesday after close of nominations and on following Thursdays and Tuesdays of each week) until two candidates left
   - Candidates can voluntarily withdraw from the contest at any time, unless only two are left, in which case no withdrawals permissible

(3) Top two candidates go forward to secret postal ballot of individual party members
   - Timetable determined by chairman of 1922 committee in consultation with party board ('as soon as practicable' after last parliamentary ballot)
   - Eligible voters: members of good standing for at least three months before announcement of confidence vote, or, if leader resigned/died, three months before close of ballot
   - To win ballot, a candidate requires majority of votes cast.

Confidence Votes

- Either: leader calls for a vote on his own initiative
- *Or*: 15% of Conservative MPs demand confidence vote in the leader by writing to chairman of 1922 committee (names not made public)
- Confidence motion can be moved at any time in calendar
- If 15% threshold passed (or if leader demands a vote), confidence motion voted on by Conservative MPs (timing decided by chairman of 1922 committee in consultation with leader). Majority of votes cast in secret ballot required to defeat leader
- If leader wins, no further confidence votes permitted for another year. If leader defeated, he is obliged to resign and a leadership contest is announced. Defeated incumbent not permitted to participate in selection ballot.

Sources: *Constitution of the Conservative Party* (London: Conservative Party, 2004), Schedule 2; 1922 Committee, *Procedure for the Election of the Leader of the Conservative Party* (n.d.).
Notes: Box shows selection and eviction rules as of 2011. Provision for re-run parliamentary ballots in the event of a tie for last place was added after this eventuality occurred in 2001 contest.

if the incumbent had survived an earlier vote, offered some protection to the leader.

The rules appeared to indicate that letters sent to the chairman of the 1922 committee requesting a confidence vote would sit on file indefinitely unless withdrawn by their senders or until the 15 percent threshold was reached. However, the policy of Sir Michael Spicer, the first chairman to operate the new system, was that letters would need to be renewed annually.[16] In contrast, the policy of his successor, Graham Brady, is that letters should indeed remain on file.[17] Brady's policy offers less security of tenure to the incumbent leader.

Finally, the processes of removing an incumbent and choosing a replacement were institutionally separated. Such separation removes some protection from incumbents because it makes it unnecessary for plotters to find an assassin and thus reduces the pressure on would-be leaders to become directly involved until the leader has been removed. The leader's senior colleagues would not need to take a risk in challenging him directly in a leadership election because such challenges were no longer possible.

New rules were set out for balloting in leadership elections (see Box 4.1). Candidates would need to be nominated by two MPs to stand; if three or more candidates secured nomination, they would participate in a series of preliminary parliamentary ballots. MPs would vote for one candidate in each ballot and the candidate with the fewest votes would be eliminated. Unlike in the past, there was no provision for candidates to enter in later ballots. That rule had enabled the incumbent's rivals to wait for him to be damaged before entering later, but that was no longer a consideration, as the confidence-vote mechanism obviated the need for stalking horses. The eliminative process would continue until only two candidates were left and they would go through to a postal ballot of party members. If only two candidates entered the contest, both would automatically go through to the OMOV ballot. If only one candidate were nominated, there would be no need for any ballots and he would be declared leader.

The final proposals on organisational reform, including the new leadership selection system, were set out in a document entitled *The Fresh Future* in February 1998.[18] It was sent to party members, who were asked to accept or reject it on a take-it-or-leave-it basis. One-third of the membership returned its ballot papers and fully 96 percent voted in favour.[19]

At the system's inception, most attention focused on the shift to OMOV because it represented a considerable break with the Conservative Party's history. However, there was some scepticism about the new rules. Alderman claimed that 'the switch to OMOV would appear to have been more of a tactical manoeuvre to preserve MPs' power than a massive surrender of it'.[20] Given that the parliamentary party could screen candidates, it could stop the members voting for the ones they most wanted. Moreover, the extra-parliamentary party would play no part in confidence votes. The system thus formally created a process whereby one group of actors, the members, would have the final say over who the leader would be, but another group, the MPs, would have the exclusive right to eject the leader. Given the widespread assumption that Tory members were right-wing, the system appeared to favour candidates from the right of the party. Indeed, it was suggested that one purpose behind the new system was to make it difficult for pro-Europeans to become leader because they would be unacceptable to the Eurosceptic mass membership.[21] As the following section shows, the first contest organised under the new rules appeared to confirm this prediction.

The Conservative Party leadership election of 2001

The effect of the new rules can be gauged by examining their operation in subsequent Tory leadership contests. This section analyses the 2001 election, while the next section examines the 2005 contest. The Conservative leadership contest of 2001 followed the party's heavy defeat in that year's general election and the subsequent resignation of Hague. It would be the first to be conducted under the new rules. Numerous possible candidates were mentioned in the press, but five formally entered the contest and secured nominations. Michael Portillo was the early favourite, having returned to the Commons in 1999 after losing his seat two years earlier. Since then, he had softened his hard-line Thatcherite image, adopting a more socially-liberal approach to such issues as homosexuality and multiculturalism. The other major candidate to declare was Kenneth Clarke, the Tories' principal pro-European in a party that had become increasingly Eurosceptic. Clarke's campaign would emphasise his electoral popularity and vast governmental experience.

Three other candidates came forward. The most significant was Iain Duncan Smith, a traditional Thatcherite and social conservative. He had been a rebel against the Major government over the Maastricht Treaty that created the European Union but he had since served in Hague's shadow cabinet. He hoped to collect the votes of the Tory right. Competing against him for the same constituency was David Davis, another right-wing Eurosceptic, while Michael Ancram presented himself as a Eurosceptic pragmatist. Of those who did not run, the most significant was Ann Widdecombe, who enjoyed some support among party activists, but hardly any support among MPs, who would determine the two candidates to go through to the OMOV ballot. She pulled out of the race just days after indicating her interest.[22]

Although Portillo and Clarke were the two 'big beasts' in the contest, each faced major problems. Clarke had already run for the leadership in 1997, but lost to Hague largely because an increasingly Eurosceptic parliamentary party would not accept a pro-European as their leader (see Chapter 2). Clarke's hope was that his greater electoral appeal would be sufficient to overcome this opposition, especially in the wake of the Conservatives' second consecutive landslide general-election defeat. He emphasised his long years in government and his reputation for economic competence. He was convinced that he could win the membership ballot if he could somehow get through the parliamentary ballots.[23]

Portillo was aligned with his party on Europe, but his political 'reinvention' after 1997 and his subsequent public acknowledgement of homosexual experiences in his youth created suspicion among social conservatives.[24] He also had a reputation for disloyalty to two previous leaders, Major and Hague.[25] Nevertheless, he quickly secured the backing of half the shadow cabinet.[26] He ran as a 'modernising' candidate, urging his party to become more socially inclusive. He indicated his support for all-women shortlists to increase the number of female Tory MPs and wanted to review the party's opposition to Section 28 of the Local Government Act (1988), which prohibited the 'promotion' of homosexuality in schools. At one point, he also appeared to signal a willingness to consider the decriminalisation of cannabis.[27]

The main beneficiary of the opposition to Portillo was Duncan Smith, who attracted support because he was socially conservative and 'sound' on Europe. Lord Tebbit, a right-wing former cabinet minister, described Duncan Smith as 'a normal family man with children', a remark widely interpreted as a slur against Portillo.[28] Questions remained over Duncan Smith's loyalty because of his anti-EU rebellions under the Major government, but that did not significantly damage his support among ardent Eurosceptics, who regarded his actions as principled.[29]

Despite the fact that opposition to Portillo was becoming more evident, the results of the parliamentary ballots were still a shock. Portillo topped the first ballot, but by only ten votes over Duncan Smith, a margin that was narrower than expected. Clarke came third. A tie for last place between Davis and Ancram saw the first ballot re-run, before Ancram was eliminated and Davis withdrew, while Portillo's lead shrunk to eight votes. With the elimination of Davis and Ancram, their supporters switched mainly to Clarke and Duncan Smith, with the former topping

Table 4.1   Conservative Party Leadership Election 2001

	Parliamentary ballots			OMOV ballot %
	First ballot MPs	Re-run first ballot MPs	Second ballot MPs	
Iain Duncan Smith	39	42	54	60.7
Kenneth Clarke	36	39	59	39.3
Michael Portillo	49	50	53	–
David Davis	21	18	–	–
Michael Ancram	21	17	–	–
Total	166	166	166	100.0

Notes: Eliminative ballots in parliamentary votes. Full details of result in Appendix B.

the final parliamentary ballot and the latter overtaking Portillo to take second place by a single vote (Table 4.1).

The OMOV ballot was thus to be between Clarke and Duncan Smith. Ideologically, the latter was much more closely attuned to Tory members, particularly on Europe. Clarke tried to make the argument that he was the more experienced candidate and the more likely to win back Tory defectors who had voted for Labour in 1997 and 2001. However, he could not dispel the belief that he was a divisive figure. Duncan Smith secured the endorsements of two previous leaders, Thatcher and Hague, while Clarke was endorsed by Major and also by Heseltine.[30] Ultimately, the membership's suspicion of the pro-European Clarke proved too great and Duncan Smith eased to a comfortable victory, winning 60.7 percent of the votes to Clarke's 39.3 percent.

Why Duncan Smith won and Clarke (and Portillo) lost

The commonest interpretation of the 2001 Conservative leadership contest is that an ideological mass membership imposed on MPs an inadequate leader who reflected their own views and disregarded an electorally appealing candidate who did not.[31] However, while ideology was important, its influence must be seen in terms of the desire for party unity rather than any lack of concern among members for electability. In a party that had become intensely ideological, only a candidate acceptable to the dominant Eurosceptic wing could preserve party unity. Clarke's pro-Europeanism made him unacceptable to most members and thus unable to maintain intra-party unity. As Norton argues:

> However popular Clarke may have been in the country, he carried too much political baggage for most Conservative Party members. It was not simply that they disagreed with him on the issue of European integration, though they did, but also that they realized that his stance on the issue was bound to split the party, certainly badly and possibly catastrophically. They were simply not prepared to take the risk. They voted for Duncan Smith.[32]

Tory members felt that, irrespective of Clarke's appeal to voters and his undoubted competence, a Clarke-led Conservative Party would be beset by endless rows over Europe. That in turn would make the party unelectable, as voters are repelled by divided parties. The pollsters, ICM, conducted a survey of party members during the OMOV phase of the campaign. Some 'buyer beware' is necessary because the sample was very small (N = 229), it was conducted in four local associations, and the results were unweighted and not claimed to be fully representative. Nevertheless, the results were highly suggestive.

The significance of Europe and the single currency was evident when members ranked it as the key issue of the campaign and 86 percent regarded it as very or quite important, while 13 percent thought it not very or not at all important. Given the Eurosceptic views of party members, it is not surprising that the same poll found that 58 percent thought it likely that Clarke would split the party if he became leader, while 28 percent thought it unlikely (net +30 percent). In contrast, only 18 percent considered it likely that Duncan Smith would split the party if he became leader, while fully 73 percent regarded it as unlikely (net –55 percent).[33]

It might appear strange that Duncan Smith, a standard-bearer of the Thatcherites with an uncompromising position on Europe, could be seen as a unifier. However, uniting a party in which one faction is much stronger than the others requires a different approach from uniting a party in which the rival factions are evenly balanced. In 1990, Major was seen as the candidate best able to hold together the warring pro- and anti-European factions.[34] After 1997, however, the Eurosceptics were dominant and by 2001 even more so. Uniting the Conservatives required recognition that the Eurosceptics had won the argument inside the party and that required a Eurosceptic leader. Ancram might have been considered as such a candidate but it was clear that he did not have much appeal to the parliamentary party and thus never had the chance to test his popularity among the membership.

Portillo, meanwhile, failed in his leadership bid largely because he too was deemed unable to unite the party. Unlike Clarke, Portillo was acceptable to his party on Europe, but on social policy (e.g. marriage, multiculturalism and gay rights), an emerging fissure within the Conservative Party, he found himself at odds with colleagues and party members.[35] He was also damaged by his perceived disloyalty. One of his most vocal critics in the parliamentary party was Widdecombe, who accused him and his allies of backbiting and destabilising the party during Hague's leadership.[36] This distrust was shared by party members.[37]

Preserving party unity became the over-riding selection criterion in the 2001 leadership contest because the two candidates initially seen as the frontrunners, Clarke and Portillo, were both deemed too divisive. Duncan Smith was far from being the ideal candidate, but he trumped both his major rivals on the criterion of acceptability, which was a more basic priority than electoral appeal or governmental experience, on both of which Clarke was the strongest candidate. Consequently, Duncan Smith was the default choice for party members: had he faced another Eurosceptic in the OMOV ballot, unity might no longer have been the major criterion, and selectors could have voted on the basis of electability. On the other hand, had he faced Portillo, the contest may again have been decided on the basis of acceptability, but this time over social and moral issues.

It is unlikely that the identity of the selectorate affected the outcome of the contest. Although Duncan Smith won only a third of MPs' votes in the parliamentary ballots, Clarke hardly won much more. Duncan Smith also won the crucial backing of the still-revered Lady Thatcher during the OMOV stage. Even Clarke's supposedly stronger electoral appeal, which might have been expected to appeal to MPs, was not as great as he implied. An ICM poll of voters for the *Daily Telegraph* in August 2001 found that only 9 percent thought the Conservatives would have a good chance of winning the next election under Clarke, with 8 percent saying the same of Duncan Smith. Electoral considerations were weak in the 2001 contest. Given that fact, and given the Eurosceptic profile of Conservative MPs,[38] it is questionable whether Clarke would have defeated Duncan Smith in a parliamentary ballot, particularly as this method of selection had delivered Hague a comfortable victory over Clarke four years earlier.

The Conservative Party leadership election of 2005

The outcome of the 2001 leadership election discredited the selection system in the eyes of many Conservative MPs. Critics believed that Duncan Smith's victory proved that individual Tory members could not be trusted to choose the leader. Duncan Smith would serve only two years before being removed by Tory MPs in a confidence vote (see below). In the contest to replace him, the parliamentary party united unanimously behind the single candidature of Michael Howard in 2003 to avoid a lengthy OMOV ballot that might elect another unsatisfactory leader. The concern of Conservative MPs was so great that, on becoming leader, Howard promised he would look into reforming the system, although not until after the general election.[39] Most wanted a return to the previous system of parliamentary ballots. The view of one MP, quoted in the *Daily Telegraph*, was typical: '[leadership selection] must be left in the hands of the MPs because we are the people who know the candidates, their strengths and weaknesses. Look what happened when we let the party decide: we got IDS.'[40]

After the Tories' defeat in the general election of May 2005, Howard announced he would step down in the autumn but first he wanted to look again at the leadership-selection rules. The party's managerial board issued a consultation paper that recommended reverting back to selection by MPs. It said the existing system was expensive, time-consuming and confusing because individual members elected the leader but only MPs had the power to remove him. Moreover, the members could not properly know the candidates, whereas MPs did. Ultimately, MPs should choose the leader because they were the people who had to work with him on a daily basis.[41] The board initially suggested that the voluntary party's national Conservative convention, consisting of party officials and senior activists, could hold a non-binding, indicative vote on leadership candidates in the future but Tory MPs objected, fearing a split between the parliamentary and voluntary wings. Instead they wanted only a vague 'consultation' with activists, followed by a ballot of MPs.[42]

In September, the proposed changes were voted on by a constitutional college, consisting of MPs, MEPs, representatives of Tory peers and members of the national Conservative convention. In order to pass, the reforms had to be supported by 66 percent of MPs voting, 66 percent of convention members voting and at least 50 percent of all those eligible to vote in the constitutional college. Ultimately, only two of these hurdles were surmounted: 54 percent of eligible voters supported change, as did 71 percent of MPs. However, only 58 percent of members of the national Conservative convention approved the measures, while 42 percent opposed them. The proposal was thereby defeated and the 2005 leadership contest, against most people's expectations, would be conducted under the existing rules.[43]

Despite failing in the task of changing the system, Howard's decision to delay his resignation was not without consequence. A five-month breathing space between the general election and the expected leadership election enabled the Conservative Party to engage in a systematic debate about its future direction, something that had not happened in 1997 or 2001. The potential leadership candidates in the autumn would be at the forefront of this debate. It was widely anticipated that David Davis, the shadow home secretary, would run on a Thatcherite ticket of tax cuts, Euroscepticism and social conservatism. A further unstated, but widely-assumed reason for delaying the contest was that Howard feared that Davis would win a ballot of the party membership.[44] There were concerns over Davis's suitability as a leader, not least because of his alleged disloyalty to Duncan Smith.[45] Nevertheless, he secured 30 endorsements from MPs over the summer, many more than any other potential candidate, and he was quickly identified as the frontrunner. There was also speculation that Clarke would participate in his third leadership contest. Other potential candidates touted early on included the former party chairman, Theresa May, the veteran ex-minister, Sir Malcolm Rifkind, Liam Fox, a right-winger who appealed to the same constituency as Davis, Alan Duncan, a Thatcherite frontbencher, Andrew Lansley from the Tory left, and David Cameron, a youthful former special advisor who had been an MP for only four years. After the general election, Howard had promoted Cameron, widely rumoured to be his preferred successor,[46] to the post of education spokesman. Cameron was on the Conservatives' 'modernising' wing, which wanted the party to broaden its electoral appeal and shift to the centre-ground.[47] The modernisers were not part of the old Tory left; like most in the Conservative Party, they were Eurosceptics and economic 'dries', but unlike most, they were liberal on social issues, such as family values, race relations and gay rights. Cameron's appeal would be similar to Portillo's in 2001 but without the doubts about his trustworthiness.

After a summer of sparring between likely and potential candidates, the campaign finally began in earnest a month before the party conference. On 31 August, Clarke formally launched his leadership campaign. A few days later, Fox declared that he too was a candidate. Towards the end of September, it was confirmed that the election would be conducted under the existing rules. Shortly afterwards, Cameron and Davis both launched their campaigns. A number of other potential candidates declared they would not run, although uncertainty still hung over the intentions of Rifkind and May.

The party conference in October was arranged as a 'beauty contest' for the leadership candidates. Six of the candidates delivered speeches: May and Rifkind on Monday, Clarke and Cameron on Tuesday, and Davis and Fox on Wednesday. The speeches of May and Rifkind were well-received but neither made much impact and they both ruled themselves out of the contest the following week. Clarke and Cameron delivered strong speeches that drew significant applause. Clarke stressed his experience and electability. Cameron delivered his speech without notes, and although it was light on policy, it showcased his modernising credentials and communication skills. Both were praised in the media, although the following day's newspapers made more of Clarke's speech than Cameron's. Fox made a strong populist speech, in which he urged the party to stop apologising for the past, and confirmed his Euro-sceptic leanings. Davis, however, performed poorly. He was not known as a good public speaker and looked ill-prepared. Television pictures appeared to show members of the audience falling asleep as he spoke. The conclusion of the speech was so low-key that many people did not realise it had ended and Davis had to motion to them to stand to applause.[48] Until then, Davis had been the frontrunner but after the conference speeches, his candidacy looked to have been damaged.

There had already emerged evidence that Cameron could be a sur-prise package. The BBC's *Newsnight* programme commissioned a focus group of core Tory voters and potential swing voters in which the par-ticipants were shown clips of speeches by the candidates. The pro-gramme was broadcast the evening before Cameron's speech to the party conference. The focus group voiced overwhelming support for Cameron. Meanwhile, there was little enthusiasm for either Clarke or Davis, the latter being compared by some participants to John Major – nice but uncharismatic. Cameron's campaign team sent DVDs of the focus group to Conservative MPs to convince them of his electoral appeal.[49]

The new-found strength of Cameron's position was demonstrated shortly after the conference. When asked by a journalist whether he had taken drugs as a student, Cameron appeared evasive.[50] Yet despite a brief flurry of stories in the press, the issue largely subsided into the background for the rest of the campaign and Cameron's candidacy was barely damaged at all. Few in the party had any appetite for exploiting the issue, particularly as it increasingly looked as though Cameron could become unstoppable.

The first parliamentary ballot was held on 18 October. Davis had already secured 66 public endorsements from MPs and was predicted to top the ballot. Although he did so, he won only 62 votes, losing the support of some of those who had endorsed him. In second place was Cameron, just six votes behind on 56. Fox managed to edge out Clarke by four votes to go through to the second ballot to be held two days later (Table 4.2). By that time, Cameron had become firmly established as the new frontrunner, rallying to his cause most of those MPs who voted for Clarke in the first ballot. Cameron duly won the second ballot with 90 votes, far ahead of Davis who dropped to 57, just six ahead of Fox. The first ballot effectively consisted of two 'primaries': a battle between Cameron and Clarke for the votes of centrist and left-leaning MPs, and a separate battle between Davis and Fox for right-wing MPs.[51] Once Clarke was the first candidate to be eliminated, it

Table 4.2 Conservative Party Leadership Election 2005

	Parliamentary ballots		OMOV ballot %
	First ballot MPs	Second ballot MPs	
David Cameron	56	90	67.6
David Davis	62	57	32.4
Liam Fox	42	51	–
Kenneth Clarke	38	–	–
Total	198	198	100.0

Notes: Eliminative ballots in parliamentary votes. Full details of result in Appendix B.

ensured that Cameron would top the second ballot, while Davis and Fox would fight to be the second name to be put to the membership. However, the second ballot would inevitably split the right-wing vote, ensuring that whichever of the two were chosen would be a long way behind Cameron.

The momentum Cameron took from the parliamentary ballots ensured that the OMOV contest, in which he faced Davis, was a sedate and predictable affair. There were few surprises during the two-month campaign and little change in the polls. BBC1 presented a special edition of *Question Time*, in which a split audience of Conservative members and ordinary voters listened to, and questioned, the two candidates. Davis was adjudged by most observers to have 'won' this debate.[52] There were a number of regional hustings open only to Tory members and closed to the media. Cameron received further endorsements from MPs, including some on the right who had backed Fox. His position as favourite also enabled him to raise over £500,000 in donations to fund his campaign, far in excess of the £291,000 raised by Davis (see Appendix L). In the end, Cameron secured a convincing two-to-one victory on a turnout of 77 percent (Table 4.2).

Selection criteria and the 2005 contest

When Howard announced his intention to resign as party leader, Davis was widely assumed to be his heir apparent. Davis had already increased his profile by contesting the 2001 leadership election and had since established himself as the torch-bearer of the Thatcherite right. The parliamentary party, like Davis, was largely economically liberal, Eurosceptical and socially conservative, as indeed was the party on the ground. Yet the contest saw him finish a long way back in second place in the parliamentary ballots before suffering a crushing defeat in the OMOV ballot to a youthful, inexperienced candidate who was light on policy details and almost unknown outside Westminster when the contest began. Why did those Conservative members who delivered Duncan Smith a landslide victory over a more electorally appealing candidate four years earlier now snub a candidate in tune with their views for one whose ideology was ambiguous at best?

Davis emerged as the frontrunner because he initially appeared to be the most credible Eurosceptic candidate, but doubts existed about his electoral appeal and competence right from the start. His fate was sealed at the party conference. It is incontrovertible that the party conference was 'a tale of two speeches'.[53] Until then, Davis had been gradually entrenching his position, with Clarke emerging as his major rival. After the conference, Davis's campaign went into reverse while Cameron's took off. These developments were evident in the candidates' support among both MPs and party members. Figure 4.1 shows the number of public endorsements the four main candidates received from MPs. At the beginning of September, Davis already had 31 endorsements, three times as many as his nearest rivals, but in the two weeks before the

Figure 4.1   Endorsements for Conservative Leadership Candidates from MPs (1 September to 17 October 2005)

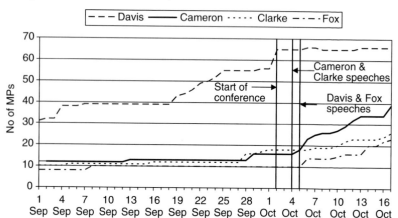

Source: A. Denham and K. O'Hara, *Democratising Conservative Leadership Selection: From Grey Suits to Grass Roots* (Manchester: Manchester University Press, 2008), pp. 212–13.
Note: Excludes endorsements for candidates who withdrew before the ballots.

party conference, this figure grew considerably, rising to 65 as the conference got under way on 2 October. The other candidates enjoyed no such pre-conference surges. In contrast, after the speeches, Davis's public support among MPs flattened whereas the other main candidates, especially Cameron, saw their support increase markedly. In the first parliamentary ballot on 18 October, Davis's 62 votes fell four short of his public endorsements. Cameron's first-ballot total of 56 votes was 17 higher than the number of his endorsements on 17 October. Fox's 42 votes were 19 higher than his number of endorsements while Clarke's 38 votes were 12 higher.

The turnaround was even more dramatic among party members. YouGov ran a series of polls throughout the contest gauging support for each candidate among party members. Figure 4.2 shows that in May, Davis was well ahead of the field on 39 percent although this figure fell over the summer. Shortly before the conference, Davis and Clarke were tied on 32 percent (28–30 September), with Cameron far behind on 17 percent. But after the conference, Davis's support plummeted to 15 percent, with Cameron surging to 42 percent and Clarke falling back to 28 percent. With Clarke's elimination from the contest on 18 October, Cameron became the runaway leader, as he appeared to attract most of his defeated rival's support. This change in fortunes is particularly apparent in the Cameron-Davis head-to-head polls (Figure 4.3), where a 60-40 Davis lead in early September was more than reversed after the conference, with Cameron eventually winning 68–32. The only narrowing of Cameron's lead during the OMOV

Figure 4.2 Support among Party Members for Leading Conservative Candidates 2005

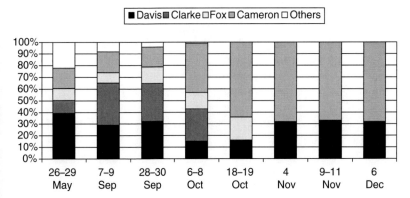

Figure 4.3 Support among Party Members for Davis and Cameron 2005 (Head-to-Head)

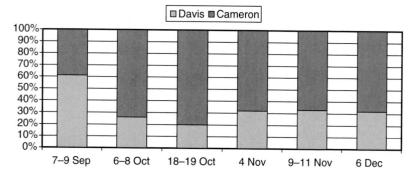

Sources for Figures 4.2 and 4.3: YouGov, 'Conservative members', poll for the *Daily Telegraph*, 12 September 2005; 'Conservative members', poll for the *Daily Telegraph*, 3 October 2005; 'Conservative members post conference', poll for the *Sunday Times*, 10 October 2005; 'Conservative leadership election', poll for the *Daily Telegraph*, 20 October 2005; 'Conservative leadership post debate', poll for the *Daily Telegraph*, 7 November 2005; 'Conservative leadership', poll for the *Daily Telegraph*, 14 November 2005. All polls available at <www.yougov.co.uk>.
Notes for both figures: Percentages recalculated to exclude respondents replying 'don't know' or 'won't vote'. Figures for 6 December are percentage of votes cast for each candidate in the OMOV ballot.

contest came after his televised debate with Davis on *Question Time* on 3 November.

Most Conservative members were not present at the party conference and received their information about the proceedings from the media. Television coverage was kind to Cameron and Clarke, but accentuated Davis's stunted performance. The verdict of the political editor of the influential *Sun* newspaper was typical: 'A couple of jokes misfired and after ten minutes of stumbling delivery, [Davis] was dying out there. By the end, he was almost pleading for a life-saving ovation.'[54] Indeed, it was press coverage that was most damaging for Davis. Table 4.3 shows national newspaper's headlines for their main stories on the Tory conference on the days following the speeches. The headlines on the day after the speeches by Cameron and Clarke were extremely positive, although Clarke took more of the plaudits. In contrast, the following day saw brickbats for Davis across the spectrum.

It seems clear that the candidates' performances at the party conference explained the turnaround in fortunes. Davis had been the undoubted frontrunner up to that point, but his poor speech and Cameron's impressive performance transformed the contest in the eyes of MPs, party

Table 4.3 Newspapers' Principal Headlines on Conservative Leadership Speeches 2005

Newspaper	5 October Headline	6 October Headline
Daily Telegraph	'"Big beast" Clarke puts pressure on Davis'	'Lacklustre Davis leaves leadership wide open'
Times	'Tory race is thrown wide open'	'Support for Davis ebbs away as his speech fails to inspire party'
Guardian	'Tories need rightwing agenda – Davis'	'Davis bid for Tory leadership stalls'
Independent	'Clarke's "big beast" performance piles pressure on Davis leadership hopes'	'MPs may be having second thoughts as Davis fails to inspire Tory faithful'
Daily Mail	'The old master v the moderniser'	'D-Day: A dismal day for Davis'
Daily Express	'Clarke wins Tory hearts'	'Tory frontrunner is a faller at the first'
Sun	'Cam on you blues'	'Out Foxed'
Daily Star	'The beast takes on the charmer: Ken wades in to ignite Tory leadership fight'	'Drippy Davis: Tory frontrunner fails to sway party faithful'
Daily Mirror	'Ken Kong: We now have to choose an even bigger beast than Blair or Brown'	'Deadly dull: David Davis delivers dismal speech in leadership contest'

Source: Nexis UK: News Search <www.lexisnexis.com>.

members and the media. On the face of it, this judgement might suggest that the selectorate (and political journalists) were overly swayed by two twenty-minute speeches that were not, in themselves, of great consequence. However, the real significance of the conference was that it amplified doubts about Davis that already existed, while offering an acceptable and electable alternative.

Why Davis lost and Cameron won

The lesson of the 1997 and 2001 leadership contests was that only a Eurosceptic leader would be acceptable to the Conservative Party, given the ideological leanings of MPs and members alike. Clarke remained the only pro-European with a realistic prospect of running for the leadership and that owed everything to his perceived electability. However, as a staunch Eurosceptic, Davis was more ideologically acceptable to the party and his participation in the 2001 contest had established him as an important figure in the party. Going into the conference, Davis and Clarke were the two leading contenders. Aside from Clarke, other potential candidates at this point were regarded mainly as also-rans, with even Cameron's candidacy seen by many in terms of setting down a marker for the future.[55]

The most efficient way of winning a contest for a vacant leadership post is for a candidate to establish himself not only as the frontrunner, but as the 'inevitable' winner. Once a candidate's victory is seen as inevitable, career-conscious MPs come out in support of the person who will shortly be allocating frontbench jobs. This strategy was attempted by Davis during the summer of 2005. Yet the number of endorsements he received from MPs, although much greater than that of his rivals, was not overwhelming. Even his peak of 66 endorsements represented only one-third of the parliamentary party. Similarly, he had not managed to break through the 40 percent barrier in polls of party members. Clearly, there remained doubts among MPs and party members about his candidacy.

The nature of those doubts was evident in a YouGov poll for the *Daily Telegraph* on the eve of the party conference (28–30 September poll in Table 4.4). At this point, Davis and Clarke were seen as the two main candidates and YouGov asked Conservative Party members to select the best candidate on five criteria that translate well into the acceptability-electability-competence framework. On electability, Clarke led Davis by 9 percentage points as the candidate best placed to boost the Tories' election chances and by 21 points as the best performer on television, which would be helpful in broadening the party's electoral appeal. On competence, Clarke led Davis by 31 points as the candidate most able to challenge Blair and Brown in parliament. The problem for Clarke, however, was that he failed to convince his party on the first-order criterion of acceptability. His pro-European views were seen as a major impediment: on the vital question of who could best unite the party, Davis led Clarke by 19 points.

The existing misgivings about Davis were confirmed by his performance at the conference. However, it was only with the emergence of Cameron as a credible candidate that Davis's fate was sealed. A poll after the elimination of Clarke gave Cameron absolute majorities on all the key leadership qualities, even after the inclusion of Fox (18–19 October poll in Table 4.4). This overwhelming advantage was confirmed during the OMOV contest (9–11 November poll in Table 4.4). Cameron's biggest leads were on electability. Most important, he also led Davis in the one crucial category that Davis had led Clarke, on being best placed to unite

Table 4.4 Conservative Members' Perceptions of Candidates' Leadership Qualities 2005

Candidate best placed to:	28–30 Sept Poll		18–19 Oct Poll			9–11 Nov Poll	
	Davis	Clarke	Davis	Cameron	Fox	Davis	Cameron
Unite Conservative Party [acceptability]	53	34	19	55	15	27	59
Boost Tories' election chances [electability]	39	48	13	63	15	21	64
Perform well on TV & radio [electability]	34	55	8	70	17	17	71
Challenge Blair & Brown in Commons [competence]	31	62	20	52	16	35	50
Make the best Prime Minister [competence]	n/a	n/a	17	56	19	32	53

Sources: YouGov, 'Conservative members survey 2', poll for the *Daily Telegraph*, 3 October 2005; 'Conservative leader election', poll for the *Daily Telegraph*, 20 October 2005; 'Conservative leadership part 5', poll for the *Daily Telegraph*, 14 November 2005. All polls available at <www.yougov.co.uk>.
Notes: All figures are percentages. Respondents replying 'neither/none' or 'don't know' excluded from table. N = 615 (Sept); N = 665 (Oct); N = 748 (Nov)

the party. Davis had acquired a reputation for plotting against Duncan Smith, and these suspicions about his loyalty, rather than ideology, created doubts about his trustworthiness and his ability to unite the party, even if these had been somewhat overlooked while Clarke was his main rival.[56] However, it would be incorrect to say that ideology no longer mattered. Continued misgivings about Clarke suggested that it did, partly because a leader who did not share the concerns of his party would struggle to unite it. Cameron, however, was seen as fairly 'sound', even if he were not as ideologically pure as the candidates of the right.

Table 4.5 shows the results of a YouGov poll of party members' stances on Europe and their perceptions of the candidates' stances,

Table 4.5   Ideological Stance of Conservative Members and Their Perceptions of Final Three Candidates

	Tory members' self-description	Tory members' descriptions of...		
		Cameron	Davis	Fox
Pro-European	7	9	3	2
Eurosceptic	80	40	65	72
Neither	13	36	19	14
Don't know	1	15	13	12

Source: YouGov, 'Conservative leader election', poll for the *Daily Telegraph*, 20 October 2005, available at <www.yougov.co.uk>.
Notes: Q. 'Conservatives these days tend to be described as being either "pro-European" or "Euro-sceptic". If you had to choose, how would you describe [yourself/Liam Fox/David Davis/David Cameron]?' All figures are percentages. N = 665

carried out after Clarke had been eliminated. Fully 80 percent of Tory members saw themselves as Eurosceptic, while just 7 percent described themselves as pro-European, with 13 percent saying they were neither. The members saw both Davis and Fox as being largely in tune with themselves, with 65 percent describing Davis and 72 percent describing Fox as Eurosceptics. Only 40 percent believed Cameron was a Eurosceptic, while 36 percent said he was neither Eurosceptic nor pro-European. Just 9 percent saw him as pro-European, so his image among party members was not that of a Europhile, but as a pragmatic, moderate Eurosceptic. Nevertheless, he sought to firm up his Eurosceptic credentials during the campaign by pledging to pull the Conservatives out of the federalist European People's Party grouping in the European parliament. That move enabled him to outflank Davis on Europe and helped him to secure support from members of the right-wing Cornerstone grouping of MPs.[57]

The Conservatives were not as badly divided in 2005 as they had been for much of the 1997–2003 period and so the need to restore party unity was not the over-riding concern it had been. Nevertheless, it remained important as long as Clarke was still in the contest because there was the risk that the party would be ungovernable with a pro-European as leader. To that extent, ideology was important in the 2005 contest, but hard-line Euroscepticism was not essential. Once Clarke was eliminated, unity was no longer a pressing concern. The contest was then decided on the second-order criterion of electability, on which Cameron was far ahead of Davis.

Assessing the role of party members in Conservative leadership selection

The 2005 leadership contest, in which a telegenic and moderate young candidate easily defeated one who was closer to the activists' hearts, suggests that some of the earlier criticisms of the Conservatives' OMOV selection system may have been misplaced. Foremost among these criticisms was that the activists had imposed Duncan Smith on the parliamentary party because he enjoyed the support of only 54 of 166 MPs in the final parliamentary ballot.[58] Yet Clarke won only 59 votes: he too would have faced questions over his legitimacy had he won the membership ballot. It is not clear, moreover, that Conservative MPs would have voted for another candidate. They had already chosen Hague over Clarke in 1997. Hague himself supported Duncan Smith in the final parliamentary ballot in 2001.[59] Given the strength of Eurosceptic feeling in the parliamentary Conservative Party, Clarke would have struggled to become leader irrespective of the selection system.

The conventional wisdom that Tory members were irrational to choose Duncan Smith overlooks the basic requirement for party unity as a prerequisite for electoral success. A pro-European would have split the party and left it vulnerable to debilitating attacks from the Labour government and the media. Deep down, Conservative members probably knew that they had little chance of winning the next general election, but their more immediate aim was to preserve party unity. Therefore, they made a logical choice in selecting Duncan Smith, irrespective of his obvious weaknesses.

Those same Conservative members went on to choose Cameron over Davis in 2005, confounding the notion that they were unthinking ideologues. They *were* ideological, but not blindly so: they understood the need for internal unity before electoral considerations. Once they were offered candidates who did not threaten the broad Eurosceptic consensus in the party in 2005, they chose on the basis of electability. If a candidate such as Cameron had been offered to them in 2001, it is highly likely they would have chosen him, certainly over Clarke and probably over Duncan Smith. Despite being a Eurosceptic, Portillo was *not* such a candidate, because he divided his party on social policy, homosexuality and (lack of) loyalty. In contrast, Cameron had no history of disloyalty and although he was more socially liberal than most Tory MPs, he did not give the impression at this stage of wanting to hector his party or force it to adopt positions that challenged its gut instincts. In this respect, it is likely that his privileged upbringing and 'high Tory' credentials neutralised fears among the membership about the direction in which he would take the party.

Members' preferences and MPs' preferences

One of the intriguing aspects of the Tories' selection system concerns the interaction between the political preferences of MPs and party members. The two-stage process ensures that the parliamentary party structures the choices of the individual members. The MPs can refuse to allow candidates to advance if they do not have sufficient support within the parliamentary party, even if they are liked by the members, such as Widdecombe in 2001. Moreover, if MPs know the members' preferences – and frequent polling nowadays ensures that they do – they may find it advantageous to vote strategically in the parliamentary ballots to maximise their preferred candidate's chances by influencing the identity of his opponent in the OMOV ballot. For example, some supporters of Fox in 2005 believed that his chances were damaged by tactical voting for Davis by some supporters of Cameron, although the Cameron camp denied this charge.[60]

A further way in which some observers have depicted the relationship between MPs and members in the Tory selection system is through the notion of 'giving a lead'. Heppell argues that '[u]nlike four years earlier, Conservative parliamentarians [in 2005] had given a clear and unambiguous lead to the party membership, who duly followed their lead [in choosing Cameron].'[61] However, although it is true that Cameron, unlike Clarke or Duncan Smith in 2001, had a big lead over his nearest rival going into the OMOV ballot, it is not entirely clear that the MPs gave a lead to the members. Indeed, it was arguably the other way round.

Cameron's fortunes changed after his own credibility-boosting speech to the party conference and Davis's lacklustre speech the following day. The biggest impression was made with party members. Before the conference, Davis led Cameron 61-39 on head-to-head polls, but immediately after the speeches, Cameron led 74-26 (see Figure 4.3). The initial shift in support among MPs was nowhere near as dramatic. A YouGov poll conducted between the first and second ballots found that Cameron's head-to-head rating against Davis had improved to 80-20 among party members. Against Fox, he led 77-23. It was clear to MPs which way the wind was blowing before they cast their votes. As the leading Conservative activist and blogger, Tim Montgomerie, put it:

> An election that could have been decided behind closed doors – with promises of jobs and arms-twisting – was being decided by the opin-

ions of grassroots members. Michael Howard had miscalculated that MPs would be less enamoured of David Davis than party members. In the end it was a tidal wave of grassroots support that led many MPs to abandon their pledges to Mr Davis and embrace the X-factor Cameron.[62]

A final point on the notion of 'giving a lead' is that, had Clarke beaten Fox to third place in the first ballot, it would have been the centre and left vote, rather than the right-wing vote, that was split in the final ballot. In that situation, Davis could easily have topped the final ballot, once again facing Cameron in the OMOV ballot but this time having won more support than his rival from MPs. If party members stuck with Cameron in these circumstances, it might then have looked as if MPs were in disagreement with the members, leading to a re-run of Duncan Smith's legitimacy problems. That is one of the weaknesses of the Conservatives' selection system, as it is of Labour's electoral college, as separate constituencies of selectors creates the possibility of rival legitimacies. If one or more of these constituencies is prepared to 'take a lead' from another, these problems of legitimacy can reduced.

The eviction of Duncan Smith

It was shown earlier that, as well as enfranchising party members in leadership elections, the Conservatives' post-1998 selection rules contained a new mechanism for evicting leaders. Formal leadership challenges were replaced by confidence votes among Tory MPs. In this section, the discussion returns to the case of Iain Duncan Smith, who became the first Tory leader to be removed under the new rules in October 2003.

Duncan Smith's two-year tenure as leader was marked by managerial shortcomings, party disunity and poor poll ratings. His leadership got off to an inauspicious start when the 9/11 terrorist attacks on the US completely overshadowed his victory in the 2001 Conservative leadership contest. The aftermath of those events, including the subsequent war in Afghanistan, ensured that Duncan Smith struggled to get himself noticed by the public.[63] He also failed to impose himself on his own party. A fissure over social policy that had emerged under Hague widened under Duncan Smith. Although he tried to maintain unity, Duncan Smith's own traditionalist instincts made that difficult. In November 2002, his leadership suffered a major crisis when he misjudged parliamentary tactics. Duncan Smith ordered a three-line whip on a parliamentary vote on the government's desire to allow unmarried couples, including gays, to adopt children. The leader and most of his party opposed 'gay adoption', but social liberals, including Portillo and Clarke, supported it. Duncan Smith denounced his opponents for seeking to undermine his leadership and he issued a call to his party to 'unite or die', inviting scorn from those who recalled Duncan Smith's own past as a persistent rebel under the Major government.[64]

There were severe criticisms of Duncan Smith's competence as a leader. His colleagues despaired of his lack of managerial skills and the chaotic state of his private office, which hindered his ability to run the party effectively.[65] In the summer of 2002, Duncan Smith demoted Davis from his job as party chairman while the latter was away on holiday, drawing critical press comment and entrenching divisions inside the party.[66] In February 2003, another bout of infighting saw Duncan Smith sack Portilloite officials in central office, accusing them of plotting against him.[67]

Duncan Smith struggled to inspire confidence that he could improve his party's fortunes. He was a poor public speaker and struggled to make an impact at Prime Minister's Questions or in set-piece speeches. Indeed, during his 2002 conference speech, he implored his audience 'never [to] underestimate the determination of a quiet man'. It had little effect other than to invite ridicule. He never looked like an alternative prime minister. Towards the end of his tenure as leader, Duncan Smith had fallen into third place behind Blair and Charles Kennedy in polls asking respondents which leader would make the best prime minister.[68]

There was little evidence of an improvement in the Conservatives' electoral fortunes and the party looked on course for another resounding election defeat, despite a narrowing of Labour's lead. It is true that, while the Tories were 17 points behind in the polls when Duncan Smith took over as leader, they were just 5 points behind Labour when he departed (Figure 4.4). However, that was still a respectable performance for a mid-term government. Moreover, the fall in Labour's lead owed more to the general unpopularity of the Blair government and in particular its decision to join the US-led invasion of Iraq in 2003. Even then, Conservatives support remained stuck in the low-30 percent range, where it had been for several years. It was the Liberal Democrats that were the main beneficiaries of the government's problems, partly because they were the only major party to oppose the Iraq War. The Conservatives supported it and so could not profit from rising anti-war sentiment. Meanwhile, Duncan Smith's own popularity ratings had started off low and fell further. His net satisfaction was positive for only two months in 2001

Figure 4.4 Conservatives' Poll Lead and Duncan Smith's Net Satisfaction Rating 2001–03

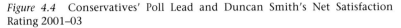

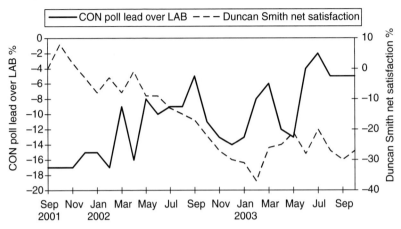

Sources: ICM Research, '*Guardian* monthly polls', available at <http://www.icmresearch.com>; Ipsos-MORI, 'Political monitor: Satisfaction ratings 1997–present', available at <http://www.ipsos-mori.com>.

Notes: Q1. 'If there were to be a general election tomorrow which party do you think you would vote for?' [CON poll lead over LAB = % Conservative minus % Labour] Q2. 'Are you satisfied or dissatisfied with the way Mr Duncan Smith is doing his job as Leader of the Opposition?' [Duncan Smith net satisfaction = % satisfied minus % dissatisfied]

before falling permanently into negative territory, reaching a low of –37 in February 2003.

Duncan Smith's poor performance and the Conservatives' failure to overhaul Labour's poll lead ensured that leadership plots were incessant. In the autumn of 2002, Duncan Smith saw off an attempted coup. In May 2003, the frontbencher, Crispin Blunt, resigned in advance of local-election results and urged his leader to go, but the results for the Tories were better than expected and Duncan Smith gained some breathing space. However, the end finally came in the autumn after it was revealed that a parliamentary investigation would examine allegations that he employed his wife, Betsy, for secretarial work, when the work she did was insufficient to merit her state-paid salary.[69] Duncan Smith would eventually be cleared of wrong-doing but it was too late. On 28 October, the chairman of the 1922 committee, Sir Michael Spicer, confirmed that he had received the requisite 25 letters from Tory MPs, representing 15 percent of the parliamentary party, demanding a confidence vote.[70] A secret ballot of MPs took place the following day and Duncan Smith was defeated by 75 votes to 90.

Method of eviction

The provision for a confidence vote provided Duncan Smith's opponents with a clear mechanism for removing him from office. That left the question of how to mobilise sufficient MPs to demand a confidence vote. There was also the problem of who would replace him. The confidence-vote procedure and subsequent leadership election sequentially separated these two stages, but they would still be connected in the minds of many of the leader's opponents. Some MPs might be prepared to join the call for a confidence vote only if they were sure that they would get the new leader of their choice. That would be less likely to happen if there were rivals to take over. Furthermore, rival candidates would necessitate a long OMOV contest that could put the party out of action for two months. In contrast, if MPs could unite behind a single candidate, it would obviate the need for a membership ballot. It would also rule out the imposition by the members of a leader who did not enjoy the respect of the MPs, one of the principal complaints against Duncan Smith.

It is risky to move against leaders and costly trying to prise them from office. There is a strong argument for claiming that the Conservative Party's eviction institutions played, if not *the* most important, then at least *an* important role in Duncan Smith's defenestration. There have been leaders whose personal ratings have been as bad as Duncan Smith's, whose parties were further behind in the polls and which were seen as just as badly divided, who nevertheless managed to survive attempts to oust them. There was enough double-dealing among Tory MPs and poor organisation among those plotting against Duncan Smith to make it far from certain that the discontent would end in his ejection. Nevertheless, the existence of an eviction mechanism ensured that widespread dissatisfaction with the leader could be directed into a move against him.

The confidence vote that ultimately removed Duncan Smith was merely the final act of a drawn-out saga. The secret ballot enabled the embattled leader's opponents, whether on the front or back benches, to vote against him free from the threat of sanction. Thus, once the decision to hold a vote had been taken, the plotters' mobilisation costs fell substantially because voting against the leader in a secret ballot was risk-free. The riskier business of securing a vote of confidence in the leader was achieved by a subset of his enemies. The rules required 15 percent of Tory MPs to write to the chairman of the 1922 committee to request a confidence vote before one would be granted. Although letter-writers were promised anonymity and many were assured by the promise, there was some concern that the names might leak out.[71] That raised the plotters' mobilisation costs to some degree and probably limited the numbers of MPs, particularly frontbenchers, who were prepared to send letters.

The 15 percent threshold gave the rebels a clear target to aim for, although they were hindered by the refusal of Sir Michael Spicer to give a running tally of the number of letters he had received. Not only was 15 percent a fairly low and eminently achievable target, the fact that it was a *formal* threshold also reduced the plotters' mobilisation costs: the certainty over what was needed to trigger a ballot made it easier to marshal opposition than it would have been had there been only subjective assessments of how many letters constituted 'enough' to force a vote.

The fact that there was an eviction mechanism enabled backbenchers to play the principal role in ousting Duncan Smith. That was just as well because senior frontbenchers were disinclined to plot openly against their leader. Despite urgings from some backbenchers, none of Duncan Smith's senior colleagues would tell him to go. At a shadow cabinet meeting days before his eviction, those present professed loyalty to the leader after he acknowledged 'rumours and speculation about plots' and insisted he would stay on. Suggestions that five members of the shadow cabinet were about to resign came to nothing.[72] Those with hopes of succeeding Duncan Smith, such as Howard, Davis and Clarke, kept a safe distance from any plotting. The only major figure who was seen as semi-publicly disloyal to Duncan Smith was Eric Forth, the shadow leader of the House of Commons. He was an ally of Davis but also widely seen as a maverick.[73] Overall, shadow-cabinet members seemed caught in a collective-action problem, preferring to wait for others to make a move.

The supporters of Duncan Smith's rivals were less constrained in their attacks on him. Derek Conway was one of the few Tory MPs who publicly revealed that he had written to Spicer to call for a confidence vote. Conway was a right-wing backbencher closely associated with Davis. He had been a whip in the Major government during which time he had clashed with Duncan Smith over the latter's Maastricht rebellions.[74] Another Duncan Smith opponent who made public his letter to Spicer was Francis Maude, a moderniser and Portillo ally. Maude had also served in the Major government but had since returned to the backbenches. Other supporters of Portillo were accused of leaking information about Duncan Smith's wife during the controversy over her paid parliamentary job.[75] A year earlier, Duncan Smith's allies had named four other back-bench MPs who they claimed were plotting to force a confidence vote. They were Andrew Mackay, a former deputy chief whip under Major and a member of Hague's shadow cabinet; Douglas Hogg, an agriculture minister under Major; Anthony Steen and Andrew Mitchell.[76] Hogg, Steen and Mitchell all supported Clarke in the 2001 leadership contest, although Mitchell would later run Davis's 2005 leadership campaign.

The fact that the various plots were instigated primarily by backbenchers, who themselves were supporters of different rivals, ensured that they appeared disorganised and not very efficient.[77] It was difficult for the rebels to mobilise their colleagues. As one MP quoted in the *Daily Telegraph* put it: 'We want it to happen but we can't see how. No one will sign a letter without first knowing how many others have signed it as well, and who they are.'[78] The political journalist, Michael Crick, argued that the situation became so bad towards the end of Duncan Smith's tenure, that the whip's office intervened to hasten the confidence vote. The whips normally show great loyalty to the leader, but they must also gauge the mood on the backbenches. In Crick's account, the whips, exasperated by Duncan Smith's performance and the level of antipathy towards him on the backbenches, were involved in encouraging MPs to send letters to the 1922 committee, or at the very least, in making it clear that they would not pursue those that did.[79] Crick quotes one Tory MP as saying, 'Towards the end of the [Duncan Smith] period, somebody in the Whips' Office said to me, "Listen you guys, for Christ's sake, get on with it. If you're going to do it, get on with it." And so I think they'd realised this was unsustainable.'[80] Even the unusual step taken by the chief whip, David Maclean, of publicly announcing that he would be summoning a number of rebel MPs for talks about their 'career development' was seen by many as a deliberate provocation designed to speed up the rebellion.[81] They had to get Duncan Smith before he got them.

The confidence-vote procedure gave senior frontbenchers an alibi for their public inaction and channelled dissent into the quest for 25 letters. There were risks involved for all rebels, but these risks were higher for frontbenchers, who had more to lose from having their identities revealed. Although the plotters nominally had to recruit 25 out of 165 MPs, in practice, it would have been more like 25 out of 80 *if* few frontbenchers were prepared to risk joining the putsch. That would have made the effective threshold nearer to one-third of *backbenchers*, which would help explain why it was not an easy obstacle to overcome. It seems that some frontbenchers did send letters to Spicer.[82] However, Duncan Smith's removal in 2003 appeared to fit the common pattern for the dethroning of Tory leaders, as evident in 1911, 1965, 1975 and 1990, whereby the main role was played not by party notables but by backbenchers fearing for the party's electoral prospects.[83]

The Conservative Party's confidence-vote mechanism was an important element in Duncan Smith's eviction. It enabled most of the plotting to be done from the backbenches and ultimately the rebels did not require high-profile resignations or other public interventions by senior members of the shadow cabinet. It is more than possible that Duncan Smith would have been removed even without the confidence-vote mechanism, but its existence facilitated the channelling of discontent into an eviction. The secret ballot during the vote itself enabled, not just discontented backbenchers, but also frontbenchers to register their desire for a change of leadership. It would have been harder to achieve that without the secret ballot.

In addition to the question of mobilising MPs for a confidence vote, there was the problem of who should replace Duncan Smith in the event of his eviction. The existence of rival factions and their own favoured crown princes initially helped Duncan Smith by presenting him with a divided internal opposition. A year into his leadership, he was under severe pressure, with rumours of an impending coup around the time of the 2002 party conference and the 'gay adoption' vote. Modernisers wanted the party to adopt a more socially-liberal stance and hoped that Portillo or Clarke might take over. There was even talk of a pact, with Portillo playing the 'kingmaker' for Clarke, who could be acclaimed leader to avoid the necessity of an OMOV ballot. However, Davis was reportedly opposed to this idea, as he still nurtured his own leadership ambitions.[84] Many MPs on the right did not want a pro-European to become leader. Similarly, a right-wing putsch against Duncan Smith risked letting in Clarke. These divisions over who should take over presented Duncan Smith's opponents with a collective-action problem and helped him survive in 2002.

By 2003, the situation had changed. Portillo was no longer considered a viable candidate, having become disenchanted with life at Westminster. Clarke was still interested but after his bruising defeat in 2001, he preferred a coronation to an election in which he might find himself again rejected by the members. However, there was still considerable opposition to him within the parliamentary party.[85] His supporters believed that, only if the Conservative Party's electoral predicament became much worse than it was at that time could Clarke hope to receive the call to leadership. Some allies of other potential candidates believed that Clarke's supporters were plotting precisely such a path to the leadership. One of Davis's key lieutenants, Conway, claimed to have discovered that 23 MPs drawn mainly from among pro-Europeans and the Tory left, met on the morning of the confidence vote to discuss tactics. At this meeting, they allegedly agreed that the party was not yet desperate enough to turn to Clarke and so it would be better to keep Duncan Smith in post. A year would need to pass before another confidence vote would be allowed, by which time a general election would probably be six months away. In these circumstances, a year of infighting and poor poll ratings throughout 2004 might be enough to make Tory MPs turn to Clarke in panic.[86] If the 23 MPs did indeed support Duncan Smith in the confidence vote, it would explain his relatively strong showing: the 75 votes he won were widely remarked upon as being well above expectations for someone who had won only 54 votes in the final parliamentary ballot in the 2001 leadership election.

On the right, Davis had his supporters but again, his opponents saw him as a divisive figure who could not easily unite the party.[87] Nevertheless, as the endgame approached for Duncan Smith, Davis was seen as one of the two major candidates likely to be in the running to take over. The other was Michael Howard, a right-wing Eurosceptic and former home secretary, who had unsuccessfully bid for the leadership in 1997. Howard had been out of frontline politics for two years before returning as shadow chancellor in 2001. His strong performances against Gordon Brown in the Commons had won him new respect.[88] He was seen as a safe pair of hands, a competent politician who could take the Tories into the next general election even if he were not a long-term prospect. Howard's stock had also risen among party members, as polls showed that they preferred him to Portillo, Clarke and Davis.[89] Unlike Davis, Howard did not have many enemies in the parliamentary party. Even Widdecombe, who had destroyed his leadership bid in 1997, was not inclined to reopen that dispute.

With astonishing speed, Howard became the consensus candidate of 2003. Once Duncan Smith was evicted on 28 October, Howard was able to secure support from Eurosceptics and modernisers, who saw him as a useful stop-gap leader.[90] On the day of the confidence vote, before the result was announced, Davis told Howard he would not run against him. Even if he felt able to win the OMOV ballot, he would do so after almost certainly finishing far behind Howard in the parliamentary ballots, experiencing the same legitimacy deficit that characterised Duncan Smith's tenure. Howard quickly secured the overwhelming support of Tory MPs and on 6 November he was declared leader unopposed.

The existence of a unity candidate was vital in 2003. It enabled Conservative MPs to short-circuit the process by uniting behind Howard and thereby avoiding a ballot. That manoeuvre was a consequence of the OMOV selection system. In the first place, Tory MPs had little faith in the ability of the mass membership to make a sensible choice. Secondly, according to Conway, the prospect of a lengthy OMOV ballot 'filled everyone with horror' and was regarded as too expensive for a party that had little money. It is much more likely that a ballot would have taken place had only MPs enjoyed the right to select their leaders because it would have been much quicker and cheaper to organise.[91] In other words, the 'party costs' of leader eviction and replacement would have been considerably lower. In the event, party costs were substantially reduced by circumventing the ballot altogether, a testament to the fact that these considerations weigh heavily in the minds of politicians. Even the legitimacy costs of removing a leader elected by the membership were lower, partly because Duncan Smith was seen not to enjoy the support of MPs and partly because by the end, over half of the membership thought it had been a mistake to elect him in the first place.[92] Those features of OMOV that were thought to protect leaders – long contests and broad legitimacy – ultimately failed to save Duncan Smith.

Conclusion

Among the many consequences of Cameron's victory in the leadership contest of 2005, one was the rehabilitation of the OMOV selection system. This system appeared to have been discredited with Duncan Smith's election in 2001, to the point that Tory MPs were not prepared to risk its use again after his removal two years later. Indeed, party members themselves seemed to have accepted that leadership selection ought to be left in the hands of the MPs and a majority of members of the national Conservative convention voted to abandon the system, albeit not by a big enough margin.

At the root of these misgivings was a misunderstanding of the 2001 leadership contest. Of the three leading candidates, only one was unencumbered by ideological and/or personal baggage and that was Duncan Smith. It is easy to dismiss his authority as resting on the shaky foundations of support from a third of the parliamentary party, but Clarke and Portillo would have been in the same position had they won. Duncan Smith's problems stemmed from his limited electoral appeal and his lack of key leadership qualities: in the absence of these problems, less would have been made of his legitimacy deficit. Even in 2005, when Cameron almost won a majority on the final parliamentary ballot, that result owed a lot to the fact that Clarke departed the contest before Fox, ensuring that the centre and left vote unified in the final parliamentary ballot, whereas the right-wing vote remained split.

This perceived legitimacy problem is a consequence of a selection system that has different selectorates. The preliminary parliamentary ballots are little more than a filtering mechanism, designed to ensure that would-be leaders can demonstrate *considerable* support among MPs, not necessarily *majority* support. However, politicians and the media inevitably look for evidence that the leader enjoys the confidence of his MPs. Consequently, the results of the parliamentary ballots in the Conservative Party end up being judged on the basis of a criterion – authority within the parliamentary party – that they were not designed to measure.

The other area of interest in this study is leaders' institutional security of tenure. Part of the purpose of introducing the new selection system was to make it harder to evict Conservative leaders. There were two principal ways in which the new system might do that. First, the threshold for instigating a contest/confidence vote was raised from 10 percent to 15 percent of Tory MPs. Second, it was expected that a cumbersome membership ballot would dissuade all but the most serious challenges to the incumbent. These two factors played a role in protecting Duncan Smith in 2002, but neither was strong enough to save him in 2003, although given the extent of dissatisfaction with his leadership, that could be taken to indicate that the rules were working properly. The eviction was not a particularly easy or well-organised operation. However, the availability of a mechanism that could bring about a confidence vote by secret ballot was an important factor in Duncan Smith's defenestration. The lack of such a mechanism would have complicated matters and in the absence of a general uprising by frontbenchers and/or backbenchers, it might even have enabled Duncan Smith to survive through to the general election.

5
The Liberal Democrats: One Member-One Vote

The shift towards the selection of leaders in all-member ballots in Britain was pioneered by the Liberal Party in 1976. One member-one vote (OMOV) became a key feature of the successor party, the Liberal Democrats, from 1988 onwards. To this day, the Liberal Democrats remain the only major British party to use a 'pure' form of OMOV, undiluted by weighted votes in an electoral college or preliminary parliamentary ballots. This preference reflected the Liberal Democrats' ethos of participatory democracy and was a natural development in a party (including its predecessors) that never won more than 23 seats in a general election between 1935 and 1992. The parliamentary wing was much weaker than in the Labour and Conservative parties, and consequently the extra-parliamentary wing enjoyed a higher status.

This situation changed in 1997 when the Liberal Democrats under Paddy Ashdown doubled their parliamentary representation. They went on to make further gains under Charles Kennedy in 2001 and won 62 seats in 2005. This greater electoral credibility, together with an influx of younger, more ambitious MPs, altered the party's internal dynamics. Now, electoral advance was expected, not just desirable, and it created a new assertiveness within the shadow cabinet. This assertiveness was exercised partly in relation to the left-leaning party membership, but also in relation to the party leader when the latter was deemed to be underperforming. This chapter examines recent leadership elections and evictions in the Liberal Democrats. It explores whether OMOV in the Liberal Democrats has been compatible with parliamentary domination, or is indicative of a powerful grassroots membership.

The structure of this chapter is similar to the previous two. It begins with a brief account of the development of the OMOV selection system, together with details of the contests conducted under it. The major focus in the chapter, however, is on the two most recent leadership contests in 2006 and 2007. These are analysed in terms of the selection criteria used by party members. Before that, the chapter examines the event that made these contests possible, namely, the forced resignation of Kennedy. This episode revealed important shifts in the balance of power between the Liberal Democrats' parliamentary and extra-parliamentary wings.

Historical antecedents

The Liberal Democrats were formed after a merger between the Liberal Party and the Social Democratic Party (SDP) in 1988.[1] The new party's leadership-selection method was based on the procedures used in its predecessor parties. As was discussed in Chapter 2, the Liberals allowed their MPs to choose their leader in 1967 before adopting a form of OMOV for the next leadership contest in 1976. That year the party had debated extending the franchise to party members because of the perceived legitimacy deficit of a party leader elected by a handful of MPs – the Liberals won 13 seats in the general election of October 1974. Before it could settle on a system, the party was shaken by a sexual scandal involving its leader, Jeremy Thorpe, who was eventually forced to resign. A former leader, Jo Grimond, took over on an interim basis until the party had decided its method of leadership selection.

A special assembly in June 1976 agreed on a complicated form of membership participation. Eligible candidates had to be MPs who had secured the nominations of five Liberal MPs or 20 percent of the parliamentary party, whichever figure was lower. If two or more candidates passed this threshold, they would go through to an indirect ballot of party members. Each constituency association was allocated a block of ten votes plus an additional ten if it had been affiliated the previous year, plus one more vote for each 500 votes cast for the Liberal candidate in its constituency at the previous general election. Each association would then hold an all-member ballot and its block of votes would be allocated to candidates in proportion to the votes cast. Meanwhile, leadership elections were not mandated on an annual basis, but would be called if the leader resigned, died, was incapacitated or lost his parliamentary seat. There could also be an election if the incumbent suffered a vote of no confidence among Liberal MPs, or if 50 constituency associations from eight regions demanded one.[2] The system was used only once when David Steel convincingly defeated John Pardoe by 64 percent to 36 percent in 1976.

The SDP was formed in 1981 after a group of centrist MPs defected from the Labour Party, alienated by its leftist drift.[3] The party went on to form an electoral alliance with the Liberals in the 1983 and 1987 general elections. One of the precipitating factors in the MPs' departure from Labour was the latter's adoption of the electoral college (see Chapter 3), which they saw as a way of allowing trade-union leaders to choose the party leader. Some of the leading figures in the SDP had argued for OMOV as an alternative to the electoral college when they were in the Labour Party and continued to argue for OMOV in their new party. The SDP spent much of its first year in existence discussing the method by which it should select its leader, with the choice mainly between OMOV or selection by MPs. OMOV eventually won out, although party members only narrowly preferred it to a compromise solution in which OMOV would be used for the party's first leadership contest in 1982 and parliamentary ballots in subsequent contests.[4] Candidates needed to be nominated by 15 percent of MPs. Elections would occur when the incumbent resigned or lost his parliamentary seat, or if more than half of the members of the SDP's parliamentary committee (its MPs and representatives of SDP peers) called for one within a month of the opening of a new parliament. The system was fully used just once, in 1982, when Roy Jenkins defeated David Owen by 55.7 percent to 44.3 percent. Owen replaced Jenkins as leader when the latter resigned in 1983, but he was elected unopposed, as was Owen's successor, Robert Maclennan, in 1987.[5]

Liberal Democrat leadership selection rules and leadership elections 1988–99

After the 1987 general election, talks commenced on a merger between the Liberals and the SDP. A minority, including Owen, opposed the move, but majorities of members of both parties voted in favour of a merger and the Liberal Democrats were born in 1988.[6] The new party adopted an OMOV system similar to the SDP's, but extended the nomination rights beyond MPs to the party on the ground. It was used for the first time in 1988, and again in 1999, 2006 and 2007.

The Liberal Democrats' leadership selection rules are set out in Article 10 of the federal party's constitution (see Box 5.1). The party uses a pure OMOV system of selection, i.e. only party members choose the leader, unlike the Conservative and Labour parties, which allow their MPs to play a significant selectoral role. Liberal Democrat MPs can vote in the membership ballot, but their votes are worth the same

Box 5.1   Liberal Democrat Leadership Election Rules

Instigation of Leadership Election

- Elections take place when one of the following occurs:
  - Leader calls an election
  - Leader dies or is incapacitated
  - Leader loses his parliamentary seat
  - Leader resigns or declares intention to resign
  - Majority of all Liberal Democrat MPs pass of motion of no confidence in leader
  - 75 local parties write to Liberal Democrat president demanding election
  - Anniversary of previous general election passed without leadership contest. Federal Executive can postpone contest for a further 12 months by two-thirds majority. Entire rule dis-applies when leader is a member of the government.

Format of Leadership Elections

- Candidates must be MPs
- Incumbent leader can stand for re-election, even if defeated in confidence vote
- Candidates must be nominated by 10 percent of other Liberal Democrat MPs (candidates cannot nominate themselves)
- Candidates must be nominated by 200 party members drawn from at least 20 local parties
- If only one candidate passes nomination thresholds, he is declared leader
- If two or more candidates pass nomination thresholds, they enter all-member postal ballot using alternative-vote electoral system: if no candidate secures overall majority of votes cast in first count, candidate with fewest votes eliminated and his votes redistributed to other candidates. Process continues until a candidate passes 50 percent mark.

Source: *The Constitutions of the Liberal Democrats: The Constitution of the Federal Party* (London: Liberal Democrats, 2009), Article 10.

as those of any other party member. The alternative vote (AV) electoral system is used, with selectors ranking the candidates in order of preference on their ballot papers, which they return by post. The winning candidate must secure a majority of votes cast; if no candidate achieves this mark on the first count, the lowest-ranked candidate is eliminated and his votes redistributed on the basis of the selectors' second preferences. This process continues until one candidate achieves an overall majority.

All candidates wishing to run for the leadership[7] must be MPs and be nominated by at least 10 percent of Liberal Democrat MPs, giving the latter some gate-keeping control over the contest. Until 2005, the nomination threshold was two MPs but was changed after the general election. Some observers suggested that the change to 10 percent, which by then would mean seven MPs, was designed to prevent a challenge to Kennedy.[8] However, party managers claimed that it was intended to prevent a repeat of the 1999 leadership contest in which, at one stage, up to nine candidates declared an interest before five finally participated, in a parliamentary party of just 46 MPs.[9] That incident was widely considered embarrassing to the party.[10] Up to, and including, the 2006 leadership election, MPs could nominate more than one candidate, but in the 2007 contest, they could nominate only one. This change was introduced after Mark Oaten looked to have secured the requisite seven nominations in 2006 but only one of them intended to vote for him. In addition to nominations from MPs, candidates must be nominated by at least 200 individual party members based in at least 20 local parties, which for the purpose includes the party's various special associated organisations. The Liberal Democrats are unique among the three major parties in requiring leadership candidates to secure nominations from outside of their parliamentary party.

There are no provisions for annual leadership elections, but the party is required to hold a contest within a year of the preceding general election, although the ruling Federal Executive can delay it for a further year. This requirement does not apply if the leader is a member of the government. Other than this provision, leadership contests occur only if the incumbent: demands a contest himself; resigns; dies; is incapacitated; loses his seat in parliament; suffers a vote of no confidence by a majority of all Liberal Democrat MPs; or is faced by a formal demand for a contest by 75 local parties.

The Liberal Democrats' first full leadership election took place in 1988. Neither of the predecessor parties' leaders, David Steel and Robert Maclennan, entered the contest. Eventually, only two candidates secured the necessary nominations: Alan Beith, the party's treasury spokesman, and Paddy Ashdown, who had been elected as an MP in 1983. Both had been members of the Liberal Party, but while Beith ran as a traditional Liberal, Ashdown emphasised the need for a new start and appealed to former SDP members.[11] In the OMOV contest, 78,000 party members were sent ballot papers, as were 55,000 former Liberal and SDP members who had not joined the successor party (their papers were a different colour and had to be accompanied by a subscription in order to be counted). Ashdown won the contest easily, receiving 41,401 votes to Beith's 16,202.[12]

Ashdown would serve for 11 years as leader, overseeing a dramatic improvement in the party's electoral performance. He doubled its number of parliamentary seats, taking the total to 46 in the 1997 general election. One reason for the Liberal Democrats' electoral growth was that it benefited greatly from tactical voting.[13] Labour supporters in seats where their party had no chance of winning turned to the Liberal Democrats in considerable numbers in 1997. Warm relations between the two parties at the leadership level had facilitated this informal electoral 'cooperation'. Ashdown had argued strongly in favour of closer links with Labour under Tony Blair, and there had even been the possibility of a coalition government in 1997, but Labour's landslide victory made that unfeasible.[14] Nevertheless, the Liberal Democrats joined Labour in a joint cabinet committee to discuss constitutional reform. The Blair government also agreed to set up a commission, chaired by the Liberal Democrat peer, Lord Jenkins, to examine electoral reform for parliamentary elections.[15]

Ashdown's close links with Labour were controversial in his own party, especially after the Blair government appeared to kick the Jenkins Report on electoral reform into the long grass. Many in the party were concerned about maintaining their identity, as cooperation with other parties in the past had compromised the independence of the old Liberal Party and led it to split.[16] The issue of Labour-Liberal Democrat relations became an increasingly divisive one, with opposition rising among both MPs and activists in the Liberal Democrat party.[17] Ashdown eventually decided to step down as leader in 1999, two years into the Labour government's first term. He insisted that he had always intended to go at that point, although other Liberal Democrats believed that he left when it became clear that his cooperative project with Labour had run its course.[18]

The contest to replace Ashdown was dominated by the issue of links with Labour. Five candidates secured nominations to enter the ballot: Charles Kennedy, Simon Hughes, Malcolm Bruce, Jackie Ballard and David Rendel. All were, to varying degrees, more sceptical than Ashdown had been of close links with Labour. Kennedy and Hughes were seen as the two principal candidates in the race, with Kennedy the front-runner. Although critical of some aspects of Lib-Lab cooperation, Kennedy was the most supportive of the candidates of the links and it was the issue on which he attracted most criticism.[19]

Kennedy ultimately won the contest. Despite being the youngest candidate, he had a considerable public profile, partly because of his frequent appearances on light television shows. He secured the endorsements of over half of the parliamentary party and won 44.6 percent of members' votes in the first count in the membership ballot. Hughes won 31.8 percent while the other three candidates each failed to reach 10 percent (see Appendix C). However, it was not until the fourth count that Kennedy eventually passed the 50 percent mark, winning 56.6 percent of the votes to Hughes's 43.4 percent.[20]

In terms of the key selection criteria, none of the candidates was deemed ideologically divisive, largely because all made sceptical noises about links with Labour. However, Kennedy was the clear choice of a majority of MPs and appeared more broadly acceptable to all sections of the party. His greater public profile also gave him the edge over the other candidates on electability, which was an important criterion in the contest.[21] Finally, on competence, Hughes, Kennedy and Bruce were the longest-serving parliamentarians – each was elected in 1983 – while Rendel was first elected in 1993 and Ballard in 1997. Of these, Bruce was the most senior, holding the post of shadow chancellor at the time of the contest. However, Hughes and Kennedy were also strongly-established figures.

The fall of Charles Kennedy

Kennedy's seven years as leader saw the Liberal Democrats increase further their parliamentary representation and entrench their position as an important player in the party system. However, towards the end of his time at the helm, Kennedy faced mounting problems. This section examines his eventual downfall, while the following sections analyse the leadership elections that took place in the two years following his departure.

On the surface, Kennedy's forced resignation as Liberal Democrat leader in January 2006 appears slightly unusual compared with the ejection of other party leaders. In the general election of May 2005, the Liberal Democrats had won 62 seats, the best third-party performance since 1923. The party's poll ratings were holding up and Kennedy's net satisfaction rating was positive.[22] Beneath the surface, however, there was deep dissatisfaction among many of the party's leading figures. The election result was disappointing given that the Liberal Democrats enjoyed the ideal conditions provided by an unpopular Labour government damaged by the Iraq War and a discredited Conservative opposition.[23] The concern of many was that the Liberal Democrats might have to wait a generation before being presented again with such favourable circumstances. The election was a missed opportunity.[24]

That fear was amplified by the resurgence of the Conservatives in the post-election period. David Cameron was elected as Tory leader in December 2005 but had been leader-in-waiting since October after his speech to the Conservative conference (see Chapter 4). Cameron appeared to represent a break with the past. In December, the Tories touched 40 percent in an Ipsos-MORI poll, the first time they had done so since 1992. A Conservative revival posed a major threat to the Liberal Democrats. The Tories, rather than Labour, were the party's principal electoral competitors: two-thirds of Liberal Democrat seats were in constituencies where the Conservatives finished second.[25] Most of the seats the Liberal Democrats had gained in 1997 and held onto in 2001 and 2005 were previously Tory seats.

Internal divisions also increasingly afflicted the Liberal Democrats. A small but influential group of economically-liberal MPs on the right of the party sought to redirect its policy and electoral strategy.[26] Many of them, including Vince Cable, Mark Oaten, Nick Clegg, Chris Huhne, Ed Davey and David Laws, had contributed to *The Orange Book*, a book of essays published in 2004, urging a greater role for markets and less statism in Liberal Democrat policy.[27] The economic liberals believed that the Liberal Democrats' reputation as a centre-left party under Kennedy had cost votes in middle-class Conservative-Liberal Democrat marginals in 2005.[28] *The Orange Book* proved controversial and its contributors attracted suspicion from others in the party. Most of the parliamentary party and almost the entire extra-parliamentary party remained committed to a more left-leaning social liberalism.[29]

Such was the political context in the months before Kennedy's resignation: dissatisfaction with the election, worries about the resurgent Tories and ideological divisions. The party was in need of firm and decisive leadership, but increasing numbers of MPs – and not only economic liberals – questioned Kennedy's ability to lead the Liberal Democrats through this turbulent period. There had long been complaints inside the party that Kennedy's leadership style was too laid back. Richard Grayson, Kennedy's former policy adviser, described the latter's style as 'more chairman than leader', a description that struck a chord.[30] Economic liberals believed he had failed to take a lead in redirecting the party's electoral and policy strategy, especially at the 2005 party conference. Instead, he was intent to play down differences between economic and social liberals.[31]

The problems were not solely related to policy. Many of the party's new MPs elected in May 2005 had given up good careers to come into politics. They quickly became disenchanted with what they perceived as the lack of direction and competence from the leadership.[32] There was also the question of Kennedy's own faltering performances. This problem pre-dated the 2005 general election: Kennedy had mysteriously missed the 2004 budget statement in parliament and he stammered his way through the launch of the Liberal Democrats' election manifesto in 2005. Unknown to most people, including most Liberal Democrat MPs, Kennedy was struggling with a serious alcohol problem.

Rumours about the security of Kennedy's position surfaced during the summer of 2005 but a successful party conference appeared to have put the issue to rest. However, speculation re-emerged in November, after he put in a number of poor public performances, which were later revealed to have been alcohol-related.[33] Matters came to a head in December when Kennedy faced a revolt by his shadow cabinet. After attempting to persuade his colleagues to stop briefing the media about his leadership, he had to endure criticism of his leadership style. Some senior figures, including Sir Menzies Campbell, the deputy leader, visited Kennedy individually and pleaded with him to consider his position for the good of his family and for his own health. Others conveyed their feelings to the chief whip.[34] The chief executive, Lord Rennard, wrote a coded memo to the chief whip noting that support for Kennedy had fallen, and that it was strongest among those MPs who were unaware of his alcohol problem.[35] However, Kennedy was able rally his supporters at a meeting of the parliamentary party and a coup was averted.

Eleven senior MPs, including Cable and many younger members of the shadow cabinet, signed a letter urging Kennedy to reflect on his position. The letter's existence was revealed to Kennedy by Cable but not formally handed to him, the intention being to give him the Christmas period to consider a suitable exit strategy. The letter was not signed by three figures regarded as most likely to run in any leadership contest to replace Kennedy: Campbell, Simon Hughes, the left-leaning party president, and Mark Oaten, the home-affairs spokesman.[36]

It was not until after Christmas that the issue was forced. After years of rumours about his drinking, the broadcaster, ITN, informed Kennedy in January 2006 that it would run a story alleging that he had received treatment for alcoholism. He pre-empted the story by confirming the allegations in a statement.[37] There was widespread sympathy for Kennedy's plight, although some of his colleagues were annoyed that it had been hidden from them. For them, it appeared to explain Kennedy's poor performances and confirmed that his position was no longer tenable.[38] In the same statement, Kennedy called for a leadership election in which he would be a candidate. However, Campbell, Hughes and Oaten had already signalled that they would not stand against him.[39] Some observers believe that Kennedy might have survived had he merely asked for time to deal with the problem and left it at that, but once he called a ballot in which it was clear that serious candidates would not challenge him, it looked as though the party's agony could be prolonged for months on end.[40] Consequently, MPs consulted among themselves and the final putsch against Kennedy was organised by Davey and Sarah Teather, the education and local-government spokespersons respectively. After initially considering resigning from the shadow cabinet, they mobilised 23 other Liberal Democrat MPs to demand Kennedy's resignation and to state that they would not be willing to serve under him.[41] Kennedy duly announced his resignation the following day on 7 January and Campbell took over as interim leader until a leadership contest could be held.[42]

Institutions, coups and Kennedy's ejection

Kennedy's eviction is interesting for the manner in which it was achieved and for the ways in which it was not. Despite the availability of eviction institutions and a number of opportunities to use them, Kennedy's removal took the form of a forced resignation after a frontbench coup, albeit one in which his potential successors kept their distance. This subsection explores the reasons why Kennedy was removed in the way he was.

The Liberal Democrats' eviction rules do not provide for a challenger to announce that he wishes to stand for election unless a contest has already been called for one of the reasons listed in Box 5.1 above. Four were potentially relevant to the party in 2005–06: (1) 75 local associations could demand an election; (2) there needed to be a contest within a year of the previous general election; (3) there could be a vote of no confidence among Liberal Democrat MPs; and (4) the leader could call an election. Given grassroots loyalty to Kennedy, the first option was highly unlikely. The second option had already gone because Kennedy moved quickly to hold the mandatory leadership contest after the 2005 general election, at a time when his critics were unprepared. The third possibility, of a confidence vote, was raised in the press. The day before Kennedy's resignation, the *Times* claimed that some Liberal Democrat MPs were considering tabling a confidence motion at the weekly meeting of the parliamentary party. It was reported that the precise rules on triggering a confidence vote were not entirely clear, but that it appeared that two Liberal Democrat MPs would need to table the motion formally. Their identities would be known and the leader's opponents would require a majority of the 62 Liberal Democrat MPs eligible to vote.[43] It was unclear whether a confidence vote would be by secret ballot.[44]

Two MPs did not seem a very high barrier for the leader's critics to surmount to instigate a vote and if the vote were by secret ballot, the identities of most of Kennedy's opponents would have been protected. Kennedy would likely have lost a confidence vote in the final week of his leadership, but it is by no means certain that he would have done so earlier, particularly if loyalists had managed to force the vote to be held on a show of hands. Many economic liberals and younger MPs in the shadow cabinet had lost confidence in him, but backbenchers and junior frontbenchers were less aware of the problems, particularly concerning Kennedy's alcoholism before he had made it public.[45] Such a vote risked being divisive and entailed high disunity costs if the leader were determined to hang on. Moreover, even had he lost a confidence vote, Kennedy would have been entitled to stand for re-election, unlike Conservative leaders who are defeated in confidence votes, in which he could have appealed over the heads of his critics to the grassroots. In short, there was a great deal of uncertainty in relation to a confidence vote. If Kennedy survived, his opponents would have shot their bolt and had no alternative but to pledge loyalty.

The fourth option, for Kennedy to call a leadership election, initially looked unfeasible. It was only after he was forced to acknowledge his alcoholism that he announced a contest. Even with an election triggered, however, his critics faced the problem that the most likely replacements had ruled out running against him. Kennedy was well-liked among party members and the latter might have shown loyalty towards him in a ballot. Equally, they could have turned on anyone who did challenge him. Kennedy reportedly preferred a leadership election to a confidence vote because he believed he stood a better chance of winning the backing of individual party members.[46] Not everyone was convinced it would come to that. A Liberal Democrat frontbencher was reported by the *Times* as saying:

> If a ballot is triggered it will be because Charles has lost the support of his MPs. It is inconceivable that he can then seek a mandate over our heads from the members in the country. If he won the ballot of the party's members we would be in an impossible position. It's bluster reminiscent of John Major's back me or sack me [in 1995].[47]

Major, however, won that contest. Similarly, Kennedy was determined to hang on, even as the scale of the revolt became clear.[48] The nightmare scenario would have been for Kennedy to win a membership ballot while being seen not to enjoy the support of his own MPs.

One of the problems with an institutional process of leader eviction from the perspective of Kennedy's critics was that it was not sufficiently divorced from the process of leader replacement. A confidence vote would not necessarily be definitive while knowledge of Kennedy's drinking was restricted. Removing Kennedy through a leadership challenge, however that contest came about, would require a challenger but his major rivals all had good reasons for keeping their distance until he had departed of his own accord. None wanted to be seen as an assassin.

The response of Kennedy's critics was to seek to create a division between eviction and replacement through the non-institutional means of a coup. The relatively small size of the Liberal Democrats' parliamentary party ensured that few MPs were out-and-out backbenchers. At the time of Kennedy's ejection, a third of Liberal Democrat MPs were members of the shadow cabinet and another half were junior spokesmen or whips. Only about a dozen Liberal Democrat MPs had no official party responsibilities in parliament. There were not enough backbenchers to do the deed. Indeed, in the special circumstances of the Kennedy resignation, the leader enjoyed *more* support among those outside the shadow cabinet than inside it because backbenchers were less informed about his shortcomings. The day after the shadow cabinet revolted in December 2005, Kennedy was able to mobilise supporters at the weekly meeting of the parliamentary party. He even declared himself 'gratified by the overwhelming level of support that was expressed for me and my continuing leadership'.[49] The general lack of awareness of Kennedy's alcoholism and its effects on party management, and the unwillingness of those who did know to publicise it, increased the mobilisation costs of Kennedy's opponents in seeking to evict him. If more people had known the full story, it might have been easier to pressurise the leader to go earlier.

If Liberal Democrats MPs were to carry out a putsch against their leader, it was inevitable that it would be led by frontbenchers and carried out collectively, not individually. The problem for Kennedy's critics in the shadow cabinet was that the *most* senior members of that body, and therefore the ones whose opinions carried the greatest weight in relation to Kennedy's authority, were determined to retain their distance. Campbell, Hughes and Oaten were not among the 11 signatories of the Cable letter or the 25 MPs who publicly called for Kennedy to go. Hughes and Oaten had other reasons for not getting directly involved in the plotting: Hughes was party president and had wider responsibilities, while Oaten was a long-standing ally of Kennedy.[50] Campbell's own account in his autobiography indicates that he was deeply conflicted over what to do because of the personal nature of Kennedy's problem and his own long relationship with the leader, although he had privately counselled Kennedy to consider his position after the shadow cabinet revolt.[51] The plot to remove Kennedy suffered from a significant collective-action problem, as senior figures stood back leaving the plotters with a lack of effective leadership. It was only later that Cable was willing to play a coordinating role and even then not all of the plotters were convinced that he would stay the course.[52] The final putsch was organised by Davey and Teather, two junior shadow-cabinet members. This lack of leadership initially deprived the coup of political weight and increased the plotters' mobilisation costs. That explained why Kennedy's ejection lacked ruthlessness and speed.[53]

In the final days of his leadership, Kennedy was, as one Liberal Democrat MEP put it, 'a dead man walking'.[54] By then, no selection system could save him. But the rules did open up opportunities for Kennedy to try to hold on. OMOV entails high decision costs because it is time-consuming, a point Kennedy initially tried to exploit to undermine support for a contest:

> It [a leadership election] could not be done quickly because we are a one member, one vote party. It would occupy the party until the May elections, which I think would be the most enormous self-inflicted distraction. Nonetheless I would stand because I have the support of my colleagues and the overwhelming endorsement of the members.[55]

Perhaps for this reason, some of Campbell's allies mooted the possibility of a 'coronation', circumventing a ballot in the way the Conservatives had done in 2003 when they selected Howard.[56] Meanwhile,

Kennedy was also able to claim the support of the members who had elected him:

> [The members] are overwhelmingly supporting my position personally and politically. That has got to be weighed in the balance by a party that is a 'one member, one vote' party. If those members feel in any sense they are being short-changed or disenfranchised on the most fundamental issue of all, we will start to lose active engagement of members.[57]

This support might have been weaker had the membership known earlier of their leader's drinking problem but as they did not, their support had the effect of imposing legitimacy costs on Kennedy's opponents in the parliamentary party.

In summary, institutions had *some* role in the ejection of Kennedy. By the end, he had little hope of survival but before that point, the institutions had hindered the plotters by not offering a clear enough separation of the processes of leader eviction and replacement. That is another way of saying that Kennedy's rivals did not want to stand against him, especially in a ballot of the party membership. As one journalist observed, 'Mr Kennedy's popularity among members, the sympathy his [drinking] problems are likely to arouse and the danger of a challenger looking "treacherous" were always likely to deter a head-to-head bid for the leadership'.[58] The history of British leadership challenges suggests that this disinclination was the wiser course of action for those individuals, even if it did prolong the party's collective agony.

The Liberal Democrat leadership election of 2006

The 2006 leadership contest followed the fall of Kennedy.[59] Kennedy had called for the election but withdrew his candidacy after the collapse in support for him among his parliamentary colleagues. It was only then that other candidates came forward to announce their intentions to participate. Campbell, who took over as interim leader, quickly established himself as the frontrunner. For a while, it seemed possible that he could secure the leadership unopposed, although two backbenchers, Phil Wills and John Hemming, contemplated standing to avoid a coronation.[60] In the event, other candidates came forward and neither backbencher secured sufficient nominations.

Campbell was the obvious choice to take over from Kennedy. He was the Liberal Democrats' elder statesman and had enjoyed 'a good war' during the Iraq conflict, being the face and voice of the party's opposition to the invasion. Under his interim leadership, the Liberal Democrats won the Dunfermline & West Fife parliamentary by-election on a 16 percent swing from Labour. Ideologically, he was seen as a centrist who could hold together the diverging socially-liberal and economically-liberal wings of the party.[61] He was quickly endorsed by Cable and a former leader, Ashdown. He also garnered significant support from young, 'modernising' MPs.[62] It was assumed that these figures, who included Teather, Laws and Clegg, saw Campbell as a stop-gap leader, who could appoint modernisers to the front bench and take the party through to the next election, by which time they would have gained valuable experience and be positioned to take over.[63] Campbell signalled his willingness to end the Liberal Democrats' commitment to raise the top rate of tax to 50 percent, a policy that had become totemic because of its redistributive nature.[64] However, aware that the membership leaned more to the left, he insisted that he would position the party to the left of Labour, with an emphasis on fighting poverty and promoting the cause of the environment.[65] The main concern about Campbell was his age: at 64, some of his opponents hinted that he was too old, especially now that the Conservatives were led by the youthful Cameron.[66]

In addition to Campbell, early attention focused on Hughes, the Liberal Democrats' president, and Oaten, the home-affairs spokesman. Hughes was on the left of the party, while Oaten was an *Orange Book* contributor. Oaten secured only one firm endorsement among his parliamentary colleagues, although he was nominated by several who wanted to enable him to stand. Despite winning support from sections of the media, on his own admission Oaten did not appeal to MPs or party members, partly for ideological reasons, partly because he was not a top parliamentary performer and partly from a failure to nurture relationships with colleagues.[67] He folded his campaign in advance of the close of nominations because of a lack of support. Days later, the contest took a farcical turn when a tabloid newspaper published lurid details about Oaten's private life.[68] Hughes then became embroiled in controversy over his sexuality, admitting to the *Sun* that he had experienced homosexual (and heterosexual) encounters, having previously said that he was not homosexual.[69] Together with the stories about Kennedy's alcoholism, these events damaged the party's credibility.

One other serious candidate to emerge was Chris Huhne, a former MEP who was first elected to parliament in 2005. Huhne's candidacy was unexpected because he was close to the modernisers who had backed Campbell. There were even rumours of a 'deal' among this group that none would challenge Campbell. Huhne was accused of reneging on it, although he denied that it amounted to a deal.[70] As an *Orange Book* contributor, Huhne was seen as right-leaning, although he also had strong environmental credentials.[71]

The OMOV contest

Nominations closed on 25 January, with Campbell, Huhne and Hughes making it on to the ballot. Campbell enjoyed the greatest support among Liberal Democrat MPs, with 35 endorsements, including most leading frontbenchers.[72] Hughes was endorsed by at least 10 MPs and Huhne by 11.[73] However, the contest then turned to the OMOV stage and there was no guarantee that the individual members would back the preferred candidate of the parliamentary party. Campbell was sceptical of the value of having so many MPs supporting him in a party with a history of an assertive grassroots.[74]

The Liberal Democrats' members had a reputation for being left-wing in their ideological leanings. A large-scale survey of the party's membership found that it was skewed to the left on questions of equality and redistribution, as well as being strongly pro-European. However, the same survey found that members were fairly centrist on the use of the market to produce goods and services. On a nine-point left-right scale of British politics, where 1 was the most left-wing position, 9 the most right-wing and 5 in the centre, the mean self-placement score was 4.1.[75] A YouGov survey carried out the following year would find that 73 percent of members preferred the party to adopt (mainly moderate) leftist positions, 19 percent wanted it in the centre and only

Figure 5.1 Liberal Democrat Members' Preferences on Party's Ideological Position

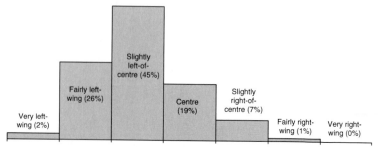

Source: YouGov, 'Lib Dem leadership contest', poll for *Sky News*, 3 December 2007, available at <http://www.yougov.co.uk>.
Notes: Q. 'Where on the political spectrum would you like the Liberal Democrat party to be?' Percentages recalculated to exclude respondents replying 'don't know'. N = 678

8 percent preferred rightist positions (Figure 5.1). It is unlikely that this distribution of opinion was much different at the time of the leadership election in 2006.

Liberal Democrat members were principally left-leaning social liberals. However, none of the leadership contenders stood outside of the mainstream of party opinion. As the nominally right-leaning candidate, Huhne supported repealing the totemic policy on raising the top rate of income tax but he was the candidate most strongly associated with green policies, which found favour with many members. Huhne and Hughes argued that British troops in Iraq should return home by the end of 2006, while Campbell rejected an 'arbitrary deadline'.[76] A majority of party members (54 percent) agreed with the Huhne-Hughes line, while 39 percent agreed with Campbell's position.[77] In short, while Campbell was the most centrist candidate, neither Hughes nor Huhne were out of step with party members, though Hughes was less attractive to modernising MPs.

The candidates embarked on a series of 11 regional hustings, as well as a number of television appearances. The latter included a joint appearance on a special edition of BBC television's *Question Time*, separate appearances on the same programme as panellists, a live televised debate with questions from viewers on *BBC News 24*, and interviews with all three candidates on BBC television's *The Daily Politics*. These hustings and media appearances offered Huhne the chance to establish a profile in front of a party membership that knew little about him.

The candidates had to raise funds to compete effectively during the campaign. The Electoral Commission listed all large donations to the candidates (see Appendix L), although small donations did not need to be declared. Campbell was ahead, attracting £44,000 in large donations. Huhne raised almost £31,000 while Hughes was some way behind, raising £26,000. In total, over £100,000 in large donations for all candidates were reported to the Electoral Commission.

Initially, media commentary assumed that the contest would be a two-horse race between Campbell and Hughes, with Huhne little more than an also-ran. However, that changed with the disclosures about Hughes's private life, revelations that proved damaging because they raised questions about the candidate's honesty and trustworthiness. The episode helped Huhne to become the main challenger to Campbell and reduced Hughes's chances of victory. However, few were prepared for a startling poll of Liberal Democrat members mid-way through the contest. The YouGov poll found that Huhne narrowly led Campbell by 32 percent to 29 percent on first preferences, with Hughes in third place on 23 percent. However, Hughes's supporters narrowly split for Campbell over Huhne on second preferences.[78]

In the event, Campbell managed to shore up his support. After a two-month campaign, he emerged victorious with a comfortable, if not overwhelming, majority (Table 5.1). He led the first count by 12 percent and when Hughes was eliminated and his votes redistributed, Campbell defeated Huhne by almost 16 percent.

Table 5.1 Liberal Democrat Leadership Election 2006

	First Count %	Second Count %
Menzies Campbell	44.7	57.9
Chris Huhne	32.1	42.1
Simon Hughes	23.2	–
Total	100.0	100.0

Notes: Alternative-vote electoral system. Full details of result in Appendix C.

Selection criteria

The favourite eventually won the prize and polling during the contest indicated the reasons why. YouGov's campaign poll of party members contained a series of statements that touched on selection criteria and leader qualities, with respondents being asked to say which candidate they applied to most (Table 5.2).

On the first-order criterion of 'acceptability', Campbell was regarded by almost half of party members as the candidate most likely to unite the Liberal Democrats, with Huhne on 26 percent and Hughes on 15 percent. The division between the economic and social liberals, although not as serious as sometimes depicted, was genuine. The fact that the membership was socially liberal ensured that this factional division had the potential to turn into a dangerous split between MPs and members. It is interesting to note, therefore, that the left-leaning Hughes was seen as unable to unite the party. During the campaign, economic liberals had briefed the press that there could be funding cuts and defections to the Conservatives among some Liberal Democrat MPs if Hughes became leader.[79] The membership was aware of the dangers and eschewed a candidate long regarded as the voice of the activists. Campbell was seen as a steadying influence at a time of upheaval in the party. In this respect, he was acceptable to both the MPs and the members, and to economic and social liberals.

On the second-order criterion of electability, Campbell and Huhne were seen as equally likely to improve the Liberal Democrats' chances

Table 5.2 Liberal Democrat Members' Assessments of Candidates on Key Selection Criteria 2006

	Campbell	Hughes	Huhne
Selection criteria: candidate best placed to...			
Lead a united Liberal Democratic Party [acceptability]	48	15	26
Boost the Liberal Democrats' chances of gaining seats at next election [electability]	30	22	30
Come over well on television & radio, and in the press [electability]	33	25	31
Challenge Blair & Cameron most effectively in the House of Commons [competence]	36	26	27
Leadership qualities			
He has the right kind of experience to lead Lib Dems	58	21	16
He knows about real life outside politics	19	23	52
He is honest	46	14	28
He is committed to the right kind of policies	27	31	34
He would make an effective government minister	50	19	25

Source: YouGov, 'Survey of Liberal Democratic party members', poll for John Stevens, 7–9 February 2006, available at <http://www.yougov.co.uk>.
Notes: Q1 (selection criteria): 'Which of the three do you think would...?' Q2 (leadership qualities): 'Here are some statements about the candidates. For each statement, and putting aside your own voting preference, please indicate which candidate you think it applies to most.' All figures are percentages. N = 401

of gaining seats at the next election. Campbell had a slight lead as the candidate most likely to perform well in the media, a key consideration for parties seeking to broaden their electoral appeal. However, on both these items, only eight percentage points separated the best and worst candidates, and no-one polled higher than 33 percent. That indicated uncertainty among party members as to which candidate would improve the party's electoral prospects at a time when the Conservatives were advancing under Cameron. On the basis of these figures, it is unlikely that Campbell won because of his perceived electoral appeal in comparison with the other candidates.[80]

On the third-order criterion of competence, Liberal Democrat leaders are not usually seen as likely to become prime minister, but there remained the prospect of joining a coalition government. Campbell was seen as the candidate most likely to make an effective government minister. Competence is also crucial in opposition because the leader is expected to challenge the prime minister and the leader of the main opposition party in the House of Commons. Campbell enjoyed a 9–10 point advantage over the other candidates on this criterion, although again, he polled only 36 percent. Campbell was also regarded as the most experienced of the candidates (58 percent) and the most honest (46 percent).

Campbell won the leadership because the Liberal Democrats were in turmoil after Kennedy's departure. The factional disagreements between economic and social liberals had the potential to become something worse and a safe pair of hands was needed at this critical juncture. The requirement for unity was thus real and that helped Campbell. Electoral considerations were a medium-term issue; if the contest had been decided on that basis, Campbell could have struggled to defeat Huhne. On competence, Campbell was again the strongest candidate and that criterion would have been an important one given the chaotic circumstances of Kennedy's downfall. At a time when the Liberal Democrats were desperate to re-establish their credibility, Campbell was the logical choice to steady the ship.[81]

The Liberal Democrat leadership election of 2007

Campbell's tenure as Liberal Democrat leader was unsuccessful and brief.[82] It became apparent from the outset that media and public perceptions of him were unfavourable. He suffered from comparisons with the Conservatives' youthful leader, Cameron: Campbell was 64 years old when he became leader, although he often seemed older because of previous health problems. Eventually, it became one of the dominant narratives in media reporting on his performance and the party struggled to counter it.[83] Campbell's parliamentary performances also attracted criticism, as he appeared nervous and uncertain.[84] During Campbell's 18-month tenure, the Liberal Democrats' poll rating declined from about 20–22 percent to 15 percent, a sharp drop for a third party. His own net satisfaction rating started off positive but fell into negative territory, settling at about – 10 (Figure 5.2).

After poor local-election results in April 2007, Campbell came under intense pressure from within his party, with negative briefings to the media and what one party insider described as a 'systematic attempt to destabilise him'.[85] The Liberal Democrats were being squeezed by the Conservatives and, from June 2007, by a resurgent Labour under Gordon Brown. Pressure built up on Campbell over the summer. At a

Figure 5.2 Liberal Democrats' Poll Rating and Campbell's Net Satisfaction Rating 2006–07

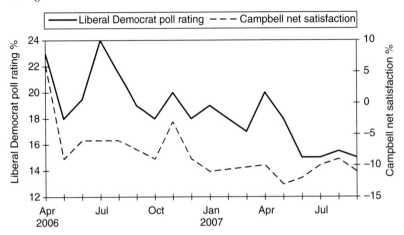

Sources: Ipsos-MORI, 'Voting intention in Great Britain: Recent trends' and 'Political monitor: Satisfaction ratings 1997–present', available at <http://www.ipsos-mori.com>.
Notes: Q1. 'How would you vote if there were a general election tomorrow?' [Liberal Democrat %] Q2. 'Are you satisfied or dissatisfied with the way Sir Menzies Campbell is doing his job as Leader of the Liberal Democrats?' [Campbell net satisfaction = % satisfied minus % dissatisfied]

dinner with Liberal Democrat peers in July, he was urged to consider his position by senior figures, including Shirley Williams and Robert Maclennan.[86] Allies of Huhne were long suspected of briefing anonymously against the leader.[87]

Brown's first few months as prime minister were relatively successful and it appeared that an early election would take place in the autumn of 2007. As long as that was the assumption, Campbell's position looked secure because it would be unfeasible to change leaders so close to a general election. However, after a surge in support for the Conservatives, Brown changed his mind. The Liberal Democrats had feared an election because of their poor poll ratings, but its 'cancellation' created space for the party to deal with the leadership issue. Hughes told journalists that Campbell had to 'raise his game'.[88] It appeared to be the prelude to a putsch, with MPs and peers briefing the press that Campbell should go quietly or face a rebellion.[89] On 15 October, Campbell learnt that two previous leaders, Steel and Ashdown, planned to visit him later in the week to ask him to think about whether he wanted to continue. Cable had told the BBC that the leader's position was 'under consideration'. Dick Taverne, a Liberal Democrat peer, also claimed that 'the overwhelming number of peers want a change [in leadership]'.[90] Later that day, Campbell announced he was stepping down with immediate effect.[91] Cable, his deputy, took over as interim leader until an election could be held.

Campbell's decision was his own but it is clear that his position was seriously in peril. Despite being the clear choice of Liberal Democrat MPs in the 2006 leadership election, he was always regarded as a caretaker leader and consequently did not have a solid base of committed supporters. Even those who endorsed him in 2006 were always looking beyond his leadership.[92] Ultimately, he jumped before he was pushed. One difference with Kennedy's removal was that the most senior members of the shadow cabinet, in the form of Hughes and Cable, appeared more willing to discuss the issue of the leadership in public. This task was made easier by their apparent lack of immediate leadership ambitions, whereas Hughes did have such ambitions at the time of Kennedy's resignation. These are the circumstances in which visits by the 'men in grey suits' are most likely to occur, and two former leaders were apparently prepared to do just that.

The leadership contest

The Liberal Democrat leadership contest that followed Campbell's resignation was, for the most part, a sedate affair. The two-month contest that took place between October and December 2007 aroused little media interest except when it showed signs of becoming antagonistic. The contest began with a stream of senior figures ruling themselves out, including Kennedy, who had been suspected of wanting to make a return, Hughes, Laws, Davey and the party's former London mayoral candidate, Susan Kramer. The 64-year-old Cable also declined to stand, citing the 'irrational prejudice' shown towards Campbell because of his age.[93] Ultimately, two candidates, Chris Huhne and Nick Clegg, secured the required seven nominations from MPs.

Although they differed in age – Huhne was 52 and Clegg 39 – the two candidates shared much in common. Both had been MPs for only two years and both had previously been MEPs. Given their relatively recent introduction to national politics, neither had been particularly well known until the 2006 leadership contest, although Huhne's participation in that contest and speculation about Clegg's possible involvement helped to boost their public profiles. Both were associated with the modernising wing of the Liberal Democrats and broadly agreed on policy. Nevertheless, Huhne was quickly established as the more left-leaning of the two candidates, with Clegg regarded as slightly more right-leaning.[94]

Huhne's perceived position was somewhat ironic given that he had been seen as the right-leaning candidate in the 2006 leadership election. His interest in green politics facilitated this shift in perceptions, as did his focus on fairness and social justice. Indeed, there were subtle differences between the two candidates. Clegg emphasised social mobility, while Huhne preferred to focus on equality. Clegg was more amenable than Huhne to market reforms of public services. Huhne also supported more green taxes. A further division that opened up during the campaign was Huhne's belief that Britain's Trident nuclear submarines should not have their lives extended, and the party should adopt either a non-nuclear defence policy or argue for a greatly scaled-down deterrent. In contrast, Clegg wanted to maintain Trident.[95]

The divergence in stances reflected the debate within the Liberal Democrats about the party's future strategy. Huhne appealed to the activists who were happy with their party's position on the centre-left. Clegg's supporters on the right of the party were sceptical that this strategy could achieve much more; it had, after all, largely failed to provide the Liberal Democrats with a breakthrough at the 2005 general election. They believed that the Liberal Democrats had to distance themselves from producer interests in the public sector, while defending the advances they had made among more libertarian voters.[96] Indeed, Huhne's supporters criticised Clegg for being a 'Cameron clone' and 'David Cameron's stunt double'.[97]

Clegg quickly became the frontrunner and secured 39 endorsements from Liberal Democrat MPs. Huhne was endorsed by 11 MPs.[98] Surprisingly, some prominent figures associated with the left of the party, including Hughes and Steve Webb, endorsed Clegg. One of the reasons for Huhne's relative lack of support among MPs was reportedly the perception that he and his allies had plotted against Campbell.[99]

Although Huhne garnered limited support among his parliamentary colleagues, he was estimated to have a stronger following among party members. The candidates had numerous opportunities to communicate with these selectors during the contest. Ten official hustings were organised in towns and cities around the country. The candidates also appeared together on BBC *Newsnight* and BBC *Question Time*. Their most contentious joint appearance was on the BBC's *The Politics Show*, when Huhne accused Clegg of 'flip-flopping' over policy. However, Huhne was forced to apologise over a briefing document drawn up by his supporters, entitled 'Calamity Clegg', in which Clegg's alleged policy shifts were detailed.[100] Late in the campaign, a YouGov poll for *Sky News* found Clegg leading Huhne by 56 percent to 44 percent among party members.[101]

Clegg's position as the frontrunner enabled him to attract more financial donations for his campaign. Clegg declared £83,500 in large donations to the Electoral Commission, with Huhne trailing on £57,000 (Appendix L). These figures did not include small donations (under £1,000). Large donations to the two candidates exceeded those to all candidates in the party's 2006 leadership contest by £40,000.

When the result of the contest was announced in December, it was much closer than anyone had anticipated. Clegg finished just 511 ahead of Huhne, out of a total of 41,465 ballots cast, a winning margin of 1.2 percent (Table 5.3). It was later reported that had 1,300 late-arriving ballots caught up in the Christmas post been counted then Huhne would have won.[102] The closeness of the outcome was partly down to Huhne's aggressive campaign and activist-friendly policies, as well as the perceived lacklustre campaign that Clegg ran.[103]

Table 5.3   Liberal Democrat Leadership Election 2007

	%
Nick Clegg	50.6
Chris Huhne	49.4
Total	100.0

Notes: Alternative-vote electoral system. Full details of result in Appendix C.

Selection criteria

Clegg's victory was largely a result of the perception that he would boost the Liberal Democrats' flagging electoral fortunes. The party had slumped alarmingly in the opinion polls under Campbell and there were fears that it would suffer major losses to the Conservatives at the following general election. Dealing with the Tory threat was thus a key issue in the leadership contest. Table 5.4 shows party members' views of the candidates' main qualities. There is no data on which candidate was most acceptable to the party and able to unify it, but it was not especially divided at any rate. Unlike the eviction of Kennedy, the resignation of Campbell created no great trauma in the party. Although the two candidates did have some differences over policy, both were modernisers.

The major factor behind Campbell's resignation was not party disunity but the need to improve its electability. Huhne edged out Clegg on competence, although a big majority of members believed there was not much difference between them. Clegg was marginally seen as

Table 5.4 Liberal Democrat Members' Perceptions of Candidates' Leadership Qualities 2007

Candidate who...	Clegg	Huhne	Not much difference
Has more voter-appeal [electability]	53	9	33
Has a better policy programme	19	28	48
Is more competent [competence]	16	21	60
Would more effectively oppose Gordon Brown [competence]	33	31	30
Would more effectively oppose David Cameron [competence/electability]	40	26	28

Source: YouGov, 'Liberal Democrat leadership contest', poll for *Sky News*, 3 December 2007, available at <http://www.yougov.co.uk>.
Notes: Q. 'Do you think one of the candidates... than the other – or is there not much difference?' All figures are percentages. N = 678

better able to oppose the Labour prime minister, but he had a much wider lead on being able to oppose the Conservative leader. Huhne's policies were viewed as better, although again, almost half of party members could not discern much difference. However, the most striking finding was in relation to the candidate judged most voter-friendly, and here Clegg led 53-9. In combination with his lead on opposing Cameron, it is clear that Clegg won the leadership on the criterion of electability. The taunts about Clegg being a 'Cameron clone' were, in their own way, recognition that the candidate's greatest appeal was his perceived ability to defend Liberal Democrat seats from the Conservatives. Nevertheless, it is noteworthy that party members came extremely close to electing Huhne, despite Clegg's advantage on electability. Doing so would have put them at loggerheads with Liberal Democrat MPs, who had clearly identified Clegg as their preferred leader.

Conclusion: MPs, party members and power in the Liberal Democrats

The Liberal Democrats have long prided themselves as a grassroots party committed to participatory democracy. It is not surprising that such an ethos should take hold given that the party and its predecessors had been out of government for the entire post-war period until 2010. However, the considerable growth in the Liberal Democrats' parliamentary representation between 1997 and 2005 increased the party's credibility with voters. The prospect of participation in a coalition government suddenly seemed realistic and was proven to be so in 2010. This enhanced credibility and public profile was responsible for a shift in power relations inside the Liberal Democrats. Despite the system of intra-party democracy set out in the party constitution, policy-making was becoming increasingly dominated by the parliamentary party.[104] Radical policies from the party conference could be tolerated as long as the Liberal Democrats' electoral hopes were modest, but that changed as they emerged as a serious political force after 1997.

The power shift was not restricted to policy-making. The downfall of Kennedy in 2006 was a seminal event in the history of the Liberal Democrats. The parliamentary party felt compelled to move against its leader because of his perceived managerial shortcomings. The Liberal Democrats' leadership-selection system formally puts great power in the hands of individual party members, but the lesson of Kennedy's eviction is that constitutional rules are but *one* source of power inside parties. Without support from his senior colleagues, Kennedy's authority was fatally damaged, although his ousting was drawn-out and messy because it was left to more junior figures to organise. Liberal Democrat members select the leader, but the length of tenure of leaders is determined by Liberal Democrat MPs, and that has become particularly evident as the party's electoral and parliamentary ambitions have grown bolder. Without any great constitutional changes, Liberal Democrat MPs have found their hand strengthened in relation to the extra-parliamentary party.[105]

Party members nevertheless remain important in leadership contests. MPs can overthrow an incumbent leader and flock behind a desired replacement, but it is still the task of the members to make the final choice. To date, the members have always chosen the preferred candidate of the parliamentary party, but in 2007 they did so by just 1.2 percent. In the 2006 and 2007 contests, Huhne greatly exceeded initial expectations, based on his limited endorsements from MPs. In 2007, he was seen as the more left-leaning of the two candidates and he clearly benefited from the votes of the activist left. Even in 2006, when he was initially pigeon-holed as a 'centre-right' candidate, he attracted the votes of those members interested in his environmental agenda. He was also preferred by those who saw Campbell as the candidate of the parliamentary elite. It is therefore important not to overstate the decline in the membership's power: if just 256 people who voted for Clegg had switched to Huhne, or if late ballots had been counted (allegedly), Huhne would have become leader in 2007.

The question of selection criteria is crucial. 'Acceptability', in terms of the ability to unite the party, is the most important criterion in divided parties. If the law of curvilinear disparity is correct, the potential exists for an ideological split between members and MPs: members would be expected to regard radical candidates as more acceptable than moderate ones, whereas MPs would think the opposite. The contests of 2006 and 2007 showed that there was a degree of this disjuncture, but only a degree. The left-leaning Hughes underperformed in 2006 on this basis, indicating that ideology was not sufficient for the members to choose him. Indeed, they believed he would not be able to unite the party. He also trailed Campbell and Huhne on electability and competence. In 2007, Huhne was a much more credible left-leaning candidate, but even then, the members ultimately chose Clegg, largely for electoral reasons. Liberal Democrat members have never been unthinking ideologues and seem to have always taken account of the specific circumstances of the time when selecting leaders. Taking into consideration some of these circumstances, such as the merged party's early struggle for survival in 1988, its relationship with the Labour government in 1999, the fight for credibility in 2006 and the necessity to boost electability in 2007, one *Orange Book* contributor opined that Liberal Democrat members have chosen the right candidate in every leadership election since the party's formation.[106] As the Liberal Democrats entered a new phase of their history when they joined the coalition government in 2010, it remained to be seen whether the membership would continue to be in tune with the parliamentary party.

6
Electing and Ejecting Party Leaders: An Assessment

Having examined the operation of selection and eviction mechanisms in the three major British parties, it is possible to draw some conclusions. This final chapter begins by assessing the impact of one member-one vote (OMOV) on the selection of leaders. It looks at the criteria that party members use when choosing leaders and shows that Stark was right to say that institutions are not *usually* crucial in this respect. However, there are a small number of cases where institutions were demonstrably important, most recently in the Labour Party in 2010. The next section asks whether institutions had any effect on the competitiveness of leadership elections. Again, the answer is largely negative, although Labour's block-vote-based electoral college exaggerated victory margins. The following section looks at recent trends in the age and experience of party leaders on assuming the job. There appears to be a shift towards younger leaders, although it is hard to say whether this trend is due to OMOV. The last main section turns to leader eviction. It argues that the evidence of attempted evictions in Britain calls into question the common assumption that leaders fall because of the withdrawal of support from party elites. It concludes that institutions can be important in evictions because they help to determine whether broader opposition to leaders in their parliamentary parties can be mobilised.

Selection criteria, 1963–2010

One of Leonard Stark's strongest claims was that institutions usually played little or no role in determining which candidate won individual leadership contests. The basis of this claim is that party notables, MPs, activists and individual members alike choose leaders using the same criteria. When parties are divided, they select the candidate deemed most acceptable to a broad range of opinion and therefore most likely to unite the party. If the party is not divided, parties discriminate between candidates on the basis of their electability, and if they are equally electable, selectors choose on the basis of perceived competence in government. According to Stark, there was only one leadership contest between 1963 and 1995 in which a candidate who was inferior to another candidate on each of these criteria ended up winning, namely, Thatcher in 1975. Likewise, Stark claimed that Thatcher was the only unambiguous case of a leader who would not have been chosen under the selection system previously used by her party.[1]

Most of the more recent leadership contests examined in this book support Stark's argument. Table 6.1 lists the winning candidates, as well as the candidates deemed the best on each of the three major selection criteria, in leadership elections between 1963 and 2010. The entries for contests between 1963 and 1995 are taken from Stark.[2] Judgements on contests from 1997 onwards are based on the analysis in the present book.

Most Labour leadership elections have been characterised by few surprises. Wilson (1963), Callaghan (1976), Kinnock (1983 and 1988), Smith (1992) and Blair (1994) were all expected to win and did. Foot's victory in 1980 was more of a surprise. He was more likely than Healey to unite a party whose centre of gravity was shifting to the left, although Healey enjoyed greater electoral popularity and had spent more time in government. Stark argues that the Parliamentary Labour Party's (PLP) selection of Foot indicates that institutions did not matter and that parliamentary ballots were not necessarily biased in favour of the Labour right.[3] He rejects the view of Punnett that Foot would not have defeated Healey in a 'normal' PLP ballot, but that the MPs chose Foot because they wanted to pick a leader in tune with the preferences of the people who would soon be selecting leaders through the emergent electoral college.[4]

There is a strong argument, nevertheless, that institutions did matter in this contest. A better explanation of why Labour MPs chose Foot is that they thought it less likely that Tony Benn would use the electoral college to challenge Foot than he would Healey, and it was Benn that the PLP most wanted to avoid. This interpretation is supported by the subsequent course of events, when Benn did indeed use the new electoral college to challenge, not Foot for the leadership, but Healey for the deputy leadership in 1981. The point is that this period was a time when the PLP was more centrist than the activists and some of the major trade unions.[5] In these circumstances, there is the potential for

Table 6.1 Selection Criteria in Contested Leadership Elections 1963–2010

Contest	System	Acceptable	Electable	Competent	Winner
Labour					
1963	PPB	Wilson	Wilson	Wilson	Wilson
1976	PPB	Callaghan	Callaghan	Callaghan	Callaghan
1980	PPB	Foot	Healey	Healey	Foot
1983	EC (BV)	Kinnock	Kinnock/Hattersley	Hattersley	Kinnock
1988	EC (BV)	Kinnock	Kinnock	Kinnock	Kinnock
1992	EC (BV)	Smith	Smith	Smith	Smith
1994	EC (OMOV)	Blair	Blair	Blair	Blair
2010	EC (OMOV)	D./E. Miliband	D. Miliband	D. Miliband	E. Miliband
Conservative					
1965	PPB	Heath/Maudling	Heath	Heath/Maudling	Heath
1975	PPB	Whitelaw	Whitelaw	Whitelaw	Thatcher
1989	PPB	Thatcher	Thatcher	Thatcher	Thatcher
1990	PPB	Major	Major/Heseltine	Major/Hurd	Major
1995	PPB	Major	Major	Major	Major
1997	PPB	Hague	Clarke	Clarke	Hague
2001	PPB/OMOV	Duncan Smith/ Ancram	Clarke	Clarke/Portillo	Duncan Smith
2005	PPB/OMOV	Cameron	Cameron	Clarke	Cameron
Liberal Democrat					
1988	OMOV	Ashdown/Beith	Ashdown	Beith	Ashdown
1999	OMOV	Kennedy	Kennedy	Kennedy/Bruce/Hughes	Kennedy
2006	OMOV	Campbell	Campbell/Huhne	Campbell	Campbell
2007	OMOV	Clegg/Huhne	Clegg	Clegg/Huhne	Clegg

Notes: PPB = Parliamentary-party ballots; OMOV = one member-one vote; EC (BV) = electoral college using block voting; EC (OMOV) = electoral college using individual voting.

ideologically-polarised MPs and activists to interpret 'acceptability' in different ways.

Similarly, Blair might not have been elected in 1994 without the reform of the electoral college the previous year. The 1994 contest was the first not to use block voting. The experience of the block-vote-based electoral college had been that trade-union leaders were usually influential in determining the trajectory of contests by offering early endorsements to particular candidates. In this way, Kinnock (1983 and 1988) and Smith (1992) quickly became unstoppable. In both cases, union leaders hoped that the chosen candidate would be sympathetic to union demands on policy, even if that did not always turn out to be the case. Many union leaders harboured deep mistrust of Blair from his time as shadow employment spokesman in 1989, when he announced Labour's abandonment of the 'closed shop', whereby employees were forced to join a union in some industries.[6] Blair famously ran as the only modernising candidate in 1994 after Brown agreed to stand aside. Given that Brown was regarded by the unions as closer to them than Blair was, it is arguable that, had the block-vote-based electoral college still been in use in 1994, union leaders would have reverted to type and endorsed Brown. In the process, the assumption would have been that those unions that nominated him would have been able to deliver their block votes at the voting stage.[7] If so, the reform of the electoral college was crucial to Blair's victory.

Institutions were undoubtedly decisive in 2010 when David Miliband, the choice of Labour MPs and party members, was defeated by his brother, Ed. The latter's victory rested on solid support from trade-union members, albeit on an extremely low turnout. Both brothers were deemed acceptable by large parts of the parliamentary and extra-parliamentary parties. However, David Miliband was not acceptable to the left-leaning union leaders, who communicated their support for Ed Miliband to their ordinary members.

In the Conservative Party, the final leadership contest conducted under the parliamentary-ballot system saw Hague win largely on the basis of his acceptability to the party. Clarke was superior on electability and competence but his pro-European views rendered him too divisive for his party. In 2001, the first contest under the new rules again produced a leader in Duncan Smith who was inferior to his major rival on electability and competence, but who was superior on acceptability. During this period, Europe was a defining issue inside the Conservative Party. Only Eurosceptic leaders were acceptable as leaders, not only to MPs but to party members too. Cameron's victory in 2005 confirmed this point, as he ran as a moderate Eurosceptic. Once the pro-European Clarke was eliminated, the contest was decided on the basis of Cameron's greater perceived electability. In prioritising unity, the party was true to form. Vernon Bogdanor observed that the experience of Robert Peel, who split the Tories twice, over Catholic emancipation in 1829 and the Corn Laws in 1846, had left a deep desire for unity in the party. 'Because of the importance of unity in the Conservative Party, candidates who are seen as divisive rarely achieve the leadership'.[8] It was on this basis that Clarke, the most electorally popular Conservative politician between 1997 and 2005, was never trusted with the leadership, either by the MPs or the membership.

The obvious conclusion to draw is that the Conservatives' shift from parliamentary ballots to a parliamentary-OMOV hybrid had less of an impact than is frequently assumed. In 2005, Cameron was the choice of both MPs and party members. Four years earlier, Duncan Smith was the definitive choice of the members, but achieved only a third of the votes of MPs. As was shown in Chapter 4, there were accusations that he had been imposed by the membership on the parliamentary party. However, that argument is unconvincing. It is irrelevant that Duncan Smith won only 54 of 166 MPs' votes in the final parliamentary ballot. The essence of the parliamentary ballots is that MPs do *not* select the leader, but merely produce a short-list for the members to do so. Only if Clarke and Duncan Smith had faced each other in a run-off parliamentary ballot would it have been possible to say who the choice of the MPs was. Given the strength of Eurosceptic opinion on the Tory backbenches and the continued divisiveness of Clarke, it is more than possible that Duncan Smith would have won a parliamentary ballot. He was, after all, endorsed by Thatcher and supported by the former leader, Hague. In 2005, the parliamentary ballots became right and centre/left 'primaries', in which the left candidate was the first to be eliminated. The effect was to exaggerate Cameron's lead among MPs, as the right-wing vote was split between Fox and Davis. Had Fox been eliminated before Clarke, then Cameron would probably not have won so many votes in the final ballot and it is possible that Davis might have finished top.

It should be noted, nevertheless, that Conservative leadership contests have regularly led to victories for candidates who were not regarded as the early favourites. Thatcher in 1975 was an example, but so was Major in 1990, Hague in 1997, Duncan Smith in 2001 and Cameron in 2005. It is likely that the desire for unity explains this phenomenon. The favourites in leadership contests tend to be the best-known candidates but also the ones who have accumulated enemies, such as Portillo (2001), Clarke (1997, 2001 and 2005), Redwood (1997) and Davis (2005). Lesser-known figures can emerge as compromise candidates, as Hague did in 1997. A low profile can signify freshness and a break with the past – important attributes in parties that have suffered electoral defeats and many of whose leading personnel are disliked or discredited. Under the post-1998 system, the favourite lost on both occasions: Portillo in 2001 and Davis in 2005. Both were seen as divisive, not least for their personal conduct towards previous leaders. Duncan Smith was also seen by some as divisive, but probably less so and by fewer people than either Clarke or Portillo.

The Liberal Democrats' OMOV system has produced leaders who were not divisive and who were deemed capable of improving the party's electoral performance. Both Ashdown and Beith could have united the post-merger party after 1988, but as Stark observes, Ashdown was thought more likely to draw attention to the party.[9] Kennedy was the choice of both the MPs and the party members in 1999. He was the strongest candidate on acceptability and electability, and was at least as strong as Malcolm Bruce and Simon Hughes on competence. His public persona was thought an advantage and likely to appeal to voters. He was acceptable to a broader range of the party than his nearest rival, Hughes, who was on the left of the Liberal Democrats. He was also more sceptical of links with Labour than Ashdown had been, though not as hostile as the other candidates.

In 2006, the Liberal Democrats required a unity candidate after Kennedy's eviction and they found one in Campbell. Huhne would have been a bolder choice, but the party needed a period of stability in order to re-establish its credibility with voters. In this respect, Campbell's perceived competence was also an important consideration. The context of Campbell's own resignation in 2007 was very different and unity was no longer the pressing concern it had been 18 months earlier when Campbell took over. Clegg defeated Huhne on the basis of his perceived electability, particularly in relation to the threat posed by the resurgent Conservatives. However, the 2007 contest was very close, the closest, in fact, in any of the three major UK parties in the post-war period, with Clegg winning by just 1.2 percent. Had Huhne won – and it was noted in Chapter 5 that late ballots allegedly favoured him sufficiently to have changed the result had they been counted – then it would have been a clear example of party members contradicting the preferences of MPs, who were overwhelmingly for Clegg.

In summary, this study provides some support for Stark's argument that selection systems are not usually decisive in determining the winner of leadership elections. The Conservative contests of 1997, 2001 and 2005, and the Liberal Democrat contests of 2006 and 2007 could all be explained on the basis of Stark's hierarchy of selection criteria. The 2010 Labour leadership contest is an exception to the rule that selection rules do not matter. Nevertheless, the three criteria of acceptability, electability and competence went a long way towards explaining the outcomes of all of the contests examined in this book. The proviso is that, when ideological differences exist between MPs, party members and in Labour's case, trade unionists, there is always the potential for the different selectorates to interpret the notion of ideological 'acceptability' in different ways. In those instances, institutions can have more of an impact on the outcome.

The competitiveness of leadership elections

Leadership elections in Britain have not, on the whole, been close-run affairs. Table 6.2 shows that, in 25 contested leadership elections in the Conservative, Labour, Liberal, Social Democratic and Liberal Democrat parties since 1960, only four were won by a candidate by a margin of victory below 10 percent: Heath in 1965, Foot in 1980, Clegg in 2007 and Miliband in 2010. Fully 14 were won with majorities over 20 percent, ten of which were over 30 percent and four of which were over 50 percent. Of these latter four, three were in Labour's electoral college in its block-vote format (1983, 1988 and 1992), emphasising how that system exaggerated the victory margin of the winners. Overwhelming victories indicate a consensus within parties over the candidate who can best achieve the party's key goals. Where such a consensus exists, it normally stretches across the parliamentary/extra-parliamentary divide. It is this consensus that explains why most leadership-election outcomes appear to be unrelated to the type of selection system used.

A further measure of the competitiveness of leadership elections is provided by the effective number of candidates (ENC) in contests. Measuring ENC entails counting the absolute number of candidates and weighting them according to the proportion of votes that they win. For example, five candidates may enter a contest but if only two of them have a realistic chance of winning, it is closer to a two-horse race than a five-horse race. The measurement of ENC is based on a similar measure for the effective number of parties (ENP).[10] It is the

Table 6.2 Effective Number of Candidates in Leadership Elections 1960–2010

Contest	System	Candidates	Laakso-Taagepera		Golosov		% win
			ENC(1)	ENC(F)	ENC(1)	ENC(F)	
Labour							
1960	PPB	2	1.8	–	1.5	–	34.4
1961	PPB	2	1.6	–	1.3	–	48.7
1963	PPB	3	2.6	1.9	2.3	1.7	16.6
1976	PPB	6	4.7	2.0	4.3	1.8	12.5
1980	PPB	4	3.2	2.0	2.7	1.9	3.7
1983	EC (BV)	4	1.8	–	1.5	–	52.0
1988	EC (BV)	2	1.3	–	1.1	–	77.2
1992	EC (BV)	2	1.2	–	1.1	–	82.0
1994	EC (OMOV)	3	2.4	–	1.9	–	32.9
2007	EC (OMOV)	1	n/a	–	n/a	–	n/a
2010	EC (OMOV)	5	3.5	2.0	3.2	2.0	1.3
Conservative							
1965	PPB	3	2.2	–	2.1	–	5.7
1975	PPB	7*	2.2	2.6	2.1	2.1	24.5
1989	PPB	2	1.2	–	1.1	–	81.0
1990	PPB	4*	2.0	2.5	1.7	2.1	14.5
1995	PPB	2	1.7	–	1.4	–	42.0
1997	PPB	5	4.5	2.0	4.0	1.8	13.6
2001	PPB/OMOV	5	4.5	1.9	4.0	1.6	21.4
2003	PPB/OMOV	1	n/a	–	n/a	–	n/a
2005	PPB/OMOV	4	3.8	1.8	3.5	1.5	35.2

Table 6.2 Effective Number of Candidates in Leadership Elections 1960–2010 – *continued*

Contest	System	Candidates	Laakso-Taagepera		Golosov		% win
			ENC(1)	ENC(F)	ENC(1)	ENC(F)	
Liberal							
1967	PPB	3	2.7	–	2.1	–	25.0
1976	OMOV	2	1.9	–	1.6	–	28.2
SDP							
1982	OMOV	2	2.0	–	1.8	–	11.4
1983	OMOV	1	n/a	–	n/a	–	n/a
1987	OMOV	1	n/a	–	n/a	–	n/a
Liberal Democrat							
1988	OMOV	2	1.7	–	1.4	–	43.7
1999	OMOV	5	3.1	2.0	2.6	1.8	13.1
2006	OMOV	3	2.8	2.0	2.4	1.7	15.8
2007	OMOV	2	2.0	–	2.0	–	1.2

Notes: ENC(1) = effective number of candidates in first round of voting. ENC(F) = effective number of candidates in final round of voting.
% win = winning candidate's margin of victory over second-placed candidate in final round of voting. Figures for Conservative parliamentary ballots exclude abstentions and spoilt ballots.
*Not all candidates participated in first ballot

inverse of the summation of the squared proportions of the vote won by the candidates:

$$ENC = 1/\Sigma V_i^2$$

where V_i is the proportion of the vote won by candidate i. An evenly-matched three-candidate contest will have an ENC of 3.0, an evenly-matched two-candidate contest 2.0, and a contest in which there are two strong candidates and one weaker one could have an ENC of 2.5.

ENC is not a perfect measure. Ofer Kenig argues that it works best in comparative analysis when each leadership contest contains the same absolute number of candidates.[11] However, the number of candidates in contested leadership elections in the major British parties since 1963 has ranged from two to seven. Kenig's solution is to divide ENC by the absolute number of candidates, N, to provide a standardised measure between 0 and 1. Yet if the aim is to measure competitiveness, this solution is also problematic. ENC/N indicates how evenly matched all the candidates are, but it is not an adequate measure of 'competitiveness' because a five-candidate race in which three candidates are no-hopers could still be competitive if the remaining two candidates were evenly matched (e.g. Labour in 2010). One solution would be to calculate ENC both for the first ballot and for the final ballot, which will often, although not always, be a run-off between two candidates.

There is, however, a broader problem with ENC, which is that it is based on the Laakso-Taagepera measure of ENP. Political scientists have increasingly noted some of the flaws with this measure.[12] One of the major problems is that it does not always perform well in contests in which one party or candidate wins an absolute majority of seats or votes. If one party or candidate is dominant, that would intuitively imply a shift in the direction of a one-party or one-candidate system and away from a two- or multi-party/candidate system. However, ENP and ENC regularly give measures of or close to 2.0 in these situations. That is especially problematical in relation to leadership elections because the winner normally claims a majority of votes.

A different measure of ENP has been offered by Grigorii Golosov.[13] Golosov's measure better reflects the dominance of parties that win overall majorities. It is, therefore, a more appropriate measure of ENC and more accurately reflects the degree of competitiveness in given leadership contests. Golosov's ENC index is given by:

$$ENC \text{ (Golosov)} = \Sigma\{\Sigma V_i/[\Sigma V_i + (V_1^2/V_i) - V_i]\}$$

where ΣV_i is simply the total number of votes cast, V_1 is the number of votes won by the candidate with the highest number of votes and V_i is the number of votes won by the ith candidate. Each candidate's score on the Golosov index is expressed in relation to that of the leading candidate. Performing the above calculation for the leading candidate gives a score of 1, with other candidates each having scores of between 0 and 1. These are then summed to produce the overall ENC.

Both the Golosov and Laakso-Taagepera measures of ENC are provided for UK party leadership contests in Table 6.2, although the following discussion refers only to the Golosov scores. Separate measures are given for the first ballot, ENC(1), and the final ballot, ENC(F). The first ballot usually shows a wider distribution of votes as there are more candidates (although not always in the Conservatives' parliamentary-ballots system), while the final ballot is usually, although not always, a run-off between the two most popular candidates. It can be seen that Golosov scores are normally lower than Laakso-Taagepera scores and in the final ballot, Golosov scores are usually lower than 2.0. In some instances, the Laakso-Taagepera scores are 2.0 for the final ballot even though the winner's margin of victory was over 10 percent.

With the partial exception of Labour's electoral college in its block-vote format, there does not appear to be any obvious relationship between selection systems and the competitiveness of leadership elections. Three of the four biggest victories in the post-war period were in the original format of the electoral college, although there was no institutional impediment to closer races. In Labour's 1981 deputy-leadership election, which saw the electoral college used for the first time, Healey defeated Benn by just 0.8 percent. However, block voting created an element of arbitrariness in the result: had the huge Transport and General Workers' Union supported Healey, as its branches wanted, instead of Benn, as its executive decided to do, then Healey would have won by 17 percent.[14] Block voting enabled frontrunners in Labour leadership elections to build early momentum and sew up contests quickly and decisively. However, big victories were also achieved in other selection systems and overall, the effect of institutions on size of victory is fairly weak.

At first glance, there appears to be an inverse relationship between the margin of victory and the absolute number of candidates entering a contest, regardless of the selection system. Of the 11 contested leadership elections with the largest margins of victory for the winner, no fewer than eight saw only two candidates formally stand. One of the remaining three, the Tory contest of 2005, had a two-candidate run-off in the OMOV ballot. These 11 elections mainly had ENCs of between 1.1 and 1.5, with only two above this range. In contrast, of the remaining 14 contested leadership elections, where the margin of victory was 25.0 percent or less, just two involved two candidates, although one of these was also the closest contest. ENC was higher in the final ballots of these contests and where there was an earlier ballot, ENC was often significantly higher, reaching 4.3 in the Labour leadership contest of 1976 and 4.0 in the Conservative contests of 1997 and 2001.

It is possible that, in two-candidate contests, the frontrunner becomes quickly established and it becomes apparent that the other candidate has little chance of victory. In contests with several candidates, selectors who are not enamoured with the frontrunner have a choice of rival candidates, and if they do not like one, they can opt for another. There is less sense of a forced choice between just two candidates and so it is often harder for the frontrunner to power to an overwhelming victory, unless he is very clearly the best candidate to unite the party and lead it to electoral success.

It is notable, however, that five of the ten leadership elections contested by only two candidates involved challenges to an incumbent. It is likely that this factor explained the large margins of victory in those five contests, ranging from 34 percent to 81 percent, especially as at least four of these challenges (Labour in 1960, 1961 and 1988 and the Conservatives in 1989) had no hope of succeeding. The remaining one, the Tory contest of 1995, also ultimately saw a comfortable victory for the winner.[15] Challenges are much more likely to involve fewer candidates than contests for vacancies because of the risks involved: on only one occasion has more than one candidate challenged an incumbent leader in the same ballot – the first ballot of the 1975 Conservative leadership contest. Given the very poor record of most leadership challengers in Britain, it is likely that the apparent inverse relationship between the number of candidates and the final margin of victory owes a lot to the preponderance of challenges within the set of two-candidate contests.

Age and experience

One of the possible effects of selection systems on party leaders is on their age and political experience. In particular, has the opening up of leadership selection to a wider selectorate led to the emergence of younger leaders? Table 6.3 provides details about the age and experience of victorious candidates in British party leadership elections since the 1960s. It also shows the age ranking of each victorious candidate compared with other candidates in their respective contests.

Labour leaders have varied considerably in their ages on assuming the leadership, although the three youngest, Kinnock, Blair and Miliband, all emerged in the era of the electoral college (Figure 6.1). One reason for that fact is that Labour frequently chooses two, or even three, consecutive leaders from the same political generation before skipping to the next generation. Thus, Wilson, Callaghan and Foot were no more than four years apart in their ages. The fact that they occupied the Labour leadership for a combined 20 years ensured that the generation of Healey, Jenkins, Crosland and Benn never became leaders, although all ran for it in 1976 and Healey did so again in 1980. It was eventually Kinnock's generation that took over but Kinnock himself was succeeded by Smith, who was four years his senior. Labour modernisers such as Blair believed that 1992 was the year when Brown should have run for the leadership. He did not and so Blair himself ran

Figure 6.1   Age of Labour Leaders on Assuming the Leadership

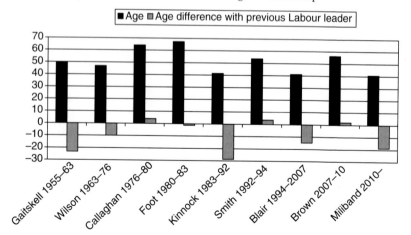

Sources: *Who's Who; Who Was Who* (various editions).

Table 6.3 Age and Experience of Victorious Candidates in Leadership Elections 1963–2010

Contest	Selection system	Winner	Age of winner*	Age ranking	Years as MP*	Years in (shadow) cabinet*	Years as leader (total)
Labour							
1963	PPB	Wilson	46	3/3	18	13	13
1976	PPB	Callaghan	64	1/6	31	25	4
1980	PPB	Foot	67	1/4	30	10	3
1983	EC (BV)	Kinnock	41	4/4	13	4	9
1988	EC (BV)	Kinnock	46	2/2	18	8	9
1992	EC (BV)	Smith	53	1/2	22	14	2
1994	EC (OMOV)	Blair	41	3/3	11	6	13
2007	EC (OMOV)	Brown	56	1/1	24	20	3
2010	EC (OMOV)	Miliband	40	4/5	5	3	–
Conservative							
1965	PPB	Heath	49	2/3	15	6	10
1975	PPB	Thatcher	49	5/7	15	7	15
1989	PPB	Thatcher	64	2/2	30	22	15
1990	PPB	Major	47	4/4	11	3	7
1995	PPB	Major	52	1/2	16	8	7
1997	PPB	Hague	36	5/5	8	2	4
2001	PPB/OMOV	Duncan Smith	47	5/5	9	4	2
2003	PPB/OMOV	Howard	62	1/1	20	10	2
2005	PPB/OMOV	Cameron	39	4/4	4	1	–

Table 6.3 Age and Experience of Victorious Candidates in Leadership Elections 1963–2010 – *continued*

Contest	Selection system	Winner	Age of winner*	Age ranking	Years as MP*	Years in (shadow) cabinet*	Years as leader (total)
Liberal							
1967	PPB	Thorpe	37	3/3	8	–	9
1976	OMOV	Steel	38	2/2	11	–	12
SDP							
1982	OMOV	Jenkins	61	1/2	29	9†	1
1983	OMOV	Owen	44	1/1	17	3†	4
1987	OMOV	Maclennan	51	1/1	21	–	<1
Liberal Democrat							
1988	OMOV	Ashdown	47	1/2	5	–	11
1999	OMOV	Kennedy	39	5/5	16	2‡	7
2006	OMOV	Campbell	64	1/3	18	9‡	2
2007	OMOV	Clegg	40	2/2	2	1	–

Sources: L. P. Stark, *Choosing a Leader: Party Leadership Contests in Britain from Macmillan to Blair* (Basingstoke: Macmillan, 1996), pp. 82–4; *Who's Who*; *Who Was Who* (various editions).

Notes: Age ranking refers to the position of the winning candidate by age among all candidates, e.g. 1/2 means the older of two candidates, 3/4 means the third-oldest of four candidates, etc.

*At time of result of leadership contest

†Jenkins and Owen served as cabinet ministers in Labour governments

‡From 1997, when their parliamentary party was larger, the Liberal Democrats appointed spokesmen to shadow all cabinet ministers. They began describing their frontbench team as a 'shadow cabinet' under Kennedy's leadership. Figures for Liberal Democrat shadow-cabinet experience date from 1997, although Kennedy and Campbell were prominent spokesmen before that.

Figure 6.2 Age of Conservative Leaders on Assuming the Leadership

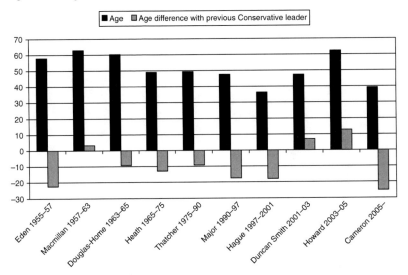

Sources: Who's Who; Who Was Who (various editions).

in 1994, only to be followed by Brown after 13 years in the post. In 2007, it was David Miliband who declined an opportunity to run but when he did eventually go for the post in 2010, he lost to his younger brother.

In general, Conservative leaders have not shown the same generational bunching as Labour leaders (Figure 6.2). Usually, there is an age difference of 10–15 years between one Tory leader and the next, although in Howard's case, he was 12 years older than his predecessor. That implies a degree of generational change when the party chooses a new leader. It also probably explains why losers in Conservative leadership contests do not normally come back in the future and win. The only one who did – Howard – did so in the unusual circumstances of a 'coronation' during a particularly bleak period for the party. This apparent lack of sentimentality helps to explain why the party was so electorally successful for so long, taking the chance to refresh itself when it changed its leader. For a party that extolled the virtues of unity, at least before the divisions over Europe in the 1990s, younger candidates often came without enemies or baggage. Tory leaders also became younger on average after the party adopted parliamentary ballots for leadership selection in the 1960s.

Liberal and Liberal Democrat leaders have usually been younger than leaders of the other two major parties (Figure 6.3). On the other hand, once they have claimed the leadership, Liberal leaders have tended to

Figure 6.3   Age of Liberal/Liberal Democrat Leaders on Assuming the Leadership

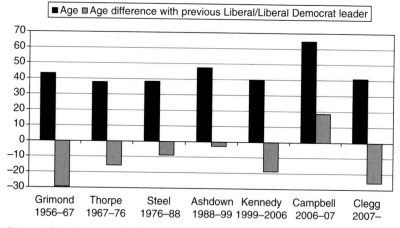

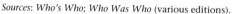

Sources: *Who's Who*; *Who Was Who* (various editions).

stay in post for a long time. Grimond was leader for 11 years, Thorpe for nine, Steel for 12, Ashdown for 11 and Kennedy for seven. The shortest-serving leader in the post-war period was also the oldest assuming the post, Campbell. Indeed, one of the principal complaints about him was precisely that he was too old.

Looking at the parties collectively, there appears to be a moderate institutional effect on leaders' ages. Table 6.4 re-orders some of the data from Table 6.3, to list the party leaders in order of age. Parliamentary ballots produced the oldest leader in this period (Foot), but also the two youngest (Hague and Thorpe). However, one of these was in the Liberal Party when it had only 12 MPs and the other was in a Conservative Party that was expected to reform its selection system soon after and may have consciously sought to 'jump a generation' to match the youthfulness of Blair.[16] OMOV and variations of it have produced young leaders in Steel, Cameron and Kennedy, but also an old one in Campbell. Howard and Brown were older on assuming the leadership and both their parties had OMOV elements in their selection systems, but both their candidacies were unopposed.

The Liberals and Liberal Democrats have regularly chosen young leaders: Clegg, Kennedy, Steel and Thorpe were all 40 or under when elected. Conservative leaders used to be chosen in their late-forties (Heath, Thatcher, Major), but Hague and Cameron were each in their thirties when selected. Labour leaders' ages show greater variation,

Table 6.4 New Party Leaders by Order of Age 1963–2010

Leader	Age	System	Year	Leader	Age	System	Year
Hague (Con)	36	PPB	1997	Duncan Smith (Con)	47	PPB/OMOV	2001
Thorpe (Lib)	37	PPB	1967	Major (Con)	47	PPB	1990
Steel (Lib)	38	OMOV	1976	Heath (Con)	49	PPB	1965
Cameron (Con)	39	PPB/OMOV	2005	Thatcher (Con)	49	PPB	1975
Kennedy (LD)	39	OMOV	1999	Maclennan (SDP)*	51	OMOV	1987
Miliband (Lab)	40	EC (OMOV)	2010	Smith (Lab)	53	EC (BV)	1992
Clegg (LD)	40	OMOV	2007	Brown (Lab)*	56	EC (OMOV)	2007
Blair (Lab)	41	EC (OMOV)	1994	Jenkins (SDP)	61	OMOV	1982
Kinnock (Lab)	41	EC (BV)	1983	Howard (Con)*	62	PPB/OMOV	2003
Owen (SDP)*	44	OMOV	1983	Callaghan (Lab)	64	PPB	1976
Wilson (Lab)	46	PPB	1963	Campbell (LD)	64	OMOV	2006
Ashdown (LD)	47	OMOV	1988	Foot (Lab)	67	PPB	1980

Notes: Excludes contests in which leaders were re-elected. Excludes Conservative leaders selected by 'magic circle'.
*Only candidate – no formal contest.

with Miliband, Blair and Kinnock chosen in their early forties, Wilson in his late-forties, Smith and Brown in their mid-fifties and Callaghan and Foot in their mid-sixties.

The New Labour era from 1997 to 2010 was particularly interesting in terms of party leaders' ages. The Conservatives chose their two youngest leaders (Hague and Cameron), as well as their oldest since Macmillan (Howard). The Liberal Democrats chose the 39-year-old Kennedy followed by the 64-year-old Campbell and the 40-year-old Clegg. Hague presented himself as a youthful leader who could modernise the Tories.[17] Cameron did much the same. Clegg appeared to represent a new generation for the Liberal Democrats. The two older leaders in this period, Howard and Campbell, both came to the leadership of their respective parties in times of crisis after the eviction of the previous leaders and the perceived need for a safe pair of hands at the tiller. Each was succeeded by a much younger man. In Blair and Miliband, Labour also chose its two youngest-ever leaders.

Young leaders offer parties the chance to 'skip a generation', break with a discredited past, move on – in short, to show that they have changed. Young leaders can also serve the internal purpose of party unity because they are less likely to have accumulated so many enemies or to have become divisive in the way that older politicians may have. Of the 22 contested leadership elections in the Conservative, Labour, Liberal and Liberal Democrat parties from 1963 to 2010, the youngest candidate in the contest won on no fewer than 13 occasions. On a further two occasions, both in the Labour Party, the age difference between the victorious and the youngest candidates was five months (in 1992) and 14 days (in 2010) respectively. In three other cases – the Conservatives in 1965 and 1975, and the Liberal Democrats in 1988 – the winner was no more than two years older than the youngest candidate. In Ashdown's case, while he was older than Beith, he also appeared the fresher of the candidates as he had been in parliament for only five years while Beith, had been an MP for 15 years. That leaves just the four outlying cases of Callaghan, Foot, Major (1995) and Campbell, three of whom were more than ten years older than the youngest candidate (Callaghan, Foot and Campbell). It would appear that parties, irrespective of the selectorate, regularly avail themselves of the opportunity to choose the candidate who appears least tainted by past failures and divisions, and that is normally one of the younger candidates.

Despite the occasional selection of older leaders, often in crisis situations, there does seem to be a trend towards the selection of younger party leaders in the period when selection was opened up. This tendency is reflected in the parliamentary experience of leaders. Of the 24 individuals elected as Labour, Conservative, Liberal, SDP and Liberal Democrat leaders since 1963, three of the four with the least parliamentary experience were chosen between 2005 and 2010: Cameron (four years), Clegg (two years) and Miliband (five years). Cameron and Clegg had each spent only one year in their respective shadow cabinets prior to becoming leader, while Miliband had spent three years in government. Other recent inexperienced leaders include Hague (eight years as an MP and two years in the cabinet before becoming leader) and to a lesser extent, Duncan Smith (nine years as an MP and four years in the shadow cabinet).

In the era of the professional politician, party leaders are often people who have already been near the centre of power long before they become leaders and frequently, long before they become MPs. Cameron was the first former 'special advisor' to become prime minister, having served Norman Lamont at the treasury in the early 1990s. Clegg was a policy advisor and speech writer for Leon Brittan at the European Commission. In Labour's 2010 leadership contest, four of the five candidates, including the victorious one, were former special advisors: one to a prime minister (David Miliband), two to a chancellor (Ed Miliband and Balls) and one to a culture secretary (Burnham).

The election of younger and less experienced (in frontbench terms) party leaders has coincided with the rise of membership ballots in British parties. It is not clear whether that is a direct consequence of widening the franchise or reflective of a new era in which the media culture values youth. Certainly, most of the negative commentary on Campbell's age came from the media and after a while, it could not but influence the way some Liberal Democrat MPs thought about their leader. The widespread belief that leaders are an important part of the 'product' that parties offer to voters ensures that parties will be conscious of candidates' voter-appeal, even if that is not always the principal criterion on which they select them.[18] Where youthfulness in politics once signified inexperience, it now symbolises freshness and a break with the past. These are important qualities in an electoral market that is more open than in previous decades.

Ejecting party leaders: An assessment

Many politicians tend to be sceptical that eviction institutions are particularly important. The former Conservative leader, Michael Howard, no doubt spoke for many when he suggested that, if a party were really determined to remove a leader, it would do so regardless of the institutions.[19] However, this belief belies the fact that all of the main UK parties have, over the last two decades, sought to make it more difficult to remove incumbent leaders. Clearly, the people who implemented these rule changes believed that they would have some effect in increasing leaders' security of tenure. Labour increased its nomination threshold for leadership challenges to 20 percent of the PLP from the previous level of 5 percent in 1988. The Conservatives had allowed contests to be instigated by a candidate securing just two nominations from MPs but changed the rules in 1991 to require 10 percent of Tory MPs to demand a contest before one could take place. In 1998, with the *Fresh Future* reforms, it was agreed that 15 percent of MPs would need to call for a confidence vote before one was granted. The Liberal Democrats raised their nomination threshold from two MPs to 10 percent of Liberal Democrat MPs in 2005.

Interestingly, these changes have not prevented parties from at least attempting to remove their leaders. Indeed, recent years appear to have seen an upsurge in attempted evictions – most likely reflecting the assumption that leaders are more important for electoral success in an increasingly 'presidential' era.[20] Nevertheless, not all of the under-pressure leaders examined earlier were forced out by their critics and it is the argument of this book that intra-party institutions played some role in determining which leaders survived and which ones did not. Eviction institutions can either exacerbate or ease the severity of the collective-action problem facing a leader's opponents. The absence of institutions compels either a frontbench coup, which would probably require agreement on a successor, or a backbench revolt. Coups and revolts are difficult to organise because individual politicians are wary of risking their positions. Institutions that make it too difficult to challenge an incumbent, such as Labour's appear to do, can have the same effect as the absence of any institutions, compelling coups or revolts as the only realistic option, despite their limitations as methods of leader eviction.

Institutions that make it relatively easy to instigate a leadership contest or confidence vote, however, significantly reduce the mobilisation costs of the incumbent's opponents. Despite being a stalking horse, Sir Anthony Meyer obtained the two nominations he required to challenge Thatcher in 1989. Once the procedures were activated, one-sixth of Tory MPs withheld their support from the prime minister in the secret leadership ballot. The following year, a further challenge under similar rules ended her tenure. In 2003, Duncan Smith's opponents managed to surmount the 15 percent hurdle for confidential letters demanding a confidence vote. The secret ballot that followed saw the leader felled by his MPs.

The conclusion of this study is that the institutional features that make it easiest for intra-party actors to evict leaders have three principal characteristics: (1) anonymity to those who wish to instigate a vote, whether at the trigger stage or at the voting stage, for example, through secret ballots; (2) relatively low thresholds for triggering a ballot; (3) the sequential separation of the processes of leader eviction and replacement. Each of these elements serves to reduce the mobilisation costs of the leader's opponents. In the event of a leadership challenge, the challenger, whether a serious one or a stalking horse, will not have his identity shielded but most of his supporters will desire anonymity. Ambitious frontbenchers and backbenchers will not want to harm their career prospects by supporting the challenger, although in a system such as Labour's, they might.

Secret ballots are crucial in extending rebellions beyond the 'usual suspects' of ex-ministers and ideological radicals on the backbenches. They provide cover for those backbenchers who want to see a change of leadership but who also hope for promotion in the future. Secret ballots safeguard frontbenchers who want a change of leadership but are not prepared to argue publicly for it. More than any other institutional device, the secret ballot reduces the risks to those who want to evict their leader. In doing so, it solves the rebels' collective-action problem for them and reduces the costs to those leading the rebellion of mobilising opposition.

Even a secret ballot may not be enough, however, if it cannot easily be instigated. Thus, nomination thresholds for challenges or activation thresholds for confidence votes are also crucial. If thresholds are low, then even small bands of critics who are unafraid of challenging the leader's authority can instigate a leadership contest or a confidence vote. The lower the threshold is, the lower the plotters' mobilisation costs will be because they need to persuade fewer people to join the first stage of the putsch. Secret ballots in combination with low thresholds make it easier for plotters to unite leadership opponents, whether they are frontbenchers or backbenchers, and whether the latter are ex-ministers, ideological radicals or erstwhile loyalists who have decided that change is essential.

Institutions that separate the processes of removing a leader and choosing a replacement generally can help to make eviction easier than those that fuse these two stages into one. Rules that fuse the two usually require a candidate to challenge the incumbent directly and play the role of 'assassin'. That is by no means impossible, but it is very risky for the challenger, as the poor record of leadership challengers in the UK demonstrates. Serious candidates who hope to take over may pay a heavy price if selectors view them as disloyal and divisive – a perennial problem for Labour's cabinet plotters during 2008–10. Similarly, in the absence of rules that permit the entry of new candidates in later ballots – which effectively separate eviction and replacement – stalking horses have less of a chance of damaging the incumbent. It is possible that the leader could fare so badly that he resigns, but then another ballot would need to be held. In the era of expensive, time-consuming OMOV ballots, that is unlikely to be tolerated and so it is more likely that the leader would get a large vote of confidence for fear that he could otherwise be left in place as a lame duck. The costs to the stalking horse of mobilising allies are thus very high.

In contrast, if leader eviction and replacement are sequentially separated, the party can first decide whether it wants to remove the leader and if so, it can choose later who it would like to replace him. Such a contest is much more likely to see the entry of a fuller range of serious candidates, free from charges of disloyalty, divisiveness and 'regicide', than would be the case in a challenge to a leader seeking re-election. It will be easier and therefore less costly for candidates to mobilise support in a contest for a vacant position than for a challenge to an incumbent. For these reasons, parties without an institutional separation between ejection and selection have sometimes sought to create such a division informally, usually by forcing the leader's resignation first, as with Kennedy in 2006.

Sequential separation of ejection and election does not always serve to make eviction easier, however. If opponents of the incumbent disagree over who they would like to see replace him, he may end up surviving. That was one of the reasons for Duncan Smith's survival in 2002: there was no consensus over the rival leadership claims of Portillo, Clarke and Davis. The fact that there was such a consensus a year later expedited Duncan Smith's removal. Similarly, Major's opponents had the chance to vote against him in the first ballot in 1995 but many pro-Europeans supported him for fear of letting in Portillo if the contest went to a second ballot. Nevertheless, systems that do not require 'assassins' generally give plotters a better chance of bringing down the leader than those that do, even if they do not necessarily make eviction easy.

In the Conservative Party, Heath in 1975 and Thatcher in 1990 were evicted through a set of institutions that combined secret ballots, low nomination thresholds and a separation of eviction and replacement. Just two MPs were required to support candidates taking part in Tory leadership contests. The necessity of a 15 percent lead in the first ballot and the provision for new candidates to enter on the second ballot were important institutional factors in the eviction of these leaders. The 15 percent rule made it harder for the incumbent to win while second-ballot entry ensured that the first ballot became a *de facto* confidence vote and thus sequentially separated the processes of leader eviction and replacement. Stalking-horse challenges would be much more difficult if there were high nomination barriers, as in the Labour Party. Similarly, a non-secret ballot, again as in the Labour Party, would make the defeat of an incumbent less likely, as MPs' votes could be monitored. That in turn would make the emergence of a challenger less likely because it would be costlier for him to mobilise support.

The removal of Duncan Smith was achieved within a somewhat tougher institutional eviction regime. The requirement for 15 percent of Tory MPs to write to the chairman of the 1922 committee to activate a confidence vote made frivolous challenges to the leader's authority much more difficult to mount. However, the move against Duncan Smith was a serious one, as demonstrated by the fact that the activation threshold of 15 percent was not only reached but comfortably passed (allegedly by almost 10 percent). Confidentiality was again crucial. Only a handful of letter-writers to Sir Michael Spicer, the chairman of the 1922 committee, publicly revealed their actions. Spicer took seriously his obligation to keep the names secret.[21] The letter-writers appeared to trust him to do so, although some frontbenchers were reportedly worried that their names might leak out if they sent letters. Confidentiality was also ensured for MPs in the confidence vote, which was by secret ballot.

There are no formal provisions for secret ballots of MPs in relation to leadership selection and eviction in the Labour Party. Not only nominations but MPs' votes in the electoral college are made public. The lack of anonymity offered to rebels appeared to be an impediment to some of those MPs who wanted to remove Brown in 2008–10. Indeed, the Hoon-Hewitt letter sought to circumvent these institutional constraints by calling for a confidence vote by secret ballot to take place among Labour MPs. In the late-1960s, Wilson's detractors tried to do the same, but with a similar lack of success. The fact that rebels in each case lobbied for such a vote was indicative of what they considered to be one of the main obstacles standing in the way of a successful eviction. A further problem was that, unlike in the Conservative Party at present, there was no constitutional means by which the rebels could force a vote of confidence. It was theoretically possible to hold such a vote at a meeting of the PLP, but it was up to the PLP chairman to decide whether to allow it. If large numbers of MPs had demanded a confidence vote, it would have been difficult for the PLP chairman to refuse. However, without such a large-scale demand, it could easily be brushed off. In 1969, Douglas Houghton, the PLP chairman, let it be known that a confidence motion would not be discussed unless the rebels could muster 120 MPs – one-third of the PLP – to request it.[22] Those MPs would have had to reveal themselves publicly. Since the entire point was that the ballot should be secret, it was never likely to happen.

The presence in a party of low trigger thresholds, secret ballots and the separation of leader eviction and replacement reduces the leader's institutional security of tenure by lowering the costs to the leader's enemies of mobilising opposition to him among MPs. Other rules can be important. Restrictions on the timing of contests can protect leaders from challenges at their moments of greatest vulnerability. Annual leadership contests enable opponents to come back each year and try again, although even then a challenger must still come forward.[23] It is also the case that membership ballots can be a strong disincentive to change leader, especially in government but also in opposition, because they usually take months to complete. In that respect, British parties have sometimes sought to circumvent the disadvantages of OMOV ballots by agreeing on a single candidate, as the Conservatives did in 2003, or by speeding up the timetable, as Labour rebels wanted to do in 2009–10. These manoeuvres indicate that politicians are aware of the potential high 'decision costs' of OMOV but have sought to devise ways of reducing these costs.

One of the most notable points about the shift to membership ballots insofar as leader-ejection is concerned is that individual members continue to play little or no role in it. In 2005, the Conservative leadership undertook a consultation exercise as a prelude, it assumed, to abandoning the post-1998 rules for leadership selection. Among various defects identified in the system, was that

> it is surely wrong in principle and certainly damaging in practice for one group of people to have the power to elect the Leader of the Party and a different group of people to have the power to remove him or her.[24]

In reality, the choosing of the leader in a membership ballot and his later ejection by MPs is a feature of the OMOV era. Only the Liberal

Democrats give their members a role in leader eviction, through the provision for a leadership election if 75 local associations call for it. However, during the eviction of Kennedy, it was widely assumed that individual members were the leader's most loyal supporters. Removing leaders has remained the prerogative of MPs because the latter have many more opportunities, and often stronger incentives, than individual members to monitor leaders' performances and to move against them when they start failing. MPs are often in daily contact with each other and so plotting and mobilising against leaders is easier than it is for members, who might never meet each other, or even for activists who usually have only local contacts. MPs can take their grievances to the media, whether on the record or in the form of anonymous criticisms. Finally, it is more important that leaders retain their authority among the majority of their fellow MPs – the people they work with closely – than among party members, whose support, though important, is less decisive on a day-to-day basis. For all these reasons, MPs remain the principal actors in leader eviction in the era of membership ballots.

The myth of the 'Men in Grey Suits'?

When a party has no institutional provisions for removing leaders or has institutions that are difficult to activate, the leader's opponents will usually look for other means to evict him. That generally means a coup or rebellion among a group of MPs, although such rebellions may also be a feature of institutional evictions. A frequent claim in academic and journalistic writing on party leaders and prime ministers is that, once they lose the confidence of their senior colleagues, they are in severe danger of being removed from their posts. These party notables, normally the most senior and respected in the (shadow) cabinet, are variously described as the 'grey beards' or more frequently, the 'men in grey suits'. Thus, it is often claimed that Thatcher was forced to resign after her cabinet told her that she could not win the second ballot in 1990. Similarly, Kennedy resigned as Liberal Democrat leader in 2006 after a revolt by his shadow cabinet.

The analysis presented in this book suggests that the role played by party notables in removing leaders has been overstated. That is not because the support of senior colleagues is unimportant. Clearly, it is of vital significance to a leader. Those observers who suggested that a delegation of cabinet ministers, including Jack Straw, Harriet Harman and Alan Johnson, could have forced out Brown in 2008–10 are almost certainly correct. The point, however, is that the chances of such delegations forming are usually low, even when a leader is performing poorly. The reasons are not hard to find. If rival crown princes covet the leader's job, there is a strong disincentive to become too closely involved in a putsch lest they become seen as disloyal and divisive or open the way for their rivals.

Even those senior politicians who do not hope to become leader will usually be dissuaded from moving against the leader because of the fear of being sacked or demoted if the coup fails. It may be many years before they manage to work their way back to their previous level – or their careers may even be over already. Career prospects are understandably a very real consideration for senior politicians and may explain why many prefer not to join attempts to remove failing leaders.[25] It will be recalled from Chapter 1 that Downs claimed that politicians were 'motivated by the desire for power, prestige, and income', which came from holding elected office. It follows that politicians who resign from office suffer a loss of these benefits. This prospect is almost certainly a major reason why more politicians, especially those in government, do not resign their positions during leadership crises. To take the case of income, any cabinet minister who might have considered resigning from Brown's government in 2008 would have forsaken a gross annual salary of £78,356 (while retaining his MP's salary of £63,291). In the event, only one minister of state resigned, losing his ministerial salary of £40,646, while an assistant government whip also resigned.[26] More ministers resigned in 2009 but several were related to the scandal over parliamentary expenses. When eight members of Blair's government resigned and called on him to go in 2006, only one was a parliamentary under-secretary, while seven were *unpaid* parliamentary private secretaries. Most were appointed to paid ministerial posts when Brown became prime minister. It ought to be noted that most shadow ministers are not paid and so there are lower financial costs in resigning, although those who do resign may reduce their chances of obtaining ministerial positions when their party returns to government.

The cases of eviction or attempted eviction examined in this book do not, on the whole, bear out the notion that party notables deliver the *coup de grace* to under-pressure leaders. Thatcher did indeed lose the confidence of her senior colleagues in 1990, but she did so only in specific circumstances. A leadership election was already under way and she called in her cabinet ministers one at a time to seek their views. But they did not organise such a visit by themselves or before the contest had been announced. Her downfall was precipitated by

Howe's resignation and both he and the former chancellor, Lawson, ultimately supported Heseltine, another former cabinet minister. The fact that Heseltine's challenge was able to gather so much support was down to the fact that the Tory back benches were in ferment, owing to the party's perilous electoral predicament. Backbenchers still had to be mobilised, which they were, by Heseltine's candidacy and through the mechanism of an easily-instigated secret ballot. Indeed, one Labour observer claimed that Thatcher's downfall was an 'accidental defenestration', a function of the Conservatives' eviction rules, which were immediately tightened by the party afterwards.[27]

Duncan Smith was another Tory leader who was evicted more because of his backbenchers than his frontbenchers. David Davis was suspected of plotting against him but Davis never went public with his criticisms. Instead, much of the active plotting was carried out by his backbench allies. One of these, Derek Conway, was one of the few Tory MPs who publicly announced that he had written to demand a confidence vote. Although some frontbenchers were rumoured to have sent letters to the 1922 committee demanding a vote, it seems clear that most letters were sent by backbenchers. Duncan Smith's senior colleagues in the shadow cabinet largely prevaricated. Suggestions that there could be mass resignations proved wide of the mark.

In the Labour Party, neither Blair nor Brown was ultimately evicted, although Blair was forced to set out a timetable for his departure. The major threat to Blair came from Brown, but the chancellor was reluctant to be seen to be moving too obviously against the prime minister. The so-called 'curry-house coup' was led by a junior minister. However, there was no generalised cabinet revolt or a series of cabinet resignations.

Brown himself would experience three attempts to remove him as prime minister. Senior members of the PLP were more prominent in these moves, although not in a coordinated way. In 2008, the most senior members of the cabinet, who were seen as being Straw, Hoon and Darling, did not join the attempt to remove Brown from his post. It was left to David Miliband to make a veiled pitch for the leadership and junior ministers to resign. Although Miliband was the foreign secretary, he did not yet have the stature or enough of a following to threaten Brown by himself. The same applied to Purnell when he resigned the following year, although had he been joined by Miliband, the putsch might have been more successful. By then, however, Miliband's card had been marked and any further act of apparent disloyalty would almost certainly have killed off his chances of taking over from Brown in the future. The final coup attempt was led by two former cabinet ministers in Hoon and Hewitt, but outside of the cabinet, neither had the weight to carry many others with them. Overall, the various attempts to overthrow Brown were characterised by Blairite and miscellaneous anti-Brown backbenchers, often ex-ministers, seeking to mobilise wider opinion on the backbenches and support from within the cabinet. With one or two exceptions, they were largely unable to do that.

The Liberal Democrats necessarily operate in a different way to the two main parties. Their parliamentary party is smaller and a bigger proportion of it holds frontbench responsibilities, especially when it is in opposition. That has ensured that, when their leaders come under pressure to resign, frontbenchers have to play a greater role. Nevertheless, the most senior members of the shadow cabinet did not become publicly involved in Kennedy's forced resignation. Campbell was widely seen as being available for the top job but he had to be careful about his public utterances and actions so as not to risk leaving him looking disloyal. Similarly, Hughes and Oaten, the other candidates frequently mentioned as possible replacements for Kennedy, maintained their distance from the coup. None of the three signed the open letter calling for their leader to stand down. It was primarily more junior and less prominent members of the shadow cabinet who led the putsch. Hughes and Cable were more public in their warnings to Campbell to raise his game in 2007 but by then neither harboured serious leadership ambitions. Campbell decided to jump before he was pushed and so in this case, it appears that senior figures played a more important role.

Overall, senior politicians tend to be cautious in moving against their leaders. Partly that is because of their fear of appearing disloyal, which can damage their own chances of taking over. It is extremely risky playing the role of assassin: intra-party actors usually disapprove of 'treachery' and they will be aware that the assassin may find it hard to demand loyalty as leader if he acquired the crown through regicide. Where there are rival crown princes, each may look to leave a putsch to the others. Only occasionally, when the most senior politicians are not after the top job for themselves but are willing to act on behalf of the party as a whole will a frontbench coup have more chance of succeeding. Otherwise, much of the plotting will be left to backbenchers.

Conclusion

The principal question under consideration in this book was whether institutions matter in the selection and ejection of British party leaders. The analysis presented above leads to two conclusions. First, as Stark argued, selection systems, and by extension the composition of the selectorate, usually have only a marginal impact on which candidate is most likely to win a given leadership contest. Of the contests analysed in this book, only that of the Labour Party in 2010 resulted in the victory of a candidate who would have been unlikely to win in a parliamentary ballot. On the other hand, Ed Miliband would also likely have lost a pure OMOV ballot and so even this contest does not provide evidence of a division between MPs and members. Only the inclusion of another category of selectors, trade-union members, led to the younger Miliband's victory, and even then on a very low turnout.

On the whole, party members and MPs use the same selection criteria when choosing leaders and that is why differences between them over candidates have been few and far between. That should not really be surprising because most MPs start out as ordinary political activists, motivated by the same ideological visions as other activists and undergoing the same processes of socialisation within parties. No doubt the need to win re-election makes them attentive to the various requirements for electability, including choosing the right leader, but few abandon all their ideological motivations. Equally, most members of mainstream parties understand that electability demands that some ideological goals be put aside. The dichotomy between moderate MPs and radical members, as highlighted by the 'law of curvilinear disparity', has always been too simplistic.

One way in which selection systems could affect the choice of candidate is when they compel challenges to the incumbent as the only institutional means of eviction. In these cases, the types of politicians who challenge leaders may be different from those who would stand for a vacancy. The obvious example is Thatcher who challenged Heath in 1975 and developed sufficient momentum to retain a lead in the second ballot. It is certainly questionable whether she could have defeated Whitelaw had the latter been in the contest from the beginning.[28]

The second conclusion to draw from this study is that institutions appear to matter more in relation to the ejection of leaders. It is difficult for atomised party members, or even more organised activists, to hold leaders to account and to remove them when they are deemed to be failing. For that reason, the removal of leaders has remained the prerogative of MPs in the era of membership ballots. The question then concerns how costly those institutions make it for a leader's opponents to mobilise against him. The conclusion from this survey of British parties is that secret ballots that are easy to set in motion, coupled with the separation of the ejection and selection phases, which obviates the need for an assassin, offer the lowest degree of institutional security of tenure for leaders. Conversely, non-secret ballots, high trigger thresholds, and the fusion of ejection and selection, increase leaders' institutional security of tenure. All-member ballots are regularly thought to protect leaders because they are time-consuming and therefore provide a disincentive for leader eviction. However, parties have sought to reduce these party costs, whether by not holding a ballot at all or by seeking to impose a speedier timetable for a leadership election.

This double conclusion is perhaps not surprising. During the period when British parties extended the franchise in leadership elections, they also tightened their rules on leadership challenges in order to protect incumbent leaders. That has not stopped several attempts to remove sitting leaders in recent years. Some of the unsuccessful attempts, especially in the Labour Party, were a testament to the importance of eviction institutions in protecting leaders. In an era when the visibility and role of party leaders has never been greater, politicians will always take a keen interest in how they can remove leaders who are under-performing, while those leaders themselves will be equally keen to protect themselves against internal plotters.

Appendix A Labour Party Leadership Election Results 1955–2010

1955 14 December

Parliamentary ballot

	MPs	%
Hugh Gaitskell	157	58.8
Aneurin Bevan	70	26.2
Herbert Morrison	40	15.0

1960 3 November

Parliamentary ballot

	MPs	%
Hugh Gaitskell*	166	67.2
Harold Wilson	81	32.8

1961 2 November

Parliamentary ballot

	MPs	%
Hugh Gaitskell*	171	74.3
Anthony Greenwood	59	25.7

1963

Parliamentary ballot

	7 February First ballot		14 February Second ballot	
	MPs	%	MPs	%
Harold Wilson	115	47.1	144	58.3
George Brown	88	36.1	103	41.7
James Callaghan	41	16.8	–	–

1976

Parliamentary ballot

	25 March First ballot		30 March Second ballot		5 April Third ballot	
	MPs	%	MPs	%	MPs	%
James Callaghan	84	26.8	141	45.2	176	56.2
Michael Foot	90	28.7	133	42.6	137	43.8
Roy Jenkins	56	17.8	–	–	–	–
Tony Benn	37	11.8	–	–	–	–
Denis Healey	30	9.6	38	12.2	–	–
Anthony Crosland	17	5.4	–	–	–	–

1980

Parliamentary ballot

	4 November First ballot		10 November Second ballot	
	MPs	%	MPs	%
Michael Foot	83	31.3	139	51.9
Denis Healey	112	42.3	129	48.1
John Silkin	38	14.3	–	–
Peter Shore	32	12.1	–	–

1983

2 October

Electoral college	PLP (30%)		CLPs (30%)		Affiliates (40%)		Total
	MPs	%	Block votes	%	Block votes	%	%
Neil Kinnock	100	49.3	571	91.5	4,389	72.6	71.3
Roy Hattersley	53	26.1	12	1.9	1,644	27.2	19.3
Eric Heffer	29	14.3	41	6.6	7	0.1	6.3
Peter Shore	21	10.3	0	0.0	5	0.1	3.1

1988

2 October

Electoral college	PLP (30%)		CLPs (30%)		Affiliates (40%)		Total
	MPs	%	Block votes	%	Block votes	%	%
Neil Kinnock*	183	82.8	489	80.4	5,605	99.2	88.6
Tony Benn	38	17.2	119	19.6	48	0.8	11.4

1992

18 July

Electoral college	PLP/EPLP (30%)		CLPs (30%)		Affiliates (40%)		Total
	MPs/ MEPs	%	Block votes	%	Block votes	%	%
John Smith	229	77.1	597	98.0	4,822	96.3	91.0
Bryan Gould	68	22.9	12	2.0	187	3.7	9.0

1994

21 July

Electoral college	PLP/EPLP (1/3) %	Members (1/3) %	Affiliates (1/3) %	Total %
Tony Blair	60.5	58.2	52.3	57.0
John Prescott	19.6	24.4	28.4	24.1
Margaret Beckett	19.9	17.4	19.3	18.9
Turnouts	*98.8%*	*69.1%*	*19.5%*	

2007

24 June

Gordon Brown   Brown declared leader after being only candidate to secure enough nominations

2010

25 September

Electoral College	PLP/EPLP (1/3)		Members (1/3)		Affiliates (1/3)		Total
	Votes	%	Votes	%	Votes	%	%
First count							
Abbott	7	2.6	9,314	7.3	25,938	12.3	7.4
Balls	40	15.0	12,831	10.1	21,618	10.2	11.8
Burnham	24	9.0	10,844	8.5	17,904	8.5	8.7
D. Miliband	111	41.7	55,905	44.1	58,189	27.5	37.8
E. Miliband	84	31.6	37,980	29.9	87,585	41.5	34.3
Total	266	100.0	126,874	100.0	211,234	100.0	100.0
EM lead	–27	–10.2	–17,925	–14.1	+29,396	+13.9	–3.5

Second count

Balls	41	15.5	14,510	11.5	26,441	12.7	13.2
Burnham	24	9.1	12,498	9.9	25,528	12.2	10.4
D. Miliband	111	42.0	57,128	45.2	61,336	29.4	38.9
E. Miliband	88	33.3	42,176	33.4	95,335	45.7	37.5
Total	264	100.0	126,312	100.0	208,640	100.0	100.0
Non-transferable	2	(0.8)	562	(0.4)	2,594	(1.2)	–
EM lead	–23	–8.7	–14,952	–11.8	+33,999	+16.3	–1.4

Third count

Balls	43	16.3	18,114	14.5	35,512	17.3	16.0
D. Miliband	125	47.3	60,375	48.2	66,889	32.6	42.7
E. Miliband	96	36.4	46,697	37.3	102,882	50.1	41.3
Total	264	100.0	125,186	100.0	205,283	100.0	100.0
Non-transferable	2	(0.8)	1,688	(1.3)	5,951	(2.8)	–
EM lead	–29	–9.0	–13,678	–10.9	+35,993	+17.5	–1.5

Fourth count

D. Miliband	140	53.4	66,814	54.4	80,266	40.2	49.3
E. Miliband	122	46.6	55,992	45.6	119,405	59.8	50.7
Total	262	100.0	122,806	100.0	199,671	100.0	100.0
Non-transferable	4	(1.5)	4,068	(3.2)	11,563	(5.5)	–
EM lead	–18	–6.9	–10,822	–8.8	+39,139	+19.6	+1.3

Turnouts	*PLP/EPLP 98.5%*	*Members 71.7%*	*Affiliates 9.0%*

Sources: D. Butler and G. Butler, *Twentieth-Century British Political Facts, 1900–2000* (Basingstoke: Palgrave, 2000), pp. 146–8 (this source provides incorrect figures for the 1960 contest; these have been corrected above); H. Drucker, 'Intra-party Democracy in Action: The Election of Leader and Deputy Leader by the Labour Party in 1983', *Parliamentary Affairs*, 37:1 (1984), 283–300, p. 295; *Report of the Eighty-Seventh Annual Conference of the Labour Party 1988*, pp. 210, 218, 221; A. McSmith, *John Smith: Playing the Long Game* (London: Verso, 1993), p. 211; K. Alderman and N. Carter, 'The Labour Party Leadership and Deputy Leadership Elections of 1994', *Parliamentary Affairs*, 48:3 (1995), 438–55, pp. 448–9; T. Heppell, *Choosing the Labour Leader: Labour Party Leadership Elections from Wilson to Brown* (London: IB Tauris, 2010), p. 188; Labour Party, 'Summary of Voting by Round', available at <http://www.labour.org.uk/votes-by-round>.

Notes: *Parliamentary ballots* (1955–80 contests): candidates needed majority of those voting to win (abstentions/spoilt ballots not included in total percentages). Exhaustive-ballot system. *Electoral college* (1983–2010 contests): Parliamentary section includes only MPs from 1983–88, but MPs and MEPs from 1992–2010. CLP/members section used block voting from 1983–92 (balloting of members to determine how to cast block votes was voluntary from 1983–88 and compulsory in 1992) and pure OMOV from 1994–2010. Affiliates section consists mainly of trade unions, with some small socialist societies. It used block voting from 1983–92 and individual voting from 1994–2010. From 1983–92, CLPs and affiliates cast one block vote for every 1,000 members they affiliated. Figures in final column for 1983–2010 are percentages of votes in the college as a whole (weighted summation of three sections). Exhaustive-ballot system 1983–92; alternative-vote system 1994–2010.
*Incumbent

Appendix B Conservative Party Leadership Election Results 1965–2005

1965

Parliamentary ballot	MPs	%	
28 July			
Edward Heath	150	50.3	Second ballot cancelled:
Reginald Maudling	133	44.6	Maudling & Powell withdrew;
Enoch Powell	15	5.0	no entry of new candidates
Abstentions/spoilt[†]	6	(2.0)	

1975

Parliamentary ballot

	First ballot (4 February)		Second ballot (11 February)	
	MPs	%	MPs	%
Margaret Thatcher	130	47.1	146	52.9
Edward Heath*	119	43.1	–	–
Hugh Fraser	16	5.8	–	–
William Whitelaw	–	–	79	28.6
Geoffrey Howe	–	–	19	6.9
James Prior	–	–	19	6.9
John Peyton	–	–	11	4.0
Abstentions/spoilt[†]	11	4.0	2	0.7

1989

Parliamentary ballot — 5 December

	MPs	%
Margaret Thatcher*	314	84.0
Anthony Meyer	33	8.8
Abstentions/spoilt[†]	27	7.2

1990

Parliamentary ballot

	First ballot (20 November)		Second ballot (27 November)		
	MPs	%	MPs	%	Third ballot
Margaret Thatcher*	204	54.8	–	–	cancelled:
Michael Heseltine	152	40.9	131	35.2	Heseltine & Hurd
John Major	–	–	185	49.7	said they would
Douglas Hurd	–	–	56	15.1	support Major
Abstentions/spoilt[†]	16	4.3	0	0	

1995

Parliamentary ballot — 4 July

	MPs	%
John Major**	218	66.3
John Redwood	89	27.1
Abstentions/spoilt[†]	22	6.7

1997	10 June		17 June		19 June	
Parliamentary ballot	First ballot		Second ballot		Third ballot	
	MPs	%	MPs	%	MPs	%
William Hague	41	25.0	62	37.8	92	56.8
Kenneth Clarke	49	29.9	64	39.0	70	43.2
John Redwood	27	16.5	38	23.2	–	–
Peter Lilley	24	14.6	–	–	–	–
Michael Howard	23	14.0	–	–	–	–
Abstentions/spoilt[†]	0	0	0	0	2	(1.2)

2001	10 July		12 July		17 July		13 September	
Parliamentary- OMOV ballots	First ballot		Re-run first ballot		Second ballot		OMOV ballot	
	MPs	%	MPs	%	MPs	%	Votes	%
Iain Duncan Smith	39	23.5	42	25.3	54	32.5	155,933	60.7
Kenneth Clarke	36	21.7	39	23.5	59	35.5	100,864	39.3
Michael Portillo	49	29.5	50	30.1	53	31.9	–	–
David Davis	21	12.7	18	10.8	–	–	–	–
Michael Ancram	21	12.7	17	10.2	–	–	–	–

Turnout: 79%

2003		29 October		
Confidence vote	Confidence		No confidence	
	MPs	%	MPs	%
Iain Duncan Smith*	75	45.5	90	54.5

| *Leadership contest* | 6 November |
| Michael Howard | Howard declared leader after being only candidate to be nominated |

2005	18 October		20 October		6 December	
Parliamentary- OMOV ballots	First ballot		Second ballot		OMOV ballot	
	MPs	%	MPs	%	Votes	%
David Cameron	56	28.3	90	45.5	134,446	67.6
David Davis	62	31.3	57	28.8	64,398	32.4
Liam Fox	42	21.2	51	25.8	–	–
Kenneth Clarke	38	19.2	–	–	–	–

Turnout: 78%

Sources: D. Butler and G. Butler, *Twentieth-Century British Political Facts, 1900–2000* (Basingstoke: Palgrave, 2000), pp. 135–6; K. Alderman and N. Carter, 'The Conservative Party Leadership Election of 2001', *Parliamentary Affairs*, 55:4 (2002), 569–85, pp. 579, 583; A. Denham and K. O'Hara, *Democratising Conservative Leadership Selection: From Grey Suits to Grass Roots* (Manchester: Manchester University Press, 2008), pp. 96, 98–9, 154, 159–60; BBC, 'Cameron chosen as new Tory leader', *BBC News*, 6 December 2005, available at <http://news.bbc.co.uk/1/hi/uk_politics/4502652.stm>.
Notes: *Parliamentary ballots* (1965–97 contests): candidates needed majority of eligible voters and 15 percent lead over nearest rival to win in first ballot (majority of votes cast and 15 percent lead needed in 1965 contest); candidates needed majority of eligible voters

to win in second ballot, during which new candidates could enter contest; candidates needed majority of votes cast to win in third ballot. *Parliamentary-OMOV ballots* (2001–05 contests): eliminative ballots of MPs to produce two candidates, who went forward to OMOV ballot. Leader ejected by confidence vote triggered by 15 percent of Conservative MPs demanding ballot in writing to chairman of 1922 committee.

*Incumbent

**Major was the incumbent in 1995 but resigned his position as party leader to instigate a leadership election

†For 1965, vote shares expressed as percentage of *votes cast* for all ballots and so abstentions and spoilt ballots not included in total percentages. Abstentions and spoilt ballots included in calculations of vote shares in first and second ballots but not third ballot for 1975–97.

Appendix C   Liberal Party, Social Democratic Party and Liberal Democrat Leadership Election Results 1967–2007

Liberal Party

1967 18 January

Parliamentary ballot	MPs	%	
Jeremy Thorpe	6	50.0	No second count –
Emlyn Hooson	3	25.0	Hooson and
Eric Lubbock	3	25.0	Lubbock withdrew

1976 7 July

OMOV ballot[†]	Votes	%
David Steel	12,541	64.1
John Pardoe	7,032	35.9

Source: D. Butler and G. Butler, *Twentieth-Century British Political Facts, 1900–2000* (Basingstoke: Palgrave, 2000), p. 165.
Notes: *Parliamentary ballot*: alternative-vote system used but tie for last place in 1967.
[†]OMOV ballots in local parties with weighted votes

Social Democratic Party

1982 2 July

OMOV ballot	Votes	%
Roy Jenkins	26,256	55.7
David Owen	20,864	44.3
Turnout: 75.6%		

1983 21 June

David Owen	Owen declared leader after being only candidate to be nominated

1987 29 August

Robert Maclennan	Maclennan declared leader after being only candidate to be nominated

Source: I. Crewe and A. King, *SDP: The Birth, Life and Death of the Social Democratic Party* (Oxford: Oxford University Press, 1995), pp. 161, 303, 411.

Liberal Democrats

1988   28 July
OMOV ballot   Votes   %
Paddy Ashdown   41,401   71.9
Alan Beith   16,202   28.1
Turnout: 71.9%

1999   9 August

OMOV ballot	First count		Second count		Third count		Fourth count	
	Votes	%	Votes	%	Votes	%	Votes	%
Charles Kennedy	22,724	44.6	23,619	46.5	25,164	49.7	28,425	56.6
Simon Hughes	16,233	31.8	17,378	34.2	19,360	38.3	21,833	43.4
Malcolm Bruce	4,643	9.1	5,241	10.3	6,068	12.0	–	–
Jackie Ballard	3,978	7.8	4,605	9.1	–	–	–	–
David Rendel	3,428	6.7	–	–	–	–	–	–
Non-transferable	–	(–)	163	(0.3)	414	(0.8)	748	(1.5)

Turnout: 61.6%

2006   2 March

OMOV ballot	First count		Second count	
	Votes	%	Votes	%
Menzies Campbell	23,264	44.7	29,697	57.9
Chris Huhne	16,691	32.1	21,628	42.1
Simon Hughes	12,081	23.2	–	–
Non-transferable	–	(–)	711	(1.4)

Turnout: 72%

2007   18 December
OMOV ballot   Votes   %
Nick Clegg   20,988   50.6
Chris Huhne   20,477   49.4
Turnout: 64%

Sources: D. Butler and G. Butler, *Twentieth-Century British Political Facts, 1900–2000* (Basingstoke: Palgrave, 2000), p. 169; H. Smith, 'The 1988 Leadership Campaign', *Journal of Liberal Democrat History*, 24 (1999), 18–22, pp. 18, 22, n. 1; K. Alderman and N. Carter, 'The Liberal Democrat Leadership Election of 1999', *Parliamentary Affairs*, 53:2 (2000), 311–27, p. 324; BBC, 'Q&A: Lib Dem election', *BBC News*, 2 March 2006, available at <http://news.bbc.co.uk/1/hi/uk_politics/4588442.stm>; T. Branigan, 'Clegg seeks new dawn for his party, and for politics', *Guardian*, 19 December 2007.
Note: Alternative-vote system

Appendix D   Green Party of England and Wales

Like ecological parties in other European countries, the Green Party of England and Wales has a strong participatory ethos and was at first ideologically opposed to the notion of a single leader. In the 1980s, it elected six speakers and three party chairs.[1] After the Greens' success in winning 15 percent of the votes (but no seats) in the 1989 UK European parliamentary elections, some in the party argued for a more centralised structure. In 1991, they persuaded the party to streamline its leadership, with two principal speakers, elected by one member-one vote (OMOV), and one party chair.[2] One of these speakers would be male and one female.

In order to capitalise on Green electoral successes in the 2004 European parliamentary elections and the 2004 London assembly elections, some modernisers argued in favour of moving to a more conventional leadership structure.[3] In 2007, an all-member ballot was held to determine whether the party should replace its principal speakers with leaders. Caroline Lucas, one of the party's incumbent principal speakers, supported it, claiming '[m]ost people don't relate to abstract concepts; rather they relate to the people who espouse and embody them. A leader and deputy leader, or two co-leaders, would act as recognisable and inspiring voices for the thousands of dedicated party activists who collectively make the party what it is.'[4] Just under half of the party's members participated in the ballot and 73 percent supported the move.[5]

The new rules for leadership elections and evictions are set out in Clause 8 of the party's constitution.[6] Provisions are made either for a single leader and deputy leader or for two co-leaders, with one from each sex. Candidates must declare whether they are running jointly to share the job or are running to be the sole leader. They cannot choose to run both as co-leaders and as sole leaders. All candidates seeking to stand for election must be nominated by 20 party members. Elections take place every two years. Voting is through an OMOV postal ballot of party members, with the result announced at the autumn conference. The votes of the leadership election are counted first. If co-leaders are elected, then the votes of the deputy leadership election are not counted, as there is no deputy role under co-leaders.

If the leader or one of the co-leaders resigned, there would be a by-election for both leader and deputy-leader positions or for both co-leader positions. However, if the deputy leader resigned, there would be a by-election for only that position. The leader or co-leaders can also be removed by the party. First, if 10 percent of party members petition the Regional Council, a central party body, to recall the leader or co-leaders, then a new election will take place. The incumbents are permitted to participate in this election. Second, the Regional Council can, by a two-thirds majority, recall the leader or deputy leader, or co-leaders and hold a new leadership election, until which the recalled official(s) would be under suspension.

The Green Party held its first leadership election under the new rules in 2008. In the OMOV ballot, Lucas overwhelmingly defeated Ashley Gunstock (Table D.1).

Table D.1   Green Party Leadership Election 2008

	5 September	
OMOV ballot	Votes	%
Caroline Lucas	2,559	92.4
Ashley Gunstock	210	7.6
Turnout: see note below table		

Source: 'Greens' new leader', *Sunday Express*, 7 September 2008.
Note: In its accounts submitted to the Electoral Commission, the Green Party reported its membership as 7,553 on 31 December 2008. On that basis, turnout in the 2008 leadership election was approximately 37%.

Appendix E United Kingdom Independence Party

The UK Independence Party (UKIP) was founded in 1993 to campaign for the withdrawal of the UK from the European Union. Since then, it has gradually grown in size, both in terms of membership (which was over 16,000 in 2009) and votes won in elections. The party won 920,000 votes in the 2010 UK general election, which left it in fourth place behind the three major parties, although it did not win any seats. However, it finished in second place, ahead of Labour and the Liberal Democrats, in the 2009 European parliamentary elections, winning 13 seats under the list-PR electoral system.

UKIP's leadership-selection rules are set out in the party's constitution.[7] Leaders serve four-year terms, although they can be extended by the party's ruling National Executive Committee (NEC) on a two-thirds majority to fight a general election or European election. Leadership elections are called when the leader either resigns, is incapacitated or dies; completes his/her four-year term; or is defeated in a no-confidence vote by the NEC. However, a leader so defeated is still entitled to stand in the subsequent leadership election. All candidates who wish to stand in a leadership contest must provide the signature of a proposer and 50 assentors, all of whom must be party members of good standing drawn from at least ten constituency associations or branches. If only one candidate is nominated, s/he is declared elected without the need for a ballot. If there are two or more candidates, they go forward to an all-member postal ballot using the plurality electoral system.

UKIP's first leader and founder was the academic, Alan Sked.[8] After a poor performance in the 1997 general election, in which UKIP was eclipsed by Sir James Goldsmith's short-lived Referendum Party in the battle for Eurosceptic votes, Sked resigned and left the party. The dissolution of the Referendum Party following Goldsmith's death gave UKIP some space to grow. Over the next few years, it suffered bouts of infighting and went through three leaders: Michael Holmes, Jeffrey Titford (both MEPs) and Roger Knapman, a former Tory MP, who led the party for four years from 2002 to 2006. In 2004, Knapman withstood an attempt by the television personality and former Labour MP, Robert Kilroy-Silk, to seize the leadership of the party. Kilroy-Silk departed to form his own short-lived Eurosceptic party, Veritas.

Knapman decided not to stand for re-election at the end of his constitutionally-prescribed four-year term and in the following leadership election, Nigel Farage, an MEP, was elected (see Table E.1). Farage led UKIP in its successful European parliamentary election campaign of 2009 but decided to stand down that year in order to concentrate on fighting for the Buckingham parliamentary seat in the 2010 general election. The leadership contest that followed was won by Lord Pearson of Rannoch, after he campaigned to broaden UKIP's focus from European affairs to include such issues as the threat posed by Islamic fundamentalism.[9] However, Pearson's reign was brief as he resigned after the 2010 general election, admitting that he was 'not much good at party politics'.[10] In the subsequent leadership election, Farage was elected as leader for the second time, claiming over 60 percent of the vote (Table E.1).

Table E.1   UKIP Leadership Elections 2006–10

2006	12 September	
OMOV ballot	Votes	%
Nigel Farage	3,329	45.0
Richard Suchorzewski	1,782	24.1
David Campbell-Bannerman	1,443	19.5
David Noakes	851	11.5
Turnout: see note below table		
2009	27 November	
OMOV ballot	Votes	%
Lord Pearson of Rannoch	4,743	47.7
Gerard Batten	2,571	25.9
Nikki Sinclaire	1,214	12.2
Mike Nattrass	1,092	11.0
Alan Wood	315	3.2
Turnout: see note below table		
2010	5 November	
OMOV ballot	Votes	%
Nigel Farage	6,085	60.5
Tim Congdon	2,037	20.3
David Campbell-Bannerman	1,404	14.0
Winston McKenzie	530	5.3
Turnout: 65.1%		

Sources: T. Branigan, 'Nigel Farage wins Ukip leadership contest', *Guardian*, 13 September 2006; BBC, 'Lord Pearson elected leader of UK Independence Party', *BBC News*, 27 November 2009, available at <http://news.bbc.co.uk/1/hi/uk_politics/8381992.stm>; Jonathan Arnott (UKIP general secretary), private communication, 2 April 2011.
Note: In its accounts submitted to the Electoral Commission, UKIP reported its membership as approximately 16,000 on 31 December 2006 and 16,252 on 31 December 2009. On those figures, turnout in the 2006 leadership election was approximately 46% while in 2009 it was approximately 61%.

Appendix F British National Party

The British National Party (BNP) is a nationalist and anti-immigration party. It is regularly described as being on the far-right of British politics and is sometimes described as a fascist party.[11] The BNP was formed in 1982 at a time when the previous major force on the British far-right, the National Front, was disintegrating amid in-fighting. Despite regularly fielding candidates in general elections, the BNP has never attained representation in the UK parliament. However, at the 2010 general election, it won 564,000 votes, its best-ever performance, and followed a period in which it had won two seats in the European parliament and one in the London assembly.

From its formation, the BNP was led by John Tyndall, a former leader of the National Front. In 1999, Tyndall was challenged by Nick Griffin, representing a younger generation seeking to 'modernise' the party.[12] Griffin won the subsequent one member-one vote (OMOV) ballot convincingly (Table F.1).

Table F.1 BNP Leadership Election 1999

	28 September	
OMOV ballot	Votes	%
Nick Griffin	1,082	72.5
John Tyndall*	411	27.5
Turnout: 80%		

Source: N. Copsey, *Contemporary British Fascism: The British National Party and the Quest for Legitimacy*, 2nd ed. (Basingstoke: Palgrave Macmillan, 2008), p. 100.
*Incumbent

Since Griffin's election, the BNP's leadership-election rules have continued to specify OMOV postal ballots using the plurality electoral system. However, there have been numerous changes over the years.[13] Previously, contests could take place annually provided that candidates came forward but as of 2011, party chairmen (i.e. leaders) would serve four-year terms. Candidates for the post of chairman must have been party members for at least five years and attained the status of 'voting member', a special category of membership bestowed on individual members who have satisfied certain criteria, such as acknowledged service to the party or attending training sessions. (Voting rights in leadership contests are not restricted to 'voting members', but extend to all individual members of two years' standing.)

There were unsuccessful challenges to Griffin in 2010 and 2011. In 2010, there was discontent within the BNP over his leadership style and the extent of the party's debts. The BNP was also embroiled in a legal dispute with the

Equality and Human Rights Commission, which argued that the party's constitution violated race-relations laws because it restricted membership to 'indi-
genous British' people, widely interpreted to mean 'white'. After the case went
to court, the BNP conceded and agreed to revise its constitution.[14] Griffin was
challenged for the leadership by three candidates, although none was able to
secure sufficient nominations to instigate a ballot (this threshold had recently
been set at 20 percent of individual members).[15]

In 2011, the party's leadership rules were modified once more and the nomination threshold was reduced to ten members of two years' standing, although
candidates also had to put up a deposit of £500, returnable if they secured
5 percent of the votes. Griffin was challenged by Andrew Brons, who, like Griffin,
was an MEP. In a contest that was much closer than expected, Griffin won by
0.4 percent, or nine votes (Table F.2).[16]

Table F.2   BNP Leadership Election 2011

	25 July	
OMOV ballot	Votes	%
Nick Griffin*	1,157	50.2
Andrew Brons	1,148	49.8

Source: BBC, 'Nick Griffin re-elected BNP leader ahead of Andrew Brons', *BBC News*, 25 July
2011, available at <http://www.bbc.co.uk/news/uk-politics-14286110>.
*Incumbent

Appendix G   Scottish National Party

The Scottish National Party (SNP) is a nationalist party that argues for Scottish independence from the UK. It was formed in 1934 but made a major electoral breakthrough in the UK general election of October 1974 when it won 30 per cent of the vote in Scotland and 11 parliamentary seats. Since then, it has won between two and six seats in the Westminster parliament. With the advent of Scottish devolution in 1999, the SNP has focused on winning Scottish parliamentary elections and in 2007, it emerged as the largest party, forming a minority Scottish executive while its leader, Alex Salmond, took the position of Scottish first minister. The SNP won an outright majority in 2011.

The SNP leader was previously elected in a ballot of delegates to the party's national conference each autumn. Salmond became leader in 1990 and remained in post until 2000. At that time, the SNP was engaged in an internal debate over its strategy in the devolution era. 'Gradualists' wanted to adopt an incremental approach to Scottish independence, whereas 'fundamentalists' preferred a more aggressive campaign to deliver independence on a quicker timescale. Many fundamentalists had opposed devolution because they believed it would hinder the campaign for full independence. In the 2000 leadership election, John Swinney, a 'realist', comfortably defeated Alex Neil, a 'fundamentalist' by 547 votes to 268 in a ballot of conference delegates.[17] Three years later, after the SNP's poor performance in Scottish parliamentary elections, Swinney was challenged by Bill Wilson but secured a resounding five-to-one margin of victory at the national conference by 577 votes to 111.[18] Nevertheless, Swinney decided to resign in 2004 after poor results in the European parliamentary elections.

The SNP changed its method of choosing leaders for the 2004 leadership election. According to the new rules, the SNP leader, who also leads the parliamentary group in the Scottish Parliament if s/he is an MSP (Member of the Scottish Parliament), would now be elected annually in an all-member postal ballot. Candidates would need to be nominated by at least 100 members drawn from at least

Table G.1   Scottish National Party Leadership Election 2004

	3 September	
OMOV ballot	Votes	%
Alex Salmond	4,952	75.8
Roseanna Cunningham	953	14.6
Mike Russell	631	9.7
Turnout: 79.2%		

Source: H. Macdonell, 'Salmond retakes SNP leadership by storm', *Scotsman*, 4 September 2004.

20 branches. The incumbent leader is automatically nominated for re-election and if there is only one candidate, no ballot is held and that candidate is declared leader.[19]

In the 2004 contest, Salmond initially indicated that he would not stand for the leadership but later changed his mind. That prompted the withdrawal from the race of Nicola Sturgeon, who instead successfully stood for the position of depute leader. Salmond won an overwhelming victory, taking three-quarters of the vote in a contest against two other candidates (Table G.1).

Appendix H   Plaid Cymru

Plaid Cymru is a Welsh nationalist party that was formed in 1925. Since 1974, it has won between two and four seats in Westminster elections, but with devolution to Wales in 1999, the party has prioritised Welsh assembly elections. It finished second to Labour in terms of both votes and seats in the first three elections to the national assembly for Wales, but came third in 2011.

Until the devolution era, Plaid Cymru's president was deemed to be the party's leader. The president was elected in a ballot of individual party members. The formation of the national assembly required the party to have a leader in the legislative body and when devolution commenced in 1999, the incumbent president, Dafydd Wigley, assumed the leadership of the Plaid group in the assembly. In 2000, Wigley stood down for health reasons and he was succeeded by Ieuan Wyn Jones. Poor results for Plaid in the 2003 assembly elections led Jones to resign but after grassroots anger at a perceived plot by Plaid assembly members to remove him, he decided to run again for the position of leader of the assembly group, but not president and therefore not formally for the overall party leadership.[20] In a postal ballot of party members using the alternative-vote system, he narrowly defeated Helen Mary Jones in the second count (Table H.1). Dafydd Iwan replaced Ieuan Wyn Jones as president. The split between the two posts was formalised in 2006 when the party's leader in the national assembly was designated as its overall leader. The separately-elected president is now the leader of the voluntary party.[21] From 2006, therefore, Ieuan Wyn Jones officially became party leader by virtue of already being its assembly-group leader, although there was no new election. Elections to both the presidency and the party leadership take place every two years provided that there is a vacancy or a candidate decides to challenge an incumbent.

Table H.1   Plaid Cymru Leadership Election 2003

	16 September			
OMOV ballot	First count		Second count	
	Votes	%	Votes	%
Ieuan Wyn Jones	2,078	40.1	2,603	50.7
Helen Mary Jones	2,089	40.3	2,532	49.3
Rhodri Glyn Thomas	1,014	19.6	–	–
Non-transferable	–	(–)	46	(0.9)
Turnout: 61%				

Sources: Plaid Cymru HQ, private communication, 16 February 2011; Roy Jones, 'Politicians' pantomime', *Morning Star*, 20 September 2003.

Appendix I Labour Party Leaders in Scotland and Wales

Labour uses tripartite electoral colleges to elect its leaders in the Scottish parliament and the Welsh assembly. In Scottish Labour leadership elections the elected representatives section consists of Scottish Labour MPs, MEPs and MSPs; in the members section, individual Scottish party members vote in a postal ballot; and the affiliates section involves a postal ballot of trade unionists and socialist-society members in Scotland. Candidates must receive the nominations of 12.5 percent of Labour MSPs to enter a contest. A similar system applies in Wales, involving Welsh party members, individual members of Welsh affiliated organisations, and Welsh Labour AMs, MPs and MEPs. The alternative vote is used in all sections of both electoral colleges. The most recently-elected leaders were Iain Gray in Scotland in 2008 and Carwyn Jones who became Welsh first minister in 2009 (Tables I.1 and I.2). Gray resigned after Labour's poor results in the 2011 Scottish elections

Table I.1 Scottish Labour Party Leadership Election 2008

Electoral college (1/3-1/3-1/3)	MSPs, MPs, MEPs %	13 September		Total %
		Individual members %	Members of affiliates %	
First count				
Iain Gray	53.7	45.2	39.2	46.0
Cathy Jamieson	26.8	30.8	42.3	33.3
Andy Kerr	19.5	24.0	18.6	20.7
Second count				
Iain Gray	67.6	57.3	48.5	57.8
Cathy Jamieson	32.4	42.7	51.5	42.2

Source: Scottish Labour Party HQ, private communication, 9 June 2011.

Table I.2 Welsh Labour Party Leadership Election 2009

Electoral college (1/3-1/3-1/3)	AMs, MPs, MEPs %	1 December		Total %
		Individual members %	Members of affiliates %	
Carwyn Jones	50.9	53.7	51.3	52.0
Edwina Hart	28.3	25.3	33.9	29.2
Huw Lewis	20.8	21.0	14.8	18.8

Source: M. Shipton and D. Williamson, 'It's Carwyn', *Western Mail*, 2 December 2009.

and at the time of writing, a leadership contest was being organised. (The result of this contest and others listed in this book can be obtained from the author's website at <http://wwwprivate.essex.ac.uk/~tquinn/>.) It was also announced that Gray's successor would become the official leader of the entire Scottish Labour Party and not only the leader of the Labour group in the Scottish parliament, as had previously been the case.

The Scottish Labour Party used an electoral college for the first time in 2008 because three of the four previous Labour leaders in the devolution era were elected unopposed. The fourth, Henry McLeish, was chosen in a ballot of Labour MSPs and Labour's Scottish Executive in 2001 because there was not enough time to organise an election in the electoral college given that McLeish was to become first minister.[22]

The Welsh Labour Party used electoral colleges in 1998 and 1999 to elect Ron Davies and Alun Michael respectively. Controversy surrounded the use of block voting by trade unions in the affiliates section, particularly in 1999, when the national party was accused of preventing Rhodri Morgan from becoming Labour's leader in Wales.[23] In the event, Michael was forced to resign after less than a year and Morgan took over unchallenged. He eventually stood down in 2009, by which time the members and affiliates sections used one member-one vote.

Appendix J Conservative Party Leaders in Scotland and Wales

Before the era of devolution, the Scottish Conservatives did not have a formal leader, although the party's national leader appointed a Scottish chairman and a (shadow) secretary of state for Scotland. However, with the advent of devolution, a leader was needed for the Tory group in the Scottish parliament. In an ad hoc secret ballot of senior party officials, including Tory candidates, constituency chairmen, area officers and the party's Scottish executive, David McLetchie defeated Phil Gallie in September 1998. McLetchie resigned after a scandal in 2005 and was replaced by fellow MSP, Annabel Goldie, who was elected unopposed.[24] Goldie served for six years but after disappointing results in the Scottish parliamentary election of May 2011 she announced her intention to step down once the party had chosen a successor. At the time of writing, the Scottish Conservatives were organising an all-member ballot (in the event of more than one candidate standing) to find Goldie's replacement. (The result of this contest and the Welsh Conservative contest of 2011 (see below) can be obtained from the author's website at <http://wwwprivate.essex.ac.uk/~tquinn/>.)

The Conservatives' first Welsh leader in the devolved era was Rod Richards, a former MP. He comfortably defeated Nick Bourne, by 3,873 votes to 2,798 in a postal ballot of party members in Wales in November 1998.[25] Richards' tenure was short-lived as he was forced to stand aside after allegations of an assault. In the leadership election that followed, Bourne was the only candidate to be nominated among the nine Conservative AMs and he was duly acclaimed leader without the need for a ballot.[26] Bourne held the post until May 2011 when he lost his seat in the Welsh assembly elections. In July 2011, the Welsh Conservatives held a postal ballot of the party's 5,000 individual members to elect Bourne's successor. Two candidates, Andrew R. T. Davies and Nick Ramsay, each secured the necessary three nominations from fellow Tory AMs to contest the election. According to incomplete figures released by the party, Davies defeated Ramsay by 53.1 percent to 46.7 percent on a turnout of 49 percent. Ramsay's campaign manager, Jonathan Morgan, claimed that Davies's margin of victory was 153 votes, although that was not officially confirmed by the party.[27]

Appendix K Liberal Democrat Leaders in Scotland and Wales

As a federal party, the Liberal Democrats had Scottish and Welsh leaders before devolution. However, the posts of leaders of the respective state parties and leaders of the party's elected representatives in the Scottish parliament and Welsh assembly have come to be combined. Scottish Liberal Democrat leaders must be MSPs and while there is no formal requirement for the Welsh party leader to be a member of the national assembly for Wales, the current leader is an AM. Both state parties select their leaders through postal ballots of members in their respective territories using the alternative vote.

Jim Wallace was the Scottish Liberal Democrats' first leader in the era of devolution having been elected unopposed in 1992. In 1999, Wallace became Scotland's deputy first minister before stepping down in 2005. He was replaced as leader and deputy first minister by Nicol Stephen, who easily defeated Mike Rumbles (Table K.1). Stephen served for three years as leader, by which time the Liberal Democrats were no longer in the executive. He stood down in 2008 and in the ensuing leadership contest, Tavish Scott won the membership ballot on the first count against two other MSPs (Table K.2). Scott resigned after the Liberal Democrats' poor showing in the 2011 Scottish parliamentary election, as the party

Table K.1   Scottish Liberal Democrat Leadership Election 2005

| OMOV ballot | 23 June | |
	Votes	%
Nicol Stephen	2,108	76.7
Mike Rumbles	642	23.3
Turnout: 65.3%		

Source: D. Fraser, 'Stephen takes aim at Labour seats after party vote', *Glasgow Herald*, 24 June 2005.

Table K.2   Scottish Liberal Democrat Leadership Election 2008

| OMOV ballot | 26 August | |
	Votes	%
Tavish Scott	1,450	59.0
Ross Finnie	568	23.1
Mike Rumbles	439	17.9
Turnout: 61%		

Source: R. Dinwoodie, 'Tavish Scott takes LibDem gold', *Glasgow Herald*, 27 August 2008.

lost 12 of its 17 seats. William Rennie was the only one of the remaining five Liberal Democrat MSPs to declare his candidacy and he was announced leader without the need for a ballot in May 2011.

From the opening of the Welsh assembly, Mike German led the six-strong group of Liberal Democrat AMs. However, he was not made official leader of the Welsh Liberal Democrats overall until November 2007, when he was the sole nominee to replace Lembit Öpik. German's intention was to hold the position only temporarily until he could oversee reviews of the party's campaigns and policy-making, and he stood down in December 2008. In the following leadership contest, Kirsty Williams became the party's first female leader when she defeated fellow AM, Jenny Randerson in a ballot of Welsh party members (Table K.3).

Table K.3 Welsh Liberal Democrat Leadership Election 2008

	8 December	
OMOV ballot	Votes	%
Kirsty Williams	910	59.8
Jenny Randerson	612	40.2
Turnout: 69.4%		

Sources: D. Williamson, 'Kirsty Williams, 37, elected to lead the Welsh Lib Dems', *Western Mail*, 9 December 2008; T. Bodden, 'Kirsty is voted Lib Dem leader', *Liverpool Daily Post*, 9 December 2008.

Appendix L Donations to Candidates in Party Leadership Contests 2001–10

The source for all tables in this appendix is the Electoral Commission's Register of Donations to Regulated Donees. Loans are reported in the Register of Borrowings by Regulated Donees. Both registers are available at <http://registers.electoral-commission.org.uk/regulatory-issues/registers.cfm>. The Electoral Commission separates donations made to politicians in their capacity as elected representatives in furtherance of their parliamentary duties and as members of registered parties in the pursuit of internal offices and similar matters. Some politicians, therefore, have two entries on the register. The data below relate solely to those entries for intra-party purposes. I thank Steven Huntingdon of the Electoral Commission for clarifying some of the entries in these tables in a private communication. Any remaining errors are mine alone. These tables include only donations of £1,000 and above for 2001–09 (£1,500 and above for 2010); donations below this level did not need to be reported to the Electoral Commission.

In the tables below, all figures are pounds sterling (£) and not adjusted for inflation. Entries are separated into cash and non-cash donations, with the latter including such things as the provision of office facilities, catering, transportation and so on. Details of loans and securities worth £1,000 or more are provided from 2006 onwards, when the law was changed to require loans to be reported (the threshold was raised to £1,500 in 2010). Any such loans and securities are provided in the notes under each table.

(1) Labour Party

2007 Leadership Contest

	Cash (£)	Non-cash (£)	Total (£)
Gordon Brown	196,700	19,005	215,705
John McDonnell	7,000	0	7,000
Total	203,700	19,005	222,705

2010 Leadership Contest

	Cash (£)	Non-cash (£)	Total (£)
Diane Abbott	13,000	0	13,000
Ed Balls	155,710	2,400	158,110
Andy Burnham	46,000	2,400	48,400
David Miliband	486,450	137,359	623,809
Ed Miliband	321,526	15,250	336,776
Total	1,022,686	157,409	1,180,095

Notes: Burnham also received £21,493 in loans and Balls received £12,925 as security against rental payments for office facilities during the leadership contest. Ed Miliband's total excludes an impermissible cash donation of £1,480 that was later returned to the donor.

(2) Conservative Party

2001 Leadership Contest

	Cash (£)	Non-cash (£)	Total (£)
Michael Ancram	30,000	3,000	33,000
Kenneth Clarke	93,000	0	93,000
David Davis	16,500	1,750	18,250
Iain Duncan Smith	88,000	12,008	100,008
Michael Portillo	91,113	4,967	96,080
Total	318,613	21,725	340,338

2003 Leadership Contest

	Cash (£)	Non-cash (£)	Total (£)
Michael Howard	75,001	0	75,001
Total	75,001	0	75,001

2005 Leadership Contest

	Cash (£)	Non-cash (£)	Total (£)
David Cameron	425,500	84,485	509,985
Kenneth Clarke	94,500	0	94,500
David Davis	284,500	6,800	291,300
Liam Fox	57,500	9,000	66,500
Malcolm Rifkind	50,000	0	50,000
Total	912,000	100,285	1,012,285

(3) Liberal Democrats

2006 Leadership Contest

	Cash (£)	Non-cash (£)	Total (£)
Menzies Campbell	43,000	1,735	44,735
Chris Huhne	30,900	0	30,900
Simon Hughes	25,000	1,000	26,000
Total	98,900	2,735	101,635

2007 Leadership Contest

	Cash (£)	Non-cash (£)	Total (£)
Nick Clegg	77,500	6,000	83,500
Chris Huhne	55,000	2,000	57,000
Total	132,500	8,000	140,500

Appendix M   Proposed Labour Leadership Election Timetable 2009

Monday November 16
Tuesday
Wednesday   *Queens Speech*
                            PLP Chair nominations open
Thursday   *European Summit*
Friday
Saturday
Sunday

Monday November 23   *PLP Chair Nominations close*
Tuesday   *Key meets/Resignation*
Wednesday   *Cabinet, NEC*
                            Timetable and Process announced
                            PLP and Supporting Nominations Open
Thursday   *PLP MEETING*
                            Queen's Speech votes
Friday   *PLP Nominations Close*
Saturday
Sunday

Monday November 30   *Confidence Motion in Parliament*
Tuesday   *All Ballot Papers distributed*
Wednesday
Thursday
Friday
Saturday
Sunday

Monday December 7
Tuesday
Wednesday   *Pre Budget Report*
Thursday
Friday
Saturday   *Closing date for ballot*
Sunday

Monday December 14   *Special Labour Party Conference, London*
                            New Leader selected
Tuesday   *PM Resigns, new PM installed*
Wednesday   *PMQs, House rises for Christmas recess*

Thursday December 17
Friday

Whole timetable is 21 days (November 23–December 15)
24 days less than Blair/Brown timetable, which was 45 days (May 10–June 25)
The changes are made up of:

- 2 days from resignation to opening of nominations (cf 4 days Blair/Brown timetable)
- Supporting nominations phase removed, so 2 days between open and close of nominations (cf 17 day gap in Blair/Brown timetable)
- 4 days from nominations close to ballot distribution (1 day less than Blair/Brown timetable)
- 11 days from issue of ballot papers to close of ballots (cf 12 days Blair/Brown timetable)
- 3 days from close of ballots to Declaration/Leadership Conference (cf 6 days Blair/Brown timetable)

The NEC needs to remove the 'supporting nominations' phase', which actually adds almost nothing to the democracy of the election process.

Source: Rt Hon. Charles Clarke, private communication, 23 February 2011. Reproduced verbatim with permission.

Notes

Introduction

1 M. Foley, *The British Presidency: Tony Blair and the Politics of Public Leadership* (Manchester: Manchester University Press, 2000); R. Heffernan and P. Webb, 'The British Prime Minister: Much More than "First Among Equals"', in T. Poguntke and P. Webb (eds), *The Presidentialization of Politics: A Comparative Study of Modern Democracies* (Oxford: Oxford University Press, 2005), pp. 26–62.

2 J. Bartle and I. Crewe, 'Party Leaders in Great Britain', in A. King (ed.), *Leaders' Personalities and the Outcomes of Democratic Elections* (Oxford: Oxford University Press, 2002), pp. 70–95; G. Evans and R. Anderson, 'The Impact of Party Leaders: How Blair Lost Labour Votes', in P. Norris and C. Wlezien (eds), *Britain Votes 2005* (Oxford: Oxford University Press, 2005), pp. 162–80.

3 N. Allen, J. Bara and J. Bartle, 'A Much Debated Campaign', in N. Allen and J. Bartle (eds), *Britain at the Polls 2010* (London: Sage, 2011), pp. 175–202.

4 For a major contribution to this debate, see G. Tsebelis, *Veto Players: How Political Institutions Work* (New York & Princeton: Russell Sage Foundation & Princeton University Press, 2002).

5 W. Cross and A. Blais, 'Who Selects the Party Leader?', *Party Politics* (2011, forthcoming).

6 P. Seyd, *The Rise and Fall of the Labour Left* (Basingstoke: Macmillan, 1987).

7 Cross and Blais, 'Who Selects the Party Leader?'

8 P. Webb, *The Modern British Party System* (London: Sage, 2000), p. 193; J. Marshall, 'Membership of UK Political Parties', *House of Commons Standard Note SN/SG/5125* (London: House of Commons Library, 2009), p. 9.

9 L. P. Stark, *Choosing a Leader: Party Leadership Contests in Britain from Macmillan to Blair* (Basingstoke: Macmillan, 1996). Another important study that informs the present one is R. M. Punnett, *Selecting the Party Leader: Britain in Comparative Perspective* (Hemel Hempstead: Harvester Wheatsheaf, 1992).

10 Stark, *Choosing a Leader*, p. 9.

Chapter 1   Electing and Ejecting Party Leaders

1 Conservative Party, *The Fresh Future* (London: Conservative Party, 1998).

2 Similar trends are evident in other countries. See L. LeDuc, 'Democratizing Party Leadership Selection', *Party Politics*, 7:3 (2001), 323–41.

3 W. Cross and A. Blais, 'Who Selects the Party Leader?', *Party Politics* (forthcoming, 2011).

4 See T. Quinn, 'Leasehold or Freehold? Leader-Eviction Rules in the British Conservative and Labour Parties', *Political Studies*, 53:4 (2005), 793–815.

5 An exception is O. Kenig, 'Classifying Party Leaders' Selection Methods in Parliamentary Democracies', *Journal of Elections, Public Opinion and Parties*, 19:4 (2009), 433–47.

6 For example, T. Heppell, *Choosing the Tory Leader: Conservative Party Leadership Elections from Heath to Cameron* (London: IB Tauris, 2008).
7 D. Kogan and M. Kogan, *The Battle for the Labour Party* (London: Fontana, 1982).
8 M. Ostrogorski, *Democracy and the Organization of Political Parties* (Chicago: Quadrangle Books, 1964).
9 J. D. May, 'Opinion Structure of Political Parties: The Special Law of Curvilinear Disparity', *Political Studies*, 21:2 (1973), 135–51.
10 H. Kitschelt, 'The Internal Politics of Parties: The Special Law of Curvilinear Disparity Revisited', *Political Studies*, 37:3 (1989), 400–21; T. Iversen, 'The Logics of Electoral Politics: Spatial, Directional, and Mobilizational Effects', *Comparative Political Studies*, 27:2 (1994), 155–89; P. Norris, 'May's Law of Curvilinear Disparity Revisited: Leaders, Officers, Members and Voters in British Political Parties', *Party Politics*, 1:1 (1995), 29–47.
11 T. Quinn, *Modernising the Labour Party: Organisational Change since 1983* (Basingstoke: Palgrave Macmillan, 2004); M. Russell, *Building New Labour: The Politics of Party Organisation* (Basingstoke: Palgrave Macmillan, 2005).
12 Quinn, *Modernising the Labour Party*, p. 28.
13 A. Downs, *An Economic Theory of Democracy* (New York: Harper & Row, 1957).
14 L. P. Stark, *Choosing a Leader: Party Leadership Contests in Britain from Macmillan to Blair* (Basingstoke: Macmillan, 1996), pp. 125–6; G. Sjöblom, *Party Strategies in a Multiparty System* (Lund: Studentlitteratur, 1968).
15 Stark, *Choosing a Leader*, p. 126.
16 H. Drucker, 'Changes in the Labour Party Leadership', *Parliamentary Affairs*, 34:4 (1981), 369–91, pp. 385–6.
17 Stark, *Choosing a Leader*, p. 128.
18 S. Walters, *Tory Wars: Conservatives in Crisis* (London: Politico's, 2001).
19 K. Alderman and N. Carter, 'The Conservative Party Leadership Election of 2001', *Parliamentary Affairs*, 55:4 (2002), 569–85, p. 582.
20 For example, May, 'Opinion Structure of Political Parties'.
21 Cited in Stark, *Choosing a Leader*, p. 128.
22 This approach has previously been used in Quinn, 'Leasehold or Freehold?', pp. 794–8.
23 Downs, *Economic Theory of Democracy*, p. 30.
24 For example, K. Strøm and W. Müller, 'Political Parties and Hard Choices', in W. Müller and K. Strøm (eds), *Policy, Office, or Votes? How Political Parties in Western Europe Make Hard Decisions* (Cambridge: Cambridge University Press, 1999), pp. 1–35.
25 M. Olson, *The Logic of Collective Action: Public Goods and the Theory of Groups* (Cambridge, MA: Harvard University Press, 1971).
26 Rt Hon. Charles Clarke, private interview, Bishopsgate, London, 22 February 2011.
27 For example, T. Quinn, 'Electing the Leader: The British Labour Party's Electoral College', *British Journal of Politics and International Relations*, 6:3 (2004), 333–52, p. 349; P. Dunleavy, 'The Westminster Model and the Distinctiveness of British Politics', in P. Dunleavy, R. Heffernan, P. Cowley and C. Hay (eds), *Developments in British Politics*, 8 (Basingstoke: Palgrave Macmillan, 2006), pp. 315–41, p. 324.
28 Quinn, 'Leasehold or Freehold?', p. 799.

29 P. Norton, 'The Party Leader', in P. Norton (ed.), *The Conservative Party* (London: Prentice Hall-Harvester Wheatsheaf, 1996), pp. 142–56; Quinn, 'Leasehold or Freehold?', pp. 801–2.

30 Strictly speaking, Redwood's candidacy was not a 'challenge' because the previous incumbent, Major, had resigned the leadership. However, for present purposes, it counts as a challenge because Major's resignation was a purely procedural manoeuvre, which was required to instigate a contest.

31 These figures exclude Roy Jenkins, who was unsuccessful in the 1976 Labour leadership contest but left the party to help form the SDP and won that party's 1982 leadership contest.

32 Stark, *Choosing a Leader*, pp. 40, 192, n. 20.

33 Mark Oaten, private interview, Vauxhall, London, 20 May 2010.

34 M. Crick, *Michael Heseltine: A Biography* (London: Hamish Hamilton, 1997), pp. 351–2.

35 K. Alderman, 'Revision of Leadership Election Procedures in the Conservative Party', *Parliamentary Affairs*, 52:2 (1999), 260–74.

36 Liberal Democrats, *The Constitutions of the Liberal Democrats: The Federal Party* (London: Liberal Democrats, 2004), Article 10.2(e).

37 K. Alderman and M. Smith, 'Can British Prime Ministers Be Given the Push by Their Parties?', *Parliamentary Affairs*, 43:3 (1990), 260–76, pp. 261–4.

38 A. Rawnsley, *The End of the Party: The Rice and Fall of New Labour* (London: Viking/Penguin, 2010), p. 400.

39 R. Heffernan, 'Prime Ministerial Predominance? Core Executive Politics in the UK', *British Journal of Politics and International Relations*, 5:3 (2003), 347–72; A. King, 'Ministerial Autonomy in Britain', in M. Laver and K. A. Shepsle (eds), *Cabinet Ministers and Parliamentary Government* (Cambridge: Cambridge University Press, 1994), pp. 203–25; A. King and N. Allen, '"Off With Their Heads": British Prime Ministers and the Power to Dismiss', *British Journal of Political Science*, 40:2 (2010), 249–78.

40 Alderman and Smith, 'Can British Prime Ministers Be Given the Push by Their Parties?', p. 269.

41 B. Pimlott, *Harold Wilson* (London: HarperCollins, 1993), p. 489.

42 P. Mandelson, *The Third Man: Life at the Heart of New Labour* (London: Harper Press, 2010), p. 21.

43 Alderman and Smith, 'Can British Prime Ministers Be Given the Push by Their Parties?', p. 264.

44 For example, P. Jenkins, *The Battle of Downing Street* (London: Charles Knight & Co., 1970), p. 109; Alderman and Smith, 'Can British Prime Ministers Be Given the Push by Their Parties?', pp. 266–7.

45 Pimlott, *Harold Wilson*, pp. 504–5.

46 Cited in V. Bogdanor, 'The Selection of the Party Leader', in A. Seldon and S. Ball (eds), *Conservative Century: The Conservative Party since 1900* (Oxford: Oxford University Press, 1994), pp. 69–96, at p. 93.

47 Alderman and Smith, 'Can British Prime Ministers Be Given the Push by Their Parties?', pp. 262–3.

48 G. Benedetto and S. Hix, 'The Rejected, the Ejected, and the Dejected: Explaining Government Rebels in the 2001–2005 British House of Commons', *Comparative Political Studies*, 40:7 (2007), 755–81.

49 Derek Conway, private interview, Victoria, London, 24 June 2010.

50 Lord Rennard of Wavertree, private interview, Westminster, 15 June 2010.

Chapter 2 Selection and Ejection by the Parliamentary Party

1 T. Bale, *The Conservative Party: From Thatcher to Cameron* (Cambridge: Polity, 2010), pp. 259–60.

2 M. Russell, *Building New Labour: The Politics of Party Organisation* (Basingstoke: Palgrave Macmillan, 2005), pp. 35–9.

3 Conservative Party, *A 21st Century Party* (London: Conservative Party, 2005), p. 15.

4 T. Quinn, 'Leasehold or Freehold? Leader-Eviction Rules in the British Conservative and Labour Parties', *Political Studies*, 53:4 (2005), 793–815, p. 809.

5 R. T. McKenzie, *British Political Parties: The Distribution of Power within the Conservative and Labour Parties*, 2nd ed. (London: Heinemann, 1964), pp. 347–52.

6 McKenzie, *British Political Parties*, pp. 612–28.

7 T. Heppell, *Choosing the Labour Leader: Labour Party Leadership Elections from Wilson to Brown* (London: IB Tauris, 2010), pp. 30–7.

8 H. Drucker, 'Leadership Selection in the Labour Party', *Parliamentary Affairs*, 29:4 (1976), 378–95; Heppell, *Choosing the Labour Leader*, pp. 54–62.

9 P. Seyd, *The Rise and Fall of the Labour Left* (Basingstoke: Macmillan, 1987), pp. 118–21, 128.

10 H. Drucker, 'Changes in the Labour Party Leadership', *Parliamentary Affairs*, 34:4 (1981), 369–81; Heppell, *Choosing the Labour Leader*, pp. 65–87.

11 R. M. Punnett, *Selecting the Party Leader: Britain in Comparative Perspective* (Hemel Hempstead: Harvester Wheatsheaf, 1992), pp. 26–9; V. Bogdanor, 'The Selection of the Party Leader', in A. Seldon and S. Ball (eds), *Conservative Century: The Conservative Party since 1900* (Oxford: Oxford University Press, 1994), pp. 69–96, at pp. 69–74.

12 Punnett, *Selecting the Party Leader*, pp. 38–49; Bogdanor, 'Selection of the Party Leader', pp. 74–80.

13 L. P. Stark, *Choosing a Leader: Party Leadership Contests in Britain from Macmillan to Blair* (Basingstoke: Macmillan, 1996), p. 21. See also A. Watkins. *A Conservative Coup: The Fall of Margaret Thatcher*, 2nd ed. (London: Duckworth, 1991), pp. 156–77.

14 Punnett, *Selecting the Party Leader*, p. 56.

15 Stark, *Choosing a Leader*, pp. 20–6.

16 Stark, *Choosing a Leader*, pp. 26–30.

17 Bogdanor, 'Selection of the Party Leader', pp. 85–6.

18 K. Alderman and M. J. Smith, 'Can British Prime Ministers be Given the Push by Their Parties?', *Parliamentary Affairs*, 43:3 (1990), 260–76, p. 272.

19 D. McSweeney, 'Changing the Rules Changed the Game: Selecting Conservative Leaders', *Party Politics*, 5:4 (1999), 471–83, p. 478.

20 M. Thatcher, *The Path to Power* (London: HarperCollins, 1995), p. 267.

21 P. Cowley and M. Bailey, 'Peasants' Uprising or Religious War? Re-examining the 1975 Conservative Leadership Contest', *British Journal of Political Science*, 30:4 (2000), 599–629.

22 Stark, *Choosing a Leader*, pp. 133–4.

23 Stark, *Choosing a Leader*, pp. 30–1.

24 Punnett, *Selecting the Party Leader*, pp. 131–5.

25 Stark, *Choosing a Leader*, pp. 70–1.

26 M. Prescott and A. Grice, 'Heseltine heart shock dashes leadership hopes', *Sunday Times*, 4 May 1997.

27 P. Webster and A. Pierce, 'Clarke rushes into race for Tory leadership', *Times*, 3 May 1997.

28 M. Garnett, 'Win or Bust: The Leadership Gamble of William Hague', in M. Garnett and P. Lynch (eds), *The Conservatives in Crisis* (Manchester: Manchester University Press, 2003), pp. 49–65, at p. 52; K. Alderman, 'The Conservative Party Leadership Election of 1997', *Parliamentary Affairs*, 51:1 (1998), 1–16, p. 5.

29 Bale, *Conservative Party*, p. 72.

30 T. Heppell and M. Hill, 'The Conservative Party Leadership Election of 1997: An Analysis of the Voting Motivations of Conservative Parliamentarians', *British Politics*, 3:1 (2008), 63–91, p. 87; S. Baxter, 'Eurosceptics hold sway in the reduced Tory ranks', *Sunday Times*, 4 May 1997.

31 P. Cowley and M. Stuart, 'The Conservative Parliamentary Party', in M. Garnett and P. Lynch (eds), *The Conservatives in Crisis* (Manchester: Manchester University Press, 2003), pp. 66–81, at pp. 67–8.

32 Alderman, 'Conservative Party Leadership Election of 1997', p. 9; Heppell and Hill, 'Conservative Party Leadership Election of 1997', p. 86.

33 P. Snowdon, *Back from the Brink: The Inside Story of the Tory Resurrection* (London: Harper Press, 2010), p. 43.

34 Alderman, 'Conservative Party Leadership Election of 1997', p. 11.

35 E. Macaskill, 'Numbers game favours Hague', *Guardian*, 11 June 1997.

36 E. Macaskill, 'Odd couple's whirlwind romance', *Guardian*, 19 June 1997.

37 Alderman, 'Conservative Party Leadership Election of 1997', p. 12.

38 A. Grice and M. Prescott, 'Hague's battle to bind Tory wounds', *Sunday Times*, 22 June 1997.

39 D. Butler and G. Butler, *British Political Facts Since 1979* (Basingstoke: Palgrave Macmillan, 2006), pp. 22–5.

40 Snowdon, *Back from the Brink*, pp. 44–5.

41 T. Heppell, *Choosing the Tory Leader: Conservative Party Leadership Elections from Heath to Cameron* (London: IB Tauris, 2008), p. 118.

42 Heppell and Hill, 'Conservative Party Leadership Election of 1997', p. 78.

43 Heppell and Hill, 'Conservative Party Leadership Election of 1997', pp. 80–2.

44 Alderman, 'Conservative Party Leadership Election of 1997', pp. 11–12; Heppell, *Choosing the Tory Leader: Conservative Party Leadership Elections from Heath to Cameron* (London: IB Tauris, 2008), p. 121.

45 Heppell and Hill, 'Conservative Party Leadership Election of 1997', p. 87.

46 Alderman, 'Conservative Party Leadership Election of 1997', pp. 9–10; Heppell, *Choosing the Tory Leader*, p. 126; Cowley and Stuart, 'Conservative Parliamentary Party', p. 67.

47 Alderman, 'Conservative Party Leadership Election of 1997', p. 11.

48 P. Cowley, 'Beyond Our Ken: The Conservative Leadership Contest of 1997', paper presented to the Centre for Legislative Studies, University of Hull (31 October 1997); Cowley and Stuart, 'Conservative Parliamentary Party', pp. 67–8.

49 Alderman, 'Conservative Party Leadership Election of 1997', p. 5.

50 P. Norton, 'The Conservative Party: Is There Anyone Out There?', in A. King (ed.), *Britain at the Polls 2001* (New York & London: Chatham House Publishers, 2002), pp. 68–94, at p. 72; Cowley, 'Beyond Our Ken'.

51 Heppell and Hill, 'Conservative Party Leadership Election of 1997', p. 88.
52 D. Butler, A. Adonis and T. Travers, *Failure in British Government: The Politics of the Poll Tax* (Oxford: Oxford University Press, 1994).
53 H. Young, *One of Us, 3ʳᵈ ed.* (London: Pan Books, 1993), pp. 549–51.
54 Young, *One of Us*, pp. 562–3.
55 Young, *One of Us*, pp. 576–82.
56 P. Norton, 'Choosing a Leader: Margaret Thatcher and the Parliamentary Conservative Party 1989–1990', *Parliamentary Affairs*, 43:3 (1990), 249–59, p. 254.
57 M. Crick, *Michael Heseltine: A Biography* (London: Hamish Hamilton, 1997), pp. 337–8.
58 G. Howe, *Conflict of Loyalty* (London: Macmillan, 1994), pp. 655–68.
59 Crick, *Michael Heseltine*, p. 344; M. Heseltine, *Life in the Jungle: My Autobiography* (London: Hodder & Stoughton, 2000), pp. 362, 369.
60 Young, *One of Us*, p. 582.
61 For example, see K. Alderman and N. Carter, 'A Very Tory Coup: The Ousting of Mrs Thatcher', *Parliamentary Affairs*, 44:2 (1991), 125–39; Heppell, *Choosing the Tory Leader*, pp. 71–93; Punnett, *Selecting the Party Leader*, pp. 63–72; M. Thatcher, *The Downing Street Years* (London: HarperCollins, 1993), pp. 829–62; Heseltine, *Life in the Jungle*, pp. 361–74; J. Major, *John Major: The Autobiography* (London: HarperCollins, 1999), pp. 167–201; Howe, *Conflict of Loyalty*, pp. 655–76; Young, *One of Us*, pp. 571–91.
62 Thatcher, *Downing Street Years*, pp. 850–5.
63 Major, *John Major*, p. 192.
64 Crick, *Michael Heseltine*, pp. 351–2.
65 P. Cowley and J. Garry, 'The British Conservative Party and Europe: The Choosing of John Major', *British Journal of Political Science*, 28:3 (1998), 473–99.
66 G. W. Jones, 'The Downfall of Margaret Thatcher', in R. A. W. Rhodes and P. Dunleavy (eds), *Prime Minister, Cabinet and Core Executive* (Basingstoke: Macmillan, 1995), pp. 87–107, at p. 101.
67 Alderman and Carter, 'A Very Tory Coup', p. 139.
68 Thatcher, *Downing Street Years*, p. 849.
69 Alderman and Carter, 'A Very Tory Coup', p. 136.
70 Bogdanor, 'Selection of the Party Leader', pp. 89–92.
71 '[W]hat this cabinet procession was doing was essentially to respond not to its own bold tendency towards rebellion, which had been shown over so many years barely to exist, but to the instinct for survival displayed by the backbench members of the party. It was, in that sense, the party and not the cabinet that pushed its leader out.' Young, *One of Us*, p. 590.
72 Lord Howard of Lympne, private interview, London School of Economics, 9 June 2010.
73 J. Tomlinson, *The Labour Governments 1964–1970, Volume 3: Economic Policy* (Manchester: Manchester University Press, 2004).
74 P. Jenkins, *The Battle of Downing Street* (London: Charles Knight & Co., 1970); B. Pimlott, *Harold Wilson* (London: HarperCollins, 1993), pp. 527–44.
75 H. Pelling and A. Reid, *A Short History of the Labour Party, 11ᵗʰ ed.* (Basingstoke: Macmillan, 1996), p. 130.
76 Pimlott, *Harold Wilson*, p. 554.

77 Pimlott, *Harold Wilson*, p. 499.
78 Pimlott, *Harold Wilson*, pp. 490–1, 504–5, 535–40; Jenkins, *Battle of Downing Street*, pp. 98–123.
79 Alderman and Smith, 'Can British Prime Ministers Be Given the Push by Their Parties?', pp. 262–3.
80 Jenkins, *Battle of Downing Street*, pp. 108–16.
81 Jenkins, *Battle of Downing Street*, p. 112.
82 Pimlott, *Harold Wilson*, p. 504.
83 Alderman and Smith, 'Can British Prime Ministers Be Given the Push by Their Parties?', p. 266; Jenkins, *Battle of Downing Street*, p. 109.
84 Pimlott, *Harold Wilson*, p. 537.
85 Pimlott, *Harold Wilson*, p. 509.
86 Thatcher, *Downing Street Years*, p. 829.
87 Alderman and Smith, 'Can British Prime Ministers Be Given the Push by Their Parties?', pp. 271, 263, 269. See also N. Allen, 'Labour's Third Term: A Tale of Two Prime Ministers', in N. Allen and J. Bartle (eds), *Britain at the Polls 2010* (London: Sage, 2011), pp. 1–36, at p. 30.
88 Heppell, *Choosing the Tory Leader*, pp. 96–100.
89 K. Alderman, 'The Conservative Party Leadership Election of 1995', *Parliamentary Affairs*, 49:2 (1996), 316–32, pp. 323–4.

Chapter 3   The Labour Party: The Electoral College

1 The most detailed account of the electoral college, and on which the following paragraph is based, is L. P. Stark, *Choosing a Leader: Party Leadership Contests in Britain from Macmillan to Blair* (Basingstoke: Macmillan, 1996), pp. 42–66.
2 Stark, *Choosing a Leader*, pp. 54–6. See also D. Kogan and M. Kogan, *The Battle for the Labour Party* (London: Fontana Paperbacks, 1982), pp. 83–97.
3 Cited in L. Minkin, *The Contentious Alliance: Trade Unions and the Labour Party* (Edinburgh: Edinburgh University Press, 1992), p. 220. See also D. Hayter, *Fightback! Labour's Traditional Right in the 1970s and 1980s* (Manchester: Manchester University Press, 2005), pp. 14–15.
4 See T. Heppell, *Choosing the Labour Leader: Labour Party Leadership Elections from Wilson to Brown* (London: IB Tauris, 2010), pp. 91–100.
5 For a detailed examination of the electoral college, see T. Quinn, 'Electing the Leader: The British Labour Party's Electoral College', *British Journal of Politics and International Relations*, 6:3 (2004), 333–52.
6 R. M. Punnett, *Selecting the Party Leader: Britain in Comparative Perspective* (Hemel Hempstead: Harvester Wheatsheaf, 1992), pp. 112–13, 124–5.
7 Quinn, 'Electing the Leader', pp. 336–9.
8 P. Wintour, 'Labour cuts fees to boost membership', *Guardian*, 29 July 1993.
9 R. M. Punnett, 'Selecting a Leader and Deputy Leader of the Labour Party: The Future of the Electoral College', *Parliamentary Affairs*, 43:2 (1990), 179–95, pp. 187–8.
10 Stark, *Choosing a Leader*, p. 60.
11 Quinn, 'Electing the Leader', pp. 339–40.

12 K. Alderman and N. Carter, 'The Labour Party and the Trade Unions: Loosening the Ties', *Parliamentary Affairs*, 47:3 (1994), 321–37, pp. 322–4.

13 P. Gould, *The Unfinished Revolution: How the Modernisers Saved the Labour Party* (London: Abacus, 1999).

14 M. Russell, *Building New Labour: The Politics of Party Organisation* (Basingstoke: Palgrave Macmillan, 2005), p. 50.

15 Alderman and Carter, 'Labour Party and the Trade Unions', pp. 324–5.

16 K. Alderman and N. Carter, 'The Labour Party Leadership and Deputy Leadership Elections of 1994', *Parliamentary Affairs*, 48:3 (1995), 438–55, pp. 439–40.

17 See Quinn, 'Electing the Leader', pp. 344–5.

18 Stark, *Choosing a Leader*, p. 129.

19 Stark, *Choosing a Leader*, p. 130.

20 Stark, *Choosing a Leader*, pp. 130–1.

21 See H. Drucker, 'Intra-Party Democracy in Action: The Election of Leader and Deputy Leader of the Labour Party in 1983', *Parliamentary Affairs*, 37:3 (1984), 283–300; K. Alderman and N. Carter, 'The Labour Party Leadership and Deputy Leadership Elections of 1992', *Parliamentary Affairs*, 46:1 (1993), 49–65; Alderman and Carter, 'Labour Party Leadership and Deputy Leadership Elections of 1994'; Heppell, *Choosing the Labour Leader*, pp. 89–152.

22 Alderman and Carter, 'Labour Party Leadership and Deputy Leadership Elections of 1994', pp. 439, 442.

23 See A. Rawnsley, *Servants of the People: The Inside Story of New Labour* (London: Penguin, 2001) and *The End of the Party: The Rise and Fall of New Labour* (London: Viking/Penguin, 2010).

24 See Alderman and Carter, 'Labour Party Leadership and Deputy Leadership Elections of 1994'; Heppell, *Choosing the Labour Leader*, pp. 153–71.

25 Stark, *Choosing a Leader*, p. 131.

26 Heppell, *Choosing the Labour Leader*, p. 188.

27 A. Denham and A. Dorey, 'Just the Ticket? The Labour Party's Deputy Leadership Election of 2007', *Political Quarterly*, 78:4 (2007), 527–35.

28 P. Mandelson, *The Third Man: Life at the Heart of New Labour* (London: Harper Press, 2010), pp. 543–51.

29 P. Curtis, 'David Miliband wins key Labour figures' support in leadership race', *Guardian*, 1 September 2010.

30 These comments are based on the author's observations of the Greenwich hustings held on 12 July 2010 and on conversations with David Miliband, Ed Balls and Diane Abbott after the debate.

31 P. Wintour and N. Watt, 'Party rifts laid bare as Labour leader result "too close to call"', *Guardian*, 25 September 2010.

32 For an outline of the candidates' policy priorities, see BBC, 'Labour Leadership Hopefuls: Policy-by-policy', *BBC News*, 1 September 2010, available at <http://www.bbc.co.uk/news/uk-politics-11150085>.

33 P. Wintour, 'Miliband brothers in bitter hustings exchange over Iraq war', *Guardian*, 30 July 2010.

34 A. Porter, 'Ed Balls: Brown failed to heed my warning on immigration', *Daily Telegraph*, 7 June 2010.

35 H. Mulholland, 'Diane Abbott accuses David Miliband of "buying" Labour leadership contest', *guardian.co.uk*, 2 August 2010, available at <http://www.

guardian.co.uk/politics/2010/aug/02/diane-abbott-david-miliband-buying-labour-leadership>.

36 N. Watt, 'Labour contenders await Blair intervention', *Guardian*, 30 August 2010.

37 A. Grice, 'Don't back me for leader, Miliband urges Blair', *Independent*, 2 September 2010.

38 'David bid got £27k Blair aid', *Sun*, 2 November 2010.

39 A. Grice, 'Unite union "ignored rules in endorsing Ed Miliband"', *Independent*, 10 September 2010; A. Stratton, N. Watt and P. Wintour, 'Ed Miliband union backers accused over Labour ballot mail-out', *Guardian*, 25 September 2010.

40 YouGov, 'Voting intention, problems + leaders', poll for the *Sun*, 24 August 2010.

41 S. Richards, 'Blairite sniping means Miliband must make a flawless start', *Independent*, 27 September 2010.

42 M. Chorley and J. Rentoul, 'David Miliband: "I can build a coalition across the party"', *Independent on Sunday*, 29 August 2010.

43 YouGov, 'Labour leaders (Labour members)', poll for the *Sunday Times*, 12 September 2010, available at <http://www.yougov.co.uk>.

44 YouGov, 'Labour leaders (Labour members)' and 'Labour leaders (trade unionists)', polls for the *Sunday Times*, 12 September 2010, available at <http://www.yougov.co.uk>.

45 J. Freedland, 'Ed Miliband won because he was neither Blair nor Brown', *guardian.co.uk*, 25 September 2010, available at <http://www.guardian.co.uk/commentisfree/2010/sep/25/ed-miliband-labour-leader-conference>.

46 P. Hennessey, 'Charlie Whelan: The puppet master who "won it for Ed"', *Sunday Telegraph*, 3 October 2010.

47 T. Quinn, 'New Labour and the Trade Unions in Britain', *Journal of Elections, Public Opinion and Parties*, 20:3 (2010): 357–80.

48 Labour Party HQ, private communication, 13 April 2011. The precise wording on the ballot papers sent to members of affiliates was: '"*I support the policies and principles of the Labour Party, and am not a supporter of any organisation opposed to it and pay a political subscription to the body that issued this ballot paper.*" Please tick [Box]. Please note: if this part of your ballot is left unmarked you will not be eligible to vote in this election.'

49 Hennessey, 'Charlie Whelan: The puppet master who "won it for Ed"'.

50 R. Sylvester and A. Thompson, '"David's attitude annoys me. It's not a disaster – get a life"', *Times*, 9 October 2010.

51 P. Wintour, 'Ed Miliband leadership: The unions had the last word', *Guardian*, 27 September 2010; Hennessey, 'Charlie Whelan: The puppet master who "won it for Ed"'.

52 For example, see A. Seldon, *Blair* (London: Free Press, 2005); A. Seldon, *Blair Unbound* (London: Pocket Books, 2008); Rawnsley, *End of the Party*; Rawnsley, *Servants of the People*; Tony Blair, *A Journey* (London: Hutchinson, 2010); Mandelson, *Third Man*.

53 Seldon, *Blair*, p. 682.

54 Seldon, *Blair Unbound*, pp. 252–3; Rawnsley, *End of the Party*, p. 235.

55   Seldon, *Blair Unbound*, p. 247; Rawnsley, *End of the Party*, p. 234.
56   See Seldon, *Blair Unbound*, pp. 483–95; Rawnsley, *End of the Party*, pp. 389–404.
57   Rawnsley, *End of the Party*, p. 400.
58   ICM, 'Guardian Labour members poll', poll for the *Guardian*, February 2004; 'Sunday Mirror leadership poll', poll for the *Sunday Mirror*, September 2006. Both polls available at <http://www.icmresearch.co.uk>.
59   Seldon, *Blair Unbound*, p. 487.
60   Seldon, *Blair Unbound*, p. 492.
61   See Rawnsley, *End of the Party*, pp. 496–514.
62   Rawnsley, *End of the Party*, pp. 532–41.
63   P. Wintour, 'Senior ministers urged: Tell battered PM it's time to go', *Guardian*, 26 July 2008; N. Morris, 'Cabinet backs Brown but "Lancashire plot" sparks open warfare', *Independent*, 29 July 2008.
64   D. Miliband, 'Against all odds we can still win, on a platform of change', *Guardian*, 30 July 2008.
65   A. McSmith, 'How Miliband started the race for No 10', *Independent*, 31 July 2008.
66   A. Porter, 'Labour at war', *Daily Telegraph*, 31 July 2008.
67   A. Grice and J. MacIntyre, 'Brown to resist backbench calls to sack Miliband', *Independent*, 1 August 2008.
68   S. Richards, 'Miliband may well have sealed Brown's fate', *Independent*, 31 July 2008.
69   A. Porter and J. Kirkup, 'I will not allow Brown to lead us to destruction, says Clarke', *Daily Telegraph*, 4 September 2008.
70   A. Seldon and G. Lodge, *Brown at 10* (London: Biteback Publishing, 2010), pp. 135–7.
71   Siobhain McDonagh MP, private interview, Westminster, 16 February 2011.
72   Rt Hon. Frank Field MP, private interview, Westminster, 1 March 2011; Rt Hon. Charles Clarke, private interview, Bishopsgate, London, 22 February 2011.
73   P. Hennessy and M. Kite, 'Labour falls into civil war', *Sunday Telegraph*, 14 September 2008.
74   P. Wintour, 'Minister quits and criticises No 10 tactics', *Guardian*, 17 September 2008.
75   Seldon and Lodge, *Brown at 10*, pp. 137–8.
76   Rawnsley, *End of the Party*, p. 571.
77   Seldon and Lodge, *Brown at 10*, p. 180.
78   See S. Birch and N. Allen, 'How Honest Do Politicians Need to Be?', *Political Quarterly*, 81:1 (2010), 49–56.
79   A. Porter and J. Kirkup, 'Brown fights for his life', *Daily Telegraph*, 4 June 2009.
80   A. Grice, 'Purnell quits and tells Brown to stand aside', *Independent*, 5 June 2009.
81   S. Coates, 'Resignation propels skirmishes into open warfare on the airwaves', *Times*, 5 June 2009.
82   Seldon and Lodge, *Brown at 10*, p. 276.
83   Seldon and Lodge, *Brown at 10*, p. 288.

84 J. Oliver, I. Oakeshott and M. Woolf, 'Night of the blunt knives', *Sunday Times*, 7 June 2009.
85 G. Hoon and P. Hewitt, 'In full: The letter from Geoff Hoon and Patricia Hewitt', *Times*, 7 January 2010.
86 M. White, 'Ballot call: What next?', *Guardian*, 7 January 2010.
87 A. Rawnsley, *The End of the Party: The Rise and Fall of New Labour*, paperback edition (London: Penguin/Viking, 2010), pp. 688, 691.
88 Clarke interview, 22 February 2011.
89 Seldon and Lodge, *Brown at 10*, pp. 385, 388–91.
90 YouGov, 'Voting Intentions and the Labour Party', poll for the *Daily Telegraph*, 22 September 2008, available at <www.yougov.co.uk>.
91 S. Coates, 'MPs fear Miliband jostling may spark early election', *Times*, 2 August 2008.
92 Rawnsley, *End of the Party*, p. 566.
93 J. Rentoul, 'That's the last challenge to Brown. Pity...', *Independent on Sunday*, 10 January 2010.
94 Seldon and Lodge, *Brown at 10*, pp. 389–90.
95 Mandelson, *Third Man*, p. 20.
96 Mandelson, *Third Man*, p. 472.
97 Clarke interview, 22 February 2011.
98 Rt Hon. George Howarth MP, telephone interview, 29 March 2011.
99 Seldon and Lodge, *Brown at 10*, pp. 124–5.
100 Rawnsley, *End of the Party*, pp. 564–5.
101 Seldon and Lodge, *Brown at 10*, p. 393.
102 Clarke interview, 22 February 2011.
103 Clarke interview, 22 February 2011.
104 Howarth interview, 29 March 2011.
105 Clarke interview, 22 February 2011.
106 Field interview, 1 March 2011.
107 Rawnsley, *End of the Party*, p. 558.
108 Rawnsley, *End of the Party*, p. 573.
109 Rawnsley, *End of the Party*, pp. 652–3.
110 J. Oliver and M. Woolf, 'Ex-ministers join Brown rebellion', *Sunday Times*, 14 September 2008.
111 Clarke interview, 22 February 2011.
112 Field interview, 1 March 2011.
113 Clarke interview, 22 February 2011.
114 Howarth interview, 29 March 2011.
115 Clarke interview, 22 February 2011. Clarke provided the author with a leadership-election schedule for a planned move against Brown in late 2009. It is reproduced in Appendix M.
116 P. Wintour, 'Ed Miliband leadership: The unions had the last word', *Guardian*, 27 September 2010.
117 S. Milne, 'Ed Miliband has to crack the whip to secure change', *Guardian*, 30 September 2010.
118 J. Rentoul, 'The party voted for David Miliband but got the Panda instead – and he won't stand a chance against Cameron', *Independent on Sunday*, 26 September 2010.
119 Clarke interview, 22 February 2011.

Chapter 4   The Conservative Party: Enfranchising the Members

1 See K. Alderman, 'The Conservative Party Leadership Election of 1997', *Parliamentary Affairs*, 51:1 (1998), 1–16.

2 Conservative Party, *A Fresh Future for the Conservative Party* (London: Conservative Party, 1997).

3 R. Kelly, 'Organisational Reform and the Extra-Parliamentary Party', in M. Garnett and P. Lynch (eds), *The Conservatives in Crisis* (Manchester: Manchester University Press, 2003), pp. 82–106, at p. 101.

4 A. McSmith, P. Wintour and P. Kellner, 'Tories force Hague into climbdown', *Observer*, 5 October 1997.

5 P. Webster, 'Rank and file vent wrath on Tory MPs', *Times*, 9 October 1997.

6 J. Landale, 'Hague wants million members by 2000', *Times*, 6 October 1997.

7 K. Alderman, 'Revision of Leadership Election Procedures in the Conservative Party', *Parliamentary Affairs*, 52:2 (1999), 260–74, p. 270.

8 P. Webster, 'Tories warm to idea of one member, one vote', *Times*, 12 December 1997.

9 Alderman, 'Revision of Leadership Election Procedures', pp. 266–8.

10 P. Webster and P. Newton, 'Tory MPs support Hague on leader's election', *Times*, 15 January 1998.

11 P. Norton, 'The Party Leader', in P. Norton (ed.), *The Conservative Party* (London: Prentice Hall-Harvester Wheatsheaf, 1996), pp. 142–56.

12 B. Brown, 'Tory MPs open leadership selection to whole party', *Independent*, 15 January 1998.

13 A. Bevins, 'Rule change may protect leader from challengers', *Independent*, 10 October 1997.

14 N. Watt, 'Backbench Tories win ballot concession', *Times*, 23 January 1998.

15 Alderman, 'Revision of Leadership Election Procedures', p. 266.

16 Lord Spicer of Cropthorne, telephone interview, 21 April 2010. The current chairman, Graham Brady, confirmed to the author that this policy was never formally incorporated into the rules. Graham Brady MP, private communication, 14 March 2011.

17 '[A] requirement to renew would be unworkable – a letter sent just before State Opening would fall almost immediately whereas one just after would be "active" for a year (or longer if State Opening was delayed). Given the relatively small number of letters that would be involved it seems to me that the most appropriate thing would be to check in person with a colleague who had written a letter a significant time beforehand whether they wished to have an opportunity to withdraw it. In practice I suspect that colleagues would in any case be keen to communicate their wishes in these circumstances.' Graham Brady MP, private communication, 4 April 2011.

18 Conservative Party, *The Fresh Future* (London: Conservative Party, 1998).

19 Kelly, 'Organisational Reform and the Extra-Parliamentary Party', p. 88.

20 Alderman, 'Revision of Leadership Election Procedures', p. 269.

21 M. d'Ancona, 'This is an unwanted battle, but one with the highest of stakes', *Sunday Telegraph*, 8 May 2005.

22 T. Heppell, *Choosing the Tory Leader: Conservative Party Leadership Elections from Heath to Cameron* (London: IB Tauris, 2008), pp. 137–40; K. Alderman

and N. Carter, 'The Conservative Party Leadership Election of 2001', *Parliamentary Affairs*, 55:4 (2002), 569–85, pp. 570–4.

23 A. Denham and K. O'Hara, *Democratising Conservative Leadership Selection: From Grey Suits to Grass Roots* (Manchester: Manchester University Press, 2008), pp. 55–6.

24 Heppell, *Choosing the Tory Leader*, pp. 139–40.

25 P. Cowley and J. Green, 'New Leaders, Same Problems: The Conservatives', in A. Geddes and J. Tonge (eds), *Britain Decides: The UK General Election 2005* (Basingstoke: Palgrave Macmillan, 2005), pp. 46–68, at p. 49.

26 S. Walters, *Tory Wars: Conservatives in Crisis* (London: Politico's, 2001), p. 210.

27 N. Watt, 'Reforming zeal pushed party too far', *Guardian*, 18 July 2001.

28 Denham and O'Hara, *Democratising Conservative Leadership Selection*, p. 55.

29 Heppell, *Choosing the Tory Leader*, p. 139.

30 P. Snowdon, *Back from the Brink: The Inside Story of the Tory Resurrection* (London: Harper Press, 2010), p. 87.

31 For example, Heppell, *Choosing the Tory Leader*, pp. 151–2; Denham and O'Hara, *Democratising Conservative Leadership Selection*, p. 65; cf. Cowley and Green, 'New Leaders, Same Problems', pp. 48–50.

32 P. Norton, 'The Conservative Party: The Politics of Panic', in J. Bartle and A. King (eds), *Britain at the Polls 2005* (Washington, DC: CQ Press, 2006), pp. 31–53, at p. 38.

33 ICM, 'Conservative Party membership poll', poll for the *Daily Telegraph*, August 2001, available at <http://www.icmresearch.co.uk>.

34 K. Alderman and N. Carter, 'A Very Tory Coup: The Ousting of Mrs Thatcher', *Parliamentary Affairs*, 44:2 (1991), 125–39.

35 P. Norton, 'The Conservative Party: Is There Anyone Out There?', in A. King (ed.), *Britain at the Polls 2001* (New York & London: Chatham House Publishers, 2002), pp. 68–94, at pp. 83–8.

36 Heppell, *Choosing the Tory Leader*, p. 143.

37 Alderman and Carter, 'The Conservative Party Leadership Election of 2001', p. 584.

38 Heppell, *Choosing the Tory Leader*, p. 152.

39 Lord Howard of Lympne, private interview, London School of Economics, 9 June 2010.

40 M. Kite, '"What are you going to do, Michael – ban people with the name David from standing?"', *Sunday Telegraph*, 8 May 2005.

41 Conservative Party, *A 21st Century Party: A Consultation Paper Setting Out Proposals to Reform the Conservative Party's Organisation* (London: Conservative Party, 2005), p. 15.

42 Denham and O'Hara, *Democratising Conservative Leadership Selection*, pp. 123, 127–8.

43 Denham and O'Hara, *Democratising Conservative Leadership Selection*, p. 129.

44 Cowley and Green, 'New Leaders, Same Problems: The Conservatives', pp. 47–8.

45 Denham and O'Hara, *Democratising Conservative Leadership Selection*, p. 94.

46 Denham and O'Hara, *Democratising Conservative Leadership Selection*, p. 108.

47 T. Bale, '"A Bit Less Bunny-Hugging and a Bit More Bunny-Boiling"? Qualifying Conservative Party Change under David Cameron', *British Politics* 3:3 (2008), 270–99.

48 T. Montgomerie, 'How Cameron Won... and Davis Lost', 6 December 2005, available at <http://conservativehome.blogs.com/toryleadership/2005/12/how_cameron_won.html>.

49 A. Rawnsley, 'New favourite, big gamble', *The Observer*, 9 October 2005.

50 F. Elliott and J. Hanning, *Cameron: The Rise of the New Conservative* (London: Harper Perennial, 2009), pp. 288–9.

51 For example, Montgomerie, 'How Cameron Won... and Davis Lost', and A. Denham and P. Dorey, 'A Tale of Two Speeches? The Conservative Leadership Election of 2005', *Political Quarterly*, 77:1 (2006), 35–42.

52 Elliott and Hanning, *Cameron*, pp. 292–3.

53 Denham and Dorey, 'A Tale of Two Speeches?'.

54 T. Kavanagh, 'A dead cert leader dies on his feet', *Sun*, 6 October 2005.

55 Denham and Dorey, 'A Tale of Two Speeches?', p. 36.

56 Heppell, *Choosing the Tory Leader*, pp. 189–90.

57 Derek Conway, private interview, Victoria, London, 24 June 2010.

58 Heppell, *Choosing the Tory Leader*, pp. 148–9; R. Kelly, 'The Extra-Parliamentary Tory Party: McKenzie Revisited', *Political Quarterly*, 75:4 (2004), 398–404, p. 399.

59 Walters, *Tory Wars*, p. 216.

60 Denham and Dorey, 'A Tale of Two Speeches', p. 37.

61 Heppell, *Choosing the Tory Leader*, p. 188.

62 Montgomerie, 'How Cameron Won... and Davis Lost'.

63 For an overview of Duncan Smith's spell as leader, see R. Hayton and T. Heppell, 'The Quiet Man of British Politics: The Rise, Fall and Significance of Iain Duncan Smith', *Parliamentary Affairs*, 63:3 (2010), 425–45.

64 Norton, 'The Conservative Party: The Politics of Panic', p. 39.

65 M. Crick, *In Search of Michael Howard* (London: Simon and Schuster, 2005), p. 423.

66 Heppell, *Choosing the Tory Leader*, p. 159.

67 Snowdon, *Back from the Brink*, pp. 108–9.

68 YouGov, 'Political trackers 2003–2005', available at <www.yougov.co.uk>.

69 Crick, *In Search of Michael Howard*, pp. 419–20.

70 According to Tim Bale, Spicer received 41 letters. T. Bale, *The Conservative Party: From Thatcher to Cameron* (Cambridge: Polity, 2010), p. 192.

71 M. Kite, 'Last-minute rush to round up the rebels', *Times*, 28 October 2003.

72 G. Jones, B. Brogan and T. Helm, 'Donor sparks off a frenzied day of plotting', *Daily Telegraph*, 23 October 2003.

73 G. Jones and A. Sparrow, 'It's a gladiatorial thing, said IDS, and then he got the thumbs down', *Daily Telegraph*, 30 October 2003.

74 Conway interview, 24 June 2010.

75 A. Sparrow and B. Brogan, 'Aide's e-mail warning of risk to IDS triggered investigation', *Daily Telegraph*, 13 October 2003.

76 G. Jones and B. Brogan, 'Duncan Smith critics named', *Daily Telegraph*, 31 October 2002.

77 Spicer interview, 21 April 2010.

78 B. Brogan and T. Helm, 'Westminster safe holds the key to Tory leader's future', *Daily Telegraph*, 9 October 2003.
79 See Crick, *In Search of Michael Howard*, pp. 418–34. Crick's argument about the role of David Maclean, the chief whip, in removing Duncan Smith and paving the way for Howard is accepted by Snowdon: 'there is no doubt that he [Maclean] presided over a very old-fashioned Tory coup in order to prevent a potentially fatal power vacuum engulfing the party'. Snowdon, *Back from the Brink*, p. 129.
80 Crick, *In Search of Michael Howard*, p. 424.
81 Crick, *In Search of Michael Howard*, p. 425.
82 Conway interview, 24 June 2010.
83 V. Bogdanor, 'The Selection of the Party Leader', in A. Seldon and S. Ball (eds), *Conservative Century: The Conservative Party since 1900* (Oxford: Oxford University Press, 1994), pp. 69–96, at p. 92. The role of backbenchers in bringing about Thatcher's downfall is discussed in Chapter 2 above.
84 G. Jones and B. Brogan, 'Portillo cast as the kingmaker for Clarke', *Daily Telegraph*, 7 November 2002.
85 G. Jones, 'Angry Clarke aims a blow at "complete rubbish" in The Times', *Daily Telegraph*, 25 October 2003.
86 Conway interview, 24 June 2010.
87 Denham and O'Hara, *Democratising Conservative Leadership Selection*, p. 94.
88 Crick, *In Search of Michael Howard*, p. 429.
89 YouGov, 'Conservative members', poll for the *Daily Telegraph*, 9 October 2003, available at <http://www.yougov.co.uk>.
90 R. Sylvester, 'It was just a battle in the war for the party's soul – the armies will return', *Daily Telegraph*, 30 October 2003.
91 Conway interview, 24 June 2010.
92 See YouGov, 'Conservative members', poll for the *Daily Telegraph*, 9 October 2003, available at <http://www.yougov.co.uk>.

Chapter 5   The Liberal Democrats: One Member-One Vote

1 See D. Dutton, *A History of the Liberal Party* (Basingstoke: Palgrave Macmillan, 2004), pp. 235–69.
2 L. P. Stark, *Choosing a Leader: Party Leadership Contests in Britain from Macmillan to Blair* (Basingstoke: Macmillan, 1996), pp. 72–4; R. M. Punnett, *Selecting the Party Leader: Britain in Comparative Perspective* (Hemel Hempstead: Harvester Wheatsheaf, 1992), pp. 137–8.
3 I. Crewe and A. King, *SDP: The Birth, Life and Death of the Social Democratic Party* (Oxford: Oxford University Press, 1995).
4 Crewe and King, *SDP*, pp. 153, 487.
5 Punnett, *Selecting the Party Leader*, pp. 138–42; Stark, *Choosing a Leader*, pp. 74–9.
6 Dutton, *History of the Liberal Party*, pp. 264–9.
7 The Liberal Democrats have a separately-elected president, who is the leader of the extra-parliamentary party.
8 J. Rentoul, 'Charles Kennedy's fate is sealed. The only question is who will wield the knife', *Independent on Sunday*, 1 January 2006.

9   Lord Rennard of Wavertree, private interview, Westminster, 15 June 2010.
10 K. Alderman and N. Carter, 'The Liberal Democrat Leadership Election of 1999', *Parliamentary Affairs*, 53:2 (2000), 311–27, p. 318.
11 Punnett, *Selecting the Party Leader*, p. 145.
12 Punnett, *Selecting the Party Leader*, pp. 145–6.
13 Dutton, *History of the Liberal Party*, pp. 284–5.
14 A. Russell and E. Fieldhouse, *Neither Left Nor Right? The Liberal Democrats and the Electorate* (Manchester: Manchester University Press, 2006), p. 41.
15 See D. Denver, 'The Liberal Democrats in "Constructive Opposition"', in A. King (ed.), *Britain at the Polls 2001* (Chatham House, NJ: Chatham House, 2002), pp. 143–63.
16 V. Bogdanor, 'The Liberal Democrat Dilemma in Historical Perspective', *Political Quarterly*, 78:1 (2007), 11–20.
17 Alderman and Carter, 'Liberal Democrat Leadership Election of 1999', pp. 312–15.
18 Russell and Fieldhouse, *Neither Left Nor Right?*, p. 43.
19 Alderman and Carter, 'Liberal Democrat Leadership Election of 1999', p. 322.
20 Alderman and Carter, 'Liberal Democrat Leadership Election of 1999', p. 324.
21 A. Denham and P. Dorey, 'The "Caretaker" Cleans Up: The Liberal Democrat Leadership Election of 2006', *Parliamentary Affairs*, 60:1 (2007), 26–45, p. 31.
22 In December 2005, the Liberal Democrats polled 21 percent in an Ipsos-MORI survey, 1 percent down on their general-election result. Kennedy's last (August 2005) net satisfaction rating was +20.
23 A. Russell, 'The Liberal Democrat Campaign', in P. Norris and C. Wlezien (eds), *Britain Votes 2005* (Oxford: Oxford University Press, 2005), pp. 87–100, at p. 87.
24 For a fuller account of the Liberal Democrats' strategic dilemmas between 2005 and 2010, see T. Quinn and B. Clements, 'Realignment in the Centre: The Liberal Democrats', in N. Allen and J. Bartle (eds), *Britain at the Polls 2010* (London: Sage, 2011), pp. 63–88.
25 P. Whiteley, P. Seyd and A. Billinghurst, *Third Force Politics: Liberal Democrats at the Grassroots* (Oxford: Oxford University Press, 2006), pp. 137–69.
26 Quinn and Clements, 'Realignment in the Centre', pp. 68–70.
27 P. Marshall and D. Laws (eds), *The Orange Book: Reclaiming Liberalism* (London: Profile Books, 2004).
28 E. Fieldhouse and D. Cutts, 'The Liberal Democrats: Steady Progress or Failure to Seize the Moment?', in A. Geddes and J. Tonge (eds), *Britain Decides: The UK General Election 2005* (Basingstoke: Palgrave Macmillan, 2005), pp. 70–88, at p. 80.
29 Richard Grayson, private interview, Goldsmiths, University of London, 1 March 2010.
30 M. Campbell, *Menzies Campbell: My Autobiography* (London: Hodder and Stoughton, 2008), p. 231.
31 G. Hurst, *Charles Kennedy: A Tragic Flaw* (London: Politico's, 2006), pp. 232–3.
32 Rt Hon. Sir Menzies Campbell MP, private interview, Westminster, 20 July 2010.

33 Hurst, *Charles Kennedy*, pp. 1–4.
34 Campbell, *Menzies Campbell*, pp. 234–5; Hurst, *Charles Kennedy*, pp. 11–13.
35 The memo is reprinted in Hurst, *Charles Kennedy*, pp. 267–8.
36 Hurst, *Charles Kennedy*, pp. 223–4.
37 A. Pierce, 'A desperate Kennedy confronts his demons', *Times*, 6 January 2006.
38 Denham and Dorey, 'The "Caretaker" Cleans Up', p. 34.
39 T. Branigan, 'Kennedy throws leadership fight into confusion', *Guardian*, 6 January 2006.
40 Rennard interview, 15 June 2010.
41 B. Carlin and G. Jones, 'Long day's journey into political oblivion', *Daily Telegraph*, 7 January 2006.
42 For differing perspectives on Kennedy's resignation, see D. Brack, 'Liberal Democrat Leadership: The Cases of Ashdown and Kennedy', *Political Quarterly*, 78:1 (2007), 78–88; S. McAnulla, 'Explaining the Forced Exit of Charles Kennedy: Pushing the Public-Private Boundary', *Politics*, 29:1 (2009), 37–44.
43 D. Charter, 'Plotters press ahead despite lack of options', *Times*, 6 January 2006.
44 Extensive efforts were made by the author to discover the precise rules governing confidence votes in the Liberal Democrat leader, including enquiries to the present and previous chief executives. No one was able to say definitively what the formal process is although the author understands that discussions were underway in 2011 to clarify the rules.
45 Hurst, *Charles Kennedy*, p. 14.
46 J. Rentoul, 'Charles Kennedy has resorted to the nuclear option and has lost in doing so', *Independent*, 6 January 2006.
47 Cited in A. Pierce, 'Kennedy accused of bluster', *Times*, 5 January 2006.
48 Hurst, *Charles Kennedy*, p. 235.
49 Hurst, *Charles Kennedy*, pp. 13–14.
50 Mark Oaten, private interview, Vauxhall, London, 20 May 2010.
51 Campbell, *Menzies Campbell*, pp. 227–41.
52 Hurst, *Charles Kennedy*, pp. 7, 17.
53 Hurst, *Charles Kennedy*, pp. 238–9.
54 Hurst, *Charles Kennedy*, p. 23.
55 Charles Kennedy cited in Pierce, 'Kennedy accused of bluster'.
56 Campbell, *Menzies Campbell*, p. 244.
57 A. Grice, '"I have been in denial. But I will fight on"' [Interview with Kennedy], *Independent*, 7 January 2006.
58 Branigan, 'Kennedy throws leadership fight into confusion'.
59 Abridged versions of this discussion of the 2006 Liberal Democrat contest can be found in Quinn and Clements, 'Realignment in the Centre', pp. 72–3, and T. Quinn, 'Membership Ballots in Party Leadership Elections in Britain', *Representation*, 46:1 (2010), 101–17, pp. 103–6.
60 A. Russell, 'Leadership contenders square up to battle over Lib Dems' top job', *Independent*, 9 January 2006.
61 Denham and Dorey, 'The "Caretaker" Cleans Up', p. 35.
62 N. Clegg, 'We need a leader with experience, not youth', *Independent*, 10 January 2006.

63 A. Miles, 'What deal? Obscure Lib Dem fends off unwelcome attention', *Times*, 2 February 2006.
64 A. Grice, 'Campbell plans to ditch 50p tax on £100,000 plus', *Independent*, 19 January 2006.
65 T. Branigan and M. White, 'Menzies Campbell: I will take Lib Dems to the left of Labour', *Guardian*, 13 January 2006.
66 B. Carlin, 'Campbell would be a stop-gap leader, hints his leadership rival', *Daily Telegraph*, 11 January 2006.
67 Oaten interview, 20 May 2010.
68 A. Russell and A. Grice, 'Oaten pulls out of Lib-Dem leadership contest', *Independent*, 20 January 2006.
69 M. White, 'Hughes comes out but stays in the race', *Guardian*, 27 January 2006.
70 Miles, 'What deal?'
71 R. Sylvester and A. Thompson, 'Lib Dem new boy aims straight for top', *Daily Telegraph*, 21 January 2006.
72 Denham and Dorey, 'The "Caretaker" Cleans Up', p. 43.
73 Russell and Grice, 'Oaten pulls out of Lib-Dem leadership contest'; 'MPs, MEPs and Peers backing Chris Huhne', available at <www.Chris2Win.org> (Huhne leadership campaign website), archived at <http://web.archive.org/web/20060422115305/http://chris2win.org/pages/supporterslist.html>.
74 Campbell interview, 20 July 2010.
75 Whiteley et al., *Third Force Politics*, pp. 49–54, 60–2.
76 Denham and Dorey, 'The "Caretaker" Cleans Up', p. 40.
77 YouGov, 'Survey of Liberal Democrat party members', poll for John Stevens, 9 February 2006, available at <http://www.yougov.co.uk>.
78 YouGov, 'Survey of Liberal Democratic party members'.
79 Denham and Dorey, 'The "Caretaker" Cleans Up', p. 42; R. Winnett and A. Taher, 'Lib Dems face funding boycott if "unfit" Hughes wins leadership', *Sunday Times*, 29 January 2006.
80 Cf. Denham and Dorey, 'The "Caretaker" Cleans Up', p. 43.
81 Oaten interview, 20 May 2010.
82 Abridged versions of this account of Campbell's resignation and the leadership election to succeed him can be found in Quinn and Clements, 'Realignment in the Centre', pp. 73–5, and Quinn, 'Membership Ballots in Party Leadership Elections in Britain', pp. 106–8.
83 Rennard interview, 15 June 2010.
84 S. Coates, 'Lib Dems face crisis as leader is told he must improve performance', *Times*, 13 October 2007.
85 D. Brack, 'Reviews: Leader out of time', *Journal of Liberal History*, No. 60 (Autumn 2008), 45–8, p. 47.
86 Campbell, *Menzies Campbell*, p. 290.
87 G. Hurst, 'Rapid exit of conference hero who defied his critics but not the polls', *Times*, 16 October 2007.
88 A. Pierce, 'Hughes: Ming must do better', *Daily Telegraph*, 13 October 2007.
89 M. Kite, 'Go gracefully, and go now, Ming told by party's MPs', *Daily Telegraph*, 14 October 2007.
90 Campbell, *Menzies Campbell*, pp. 303–4.

91 A. Grice and C. Brown, 'Campbell quits, the loser of the election that never was', *Independent*, 16 October 2007.

92 Brack, 'Reviews: Leader out of time', p. 47.

93 P. Wintour and T. Branigan, 'Huhne points to his economic expertise in leadership fight', *Guardian*, 18 October 2007.

94 C. Brown, 'Clegg rejects Huhne supporters' claim that he is a "Cameron clone"', *Independent*, 20 October 2007.

95 A. Grice, 'Huhne's coded attack on Clegg: "We don't need a third Tory party"', *Independent*, 1 November 2007.

96 J. Gerard, 'The interview: Nick Clegg', *Guardian*, 21 October 2007; and N. Clegg, 'Time for a power shift', *Guardian*, 22 November 2007.

97 Grice, 'Huhne's coded attack on Clegg'.

98 T. Branigan, 'All still to play for in Liberal Democrats' leadership race', *Guardian*, 23 November 2007.

99 D. Foggo and R. Waite, 'LSD article plays tricks on Huhne's mind', *Sunday Times*, 21 October 2007.

100 P. Wintour, 'Contest to lead Lib Dems turns nasty', *Guardian*, 19 November 2007.

101 YouGov, 'Liberal Democrat leadership contest', poll for *Sky News*, 3 December 2007, available at <http://www.yougov.co.uk>.

102 J. Merrick, 'Meet the real leader of the Liberal Democrats', *Independent on Sunday*, 6 April 2008.

103 T. Branigan, 'Clegg seeks new dawn for his party, and for politics', *Guardian*, 19 December 2007.

104 A. Russell, E. Fieldhouse and D. Cutts, '*De facto* Veto? The Parliamentary Liberal Democrats', *Political Quarterly*, 78:1 (2007), 89–98; Quinn and Clements, 'Realignment in the Centre', pp. 76–9.

105 E. Evans and E. Sanderson-Nash, 'From Sandals to Suits: Professionalisation, Coalition and the Liberal Democrats', *British Journal of Politics and International Relations*, 13:4 (2011), 459–73.

106 Oaten interview, 20 May 2010.

Chapter 6   Electing and Ejecting Party Leaders: An Assessment

1 L. P. Stark, *Choosing a Leader: Party Leadership Contests in Britain from Macmillan to Blair* (Basingstoke: Macmillan, 1996), pp. 132–3.

2 Stark, *Choosing a Leader*, pp. 129–32, 169–70.

3 Stark, *Choosing a Leader*, p. 136.

4 R. M. Punnett, *Selecting the Party Leader: Britain in Comparative Perspective* (Hemel Hempstead: Harvester Wheatsheaf, 1992), pp. 165–6.

5 D. Hayter, *Fightback! Labour's Traditional Right in the 1970s and 1980s* (Manchester: Manchester University Press, 2005).

6 A. Seldon, *Blair* (London: Free Press, 2005), pp. 103–7.

7 T. Quinn, 'Leasehold or Freehold? Leader-Eviction Rules in the British Conservative and Labour Parties', *Political Studies*, 53:4 (2005), 793–815, p. 808.

8 V. Bogdanor, 'The Selection of the Party Leader', in A. Seldon and S. Ball (eds), *Conservative Century: The Conservative Party since 1900* (Oxford: Oxford University Press, 1994), pp. 69–96, at p. 95.

9   Stark, *Choosing a Leader*, pp. 129–30.
10 M. Laakso and R. Taagepera, '"Effective" Number of Parties: A Measure with Application to West Europe', *Comparative Political Studies*, 12:1 (1979), 3–27.
11 O. Kenig, 'Democratization of Party Leadership Selection: Do Wider Selectorates Produce More Competitive Contests?', *Electoral Studies*, 28:2 (2009), 240–7, pp. 245–6.
12 P. Dunleavy and F. Boucek, 'Constructing the Number of Parties', *Party Politics*, 9:3 (2003), 291–315.
13 G. Golosov, 'The Effective Number of Parties: A New Approach', *Party Politics*, 16:2 (2010), 171–92.
14 T. Quinn, *Modernising the Labour Party: Organisational Change since 1983* (Basingstoke: Palgrave Macmillan, 2004), p. 132.
15 In the 1990 Conservative leadership election, there were only two candidates in the first ballot, when Heseltine challenged Thatcher, but two more candidates entered the second ballot.
16 K. Alderman, 'The Conservative Party Leadership Election of 1997', *Parliamentary Affairs*, 51:1, 1–16, p. 5.
17 P. Snowdon, *Back from the Brink: The Inside Story of the Tory Resurrection* (London: Harper Press, 2010), pp. 43–4.
18 J. Lees-Marshment, 'The Marriage of Politics and Marketing', *Political Studies*, 49:4 (2001), 692–713.
19 Lord Howard of Lympne, private interview, London School of Economics, 9 June 2010.
20 Rt Hon. Charles Clarke, private interview, Bishopsgate, London, 22 February 2011.
21 Derek Conway, private interview, Victoria, London, 24 June 2010; Sir Michael Spicer, telephone interview, 21 April 2010.
22 P. Jenkins, *The Battle of Downing Street* (London: Charles Knight & Co., 1970), p. 112.
23 P. Norton, 'The Party Leader', in P. Norton (ed.), *The Conservative Party* (London: Prentice Hall-Harvester Wheatsheaf, 1996), pp. 142–56, at p. 146.
24 Conservative Party, *A 21ˢᵗ Century Party* (London: Conservative Party, 2005), p. 15.
25 Clarke interview, 22 February 2011; Siobhain McDonagh MP, private interview, Westminster, 16 February 2011.
26 The source for these figures is House of Commons Information Office, 'Ministerial Salaries', *Factsheet M6: Members Series*, Revised September 2010 (London: House of Commons, 2010), pp. 8–9.
27 Clarke interview, 22 February 2011.
28 Stark, *Choosing a Leader*, p. 134.

Appendices

1 N. Carter, 'The Green Party: Emerging from the Political Wilderness?', *British Politics*, 3:2 (2008), 223–40, p. 232.
2 Carter, 'Green Party', pp. 232–3.
3 Carter, 'Green Party', p. 233.
4 'Leading edge', *Guardian: Society Guardian*, 12 September 2007.
5 Carter, 'Green Party', pp. 234, 239, n.12.

6   *Constitution of the Green Party* (London: Green Party, 2010).
7   *UKIP Constitution*, available at <http://www.ukip.org/page/ukip-constitution>.
8   The events described in the following paragraph are recounted in M. Daniel, *Cranks and Gadflies: The Story of UKIP* (London: Timewell Press, 2005).
9   N. Morris, 'Lord Pearson plays the Islam card to win leadership of Ukip', *Independent*, 28 November 2009.
10 K. Dutta, 'I wasn't up to the job, says ex-Ukip leader', *Independent*, 18 August 2010.
11 N. Copsey, *Contemporary British Fascism: The British National Party and the Quest for Legitimacy*, 2nd *ed.* (Basingstoke: Palgrave Macmillan, 2008).
12 On the BNP's development under Griffin, see M. Goodwin, 'In Search of the Winning Formula: Nick Griffin and the "Modernization" of the British National Party', in R. Eatwell and M. Goodwin (eds), *The New Extremism in 21st Century Britain* (London: Routledge, 2010), pp. 169–90.
13 Nigel Copsey (Teesside University), private communication, 4 April 2011.
14 O. Bowcott, 'BNP and equality group both claim victory in legal wrangle', *Guardian*, 18 December 2010.
15 BBC, 'Challengers fail to get backing to force BNP contest', *BBC News*, 11 August 2010, available at <http://www.bbc.co.uk/news/uk-politics-10929903>.
16 British National Party, 'D-Day – the British National Party leadership election 2011 – the count starts at 1.30pm today', 25 July 2011; 'Party leadership election result: Nick Griffin re-elected party chairman', 25 July 2011, both available at <http://www.bnp.org.uk>.
17 J. Robertson and K. Farquharson, 'Swinney to stamp out SNP bickering', *Sunday Times*, 24 September 2000.
18 J. Quinn, 'SNP leader fires warning at his rebels', *Sunday Mirror*, 28 September 2003.
19 *Constitution of the Scottish National Party* (Edinburgh: Scottish National Party, 2009), Clauses 15.5(b) and 15.7.
20 BBC, 'Jones the comeback kid', *BBC News*, 15 September 2003, available at <http://news.bbc.co.uk/1/hi/wales/3110168.stm>.
21 *Plaid Cymru Constitution* (Cardiff: Plaid Cymru, 2009), Section 1.1, Clauses 14.1.i and 14.1.iii.
22 K. Scott, 'Dewar's successor to seek more power for parliament', *Guardian*, 23 October 2000.
23 P. Flynn, *Dragons Led by Poodles: The Inside Story of a New Labour Stitch-Up* (London: Politico's, 1999).
24 A. Macleod, 'No contest as Scottish Tories go for Goldie', *Times*, 3 November 2005.
25 S. Buchanan, 'Tory Rod's victory attacked by rivals', *South Wales Evening Post*, 11 November 1998.
26 'Nick is Tories' choice', *South Wales Evening Post*, 19 August 1999.
27 BBC, 'Andrew RT Davies elected Tory Welsh assembly leader', *BBC News*, 14 July 2011, available at <http://www.bbc.co.uk/news/uk-wales-politics-14143317>; B. Wright, 'Davies elected new Welsh Tory chief', *Press Association*, 14 July 2011.

Index

Note: references to tables and boxes appear in *italics*, and those to figures in **bold**.